MARK STEYN

Lights Out

ALSO BY MARK STEYN

Broadway Babies Say Goodnight:
Musicals Then And Now
(1997)

The Face Of The Tiger
And Other Tales From The New War
(2002)

Mark Steyn From Head To Toe:
An Anatomical Anthology
(2004)

America Alone:
The End Of The World As We Know It
(2006)

Mark Steyn's Passing Parade:
Obituaries & Appreciations
(2006)

Mark Steyn's American Songbook:
Words, Music, Song
(2008)

A Song For The Season
(2008)

MARK STEYN

Lights Out

ISLAM, FREE SPEECH AND
THE TWILIGHT OF THE WEST

STOCKADE
BOOKS

Published in the United States by
Stockade Books
PO Box 30
Woodsville, New Hampshire
03785

Printed and bound in the Province of Québec (Canada)

ISBN 978-0-9731570-5-5

First Edition

Live free or die

General John Stark
July 31st 1809

AUTHOR'S NOTE

I would like to thank Kenneth Whyte, my publisher at *Maclean's*, Canada's biggest selling news weekly, and his colleagues at Rogers Publishing, for standing firm against the attempted appropriation of their property by the Canadian Islamic Congress and various "human rights" commissions.

I would also like to salute Ezra Levant, Kate McMillan of Small Dead Animals, Kathy Shaidle of Five Feet Of Fury, and Mark and Connie Fournier of Free Dominion. "These bloggers, long before the mainstream media, recognized the complaints as a politically-motivated threat to free expression," said Ken Whyte in 2009. "They did a great service to Canadian journalism." For their courage in standing up for freedoms too many citizens are willing to trade away, they've been subject to multiple nuisance lawsuits from the self-proclaimed heroes of Canada's "human rights" racket. They deserve your support.

I thank the editors of the publications in which these columns originally appeared: Ken Whyte and Dianne de Gayardon de Fenoyl at *Maclean's*; Ezra Levant and Kevin Libin at *The Western Standard*; Charles Moore and Martin Newland at Britain's *Daily Telegraph*; Peter Murtagh at *The Irish Times*; and Rich Lowry, Kathryn Lopez and Jay Nordlinger at America's *National Review*. As always, I am indebted to my assistants Tiffany Cole and Chantal Benoît. As on previous occasions, we have retained the spellings of the originating publication, whether American, Canadian, Irish, or Waziristani. So, if you don't like the case for the defence, the case for the defense should be along a couple of pages later. We do, however, have a preference for Britannic punctuation.

New Hampshire
March 2009

CONTENTS

OPENING
STATEMENTS

Free speech is the whole thing, the whole ball game.
Free speech is life itself.
SALMAN RUSHDIE
speaking at Columbia University, December 11th 1991

INTRODUCTION

Steyn in the dock

D O YOU REMEMBER a cover story run by *Maclean's*, Canada's bestselling news magazine, on October 23rd 2006? No? Me neither, and I wrote it. Such is life in the weekly mag biz. The hacks bark and the caravan moves on. But it was an excerpt on various geopolitical and demographic trends from my then brand new tome, *America Alone: The End Of The World As We Know It.* Flash forward just over a year: It's the end of 2007, and my Number One bestseller is suddenly back in the news. *America Alone*: coming soon to a Canadian "courtroom" near you! You've read the book, now read the legal briefs!

The Canadian Islamic Congress and a handful of Osgoode Hall law students had got, somewhat belatedly, worked up about the *Maclean's* excerpt and decided it was "flagrantly Islamophobic". So they filed complaints with three of Canada's many "human rights" commissions, two of which agreed to hear the "case". It would be nice to report that the third sent the plaintiffs away with a flea in their ears saying that in a free society it's no business of the state to regulate the content of privately owned magazines. Alas, it was only bureaucratic torpor that (temporarily) delayed the Province of Ontario's enthusiastic leap upon the bandwagon. Neither the Canadian Islamic Congress nor the aggrieved students were cited in the offending article. Canadian Muslims were not the subject of the piece. Indeed, Canada was barely mentioned at all, except *en passant*. Yet Canada's "human rights" commissions accepted the premise of the plaintiffs – that the article potentially breached these students' "human rights".

When the CIC launched its complaint, I was asked by a zillion correspondents what my defense is. My defense is I shouldn't have to have a defense. The plaintiffs have never asserted that the article is false, or libelous, or seditious, for all of which there would be appropriate legal remedy. Their complaint is essentially emotional: it "offended" them. And as offensiveness is in the eye of the offended, there's not a lot I can do about that.

But, given that the most fundamental "human right" in the western world is apparently the right not to be offended, perhaps I could be permitted to say what offends me. I'm offended by the federal and British Columbia "human rights" regimes' presumption that the editing decisions of privately owned magazines fall within their jurisdiction. Or to put it another way, I don't accept that free-born Canadian citizens require the permission of the Canadian state to read my columns. The eminent Queen's Counsel who heads the Canadian "Human Rights" Commission may well be a shrewd and insightful person but I don't believe her view of *Maclean's* cover stories should carry any more weight than that of Mrs Mabel Scroggins of 47 Strathcona Gardens. And it is slightly unnerving that large numbers of Canadians apparently think there's nothing wrong in subjecting the contents of political magazines to the approval of agents of the state.

Let's take it as read that I am, as claimed, "offensive". That's the point. It's offensive speech that requires legal protection. As a general rule, Barney the Dinosaur singing "Sharing Is Caring" can rub along just fine. So, if you don't believe in free speech for people you loathe, you don't believe in free speech at all.

By the way, granted that I'm loathsome and repellent, so evidently are significant numbers of other Canadians. *America Alone* was a Number One book in Canada; excerpts appeared not only in the country's oldest and most respectable news magazine, a mainstay of dentists' waiting rooms for the best part of a century, but also in the country's national newspaper, *The National Post*. The justification the inattentive citizen makes when the censors get to work is that they're obviously only targeting extremists at the very fringes of society. Yet in this case Canada's kangaroo courts were proposing to criminalize a Number One book and the Number One news weekly. And the statutory remedy for the "crime" would have been in effect to render a Number One bestselling author unpublishable in Canada.

As for "Islamophobia", that word appears nowhere in the Canadian criminal code, and indeed barely anywhere in the English language until the 1990s. It was introduced formally into the grievance culture in 1998 in a report by Britain's Runnymede Trust, which, with genuine racial prejudice on the decline in the UK, was in need of some new horrors to justify its sinecure. Islamophobia means an "irrational fear of Islam" – ie, a mental illness, like agoraphobia or arachnophobia. As a friend of mine likes to say, Islamophobia is one of those illnesses of which the only symptom is to be accused of having it. There is nothing "irrational" about wanting to examine the fastest growing religion and population demographic in the world and its relationship with western ideas of liberty and pluralism.

During the early skirmishes, a colleague who's also been called up before one of these "human rights" star chambers mused in an e-mail about the difference between his lawyer's advice - that he should be "reasonable" in order to "get off the hook" - and his own feeling that the hook itself needs to be done away with. *The Economist* reprinted my response to him:

> *I don't want to get off the hook. I want to take the hook and stick it up the collective butt of these thought police.*

Hence, this book. It reprints the essays of mine that the Canadian Islamic Congress and their stooges in the "human rights" racket attempted to criminalize: When an Islamist bully or a dimwitted PC apparatchik says you can't say something, that's all the more reason to say it again. So here's the offending material, plus some additional essays exploring the relationship between Islam and the west; my thoughts on the civilizational self-loathing of which the Muslim lobby groups are merely opportunist beneficiaries; and, finally, some snapshots of a year under the Canadian "human rights" microscope. We made headway in the campaign to repeal Section 13 and restore freedom of speech to Canada, but there's still a long way to go. And in the broader global battle to end one-way multiculturalism we are still losing turf. Indeed, the Organization of the Islamic Conference (a kind of Muslim Commonwealth, representing just under 60 nations) may well succeed in its drive to impose a de facto global law against Islamic "blasphemy". Increasingly, in the public square, in the marketplace of ideas, in ancient nations that have been the crucible of freedom, the Muslim world's prohibitions on intellectual inquiry now apply to all.

In February 2009, the British Government banned a Dutch parliamentarian, Geert Wilders, from entry to the United Kingdom, had him arrested at Heathrow, and deported. Minheer Wilders had made a "controversial" film about Islam called *Fitna*, and the Foreign Secretary, David Miliband, justified the decision by drearily regurgitating the old no-right-to-shout-fire-in-a-theatre line (see page 309). He then revealed he hadn't seen *Fitna*. As the commentator Edmund Standing asked: "How is Miliband any better than Muslims who screamed about *The Satanic Verses* without bothering to read it?"

February was also the 20th anniversary of the Ayatollah's fatwa against Salman Rushdie over *The Satanic Verses*. Two decades on, who needs the mullahs? These days western nations are happy to fatwa their own. It's now a familiar pattern. If you threaten violence (as Muslims do to Wilders), the authorities cave in, and do the mob's bidding in the interests of "public order". If you're a "moderate Muslim" who gets death threats and complains to the police, they send round two Muslim officers to advise you to zip it lest you provoke more trouble. If Muslim girls in Ontario are being murdered in "honor killings", the "Human Rights" Commissar of the "Human Rights" Commission will explain that they're only a "small commission" and they have to be able to prioritize and that Mark Steyn is a far greater threat to the Queen's peace than killers of Muslim women.

But, if you don't threaten violence, if you don't issue death threats, if you don't kill anyone, if you just make a movie or write a book or try to give a speech, the state will prosecute you, ban you or (in the case of Ayaan Hirsi Ali) force you to flee your own country. In their appeasement of thugs, western governments are making it very clear that the state accords more respect to violence than to debate. That's a dangerous lesson to teach.

Midway through my troubles, I was asked on the radio in the United States why I was bothering to defend myself. Who cares about Canada? Why not just write it off? Here's my self-interested answer: I write for a living. If I go to my American publisher to pitch a book, she'll listen to my précis and then figure, "Well, we won't be able to sell it in Canada, so there goes ten per cent of the North American market. And we won't be able to license a British edition, because some bigshot Saudi prince will sue in a London court. And we won't be able to sell French and German translation rights because it runs afoul of European Union xenophobia legislation…" And pretty soon your little book is looking a lot less commercially viable. So it's easy to say write off Canada, Britain, Europe, Australia, but at the end of the day there'll be a lot of American authors affected by this and a lot of American books that will go unpublished in America.

As I said, that's my self-interested answer as to why I'm fighting this thing. But here's my high-falutin' one. When my children are my age, I want western civilization still to be in business. The idea that America can survive as a lonely beacon of light on a dark planet is absurd. The United States is part of a global economy, a signatory to global agreements, a member of transnational bodies. To accept these brutish assaults on free speech in the rest of the west is to make inevitable a world in which one day they will be under assault in the heart of the superpower, too. Six months after my battle in Canada began, my book was published in France, and, if some French Muslim group wants to do the same as the Canadian Islamic Congress, I'll defend it in court in my lousy Québécois-accented French (which I believe is a capital offence in the Fifth Republic). And I'll do that in every western jurisdiction where bullies who can't withstand honest, open debate decide instead to use the legal system to shut down that debate. President Bush liked to say about Iraq that we're fighting them over there so we don't have to fight them over here. Same with me and the legal jihadists: I'm going to fight them over there because otherwise we're going to be fighting them over here, and sooner than you think.

THE WEST AT TWILIGHT
Lights out on liberty

ON AUGUST 3rd 1914, on the eve of the Great War, Sir Edward Grey, the British Foreign Secretary, stood at the window of his office in the summer dusk and observed: "The lamps are going out all over Europe." Today the lamps are going out on liberty all over the western world in a more subtle and elusive and profound way. The rest of the west doesn't have a US-style First Amendment. British Commonwealth countries have robust instruments of freedom going back to Magna Carta; Continental Europe has a rather more erratic inheritance, but they are supposedly supporters of things like the UN's Universal Declaration of Human Rights. Unfortunately, a lot of them are far too comfortable with the proposition that in free societies it is right and proper for the state to regulate speech. For example:

- The response of the EU Commissioner for Justice, Freedom and Security to the Danish cartoons crisis a couple of years ago was to propose a press charter that would oblige newspapers to exercise "prudence" on, ah, certain controversial subjects.

- The response of Tony Blair's ministry to the problems of his own restive Muslim populations was to propose a sweeping law dramatically constraining free discussion of religion.

- At the end of her life, Oriana Fallaci was being sued in her native Italy and in Switzerland, Austria and sundry other jurisdictions by groups who believed her opinions were not merely disagreeable but criminal.

- In 2009, the Amsterdam Court of Appeal ordered that Geert Wilders, the Dutch politician and film-maker, be put on trial for statements that "harm the religious esteem of Islamic worshippers".

~ In France, Michel Houellebecq was sued by Muslim and other "anti-racist" groups who believed opinions held by a *fictional character* in one of his *novels* were not merely disagreeable but criminal.

But it gets better. Among the "flagrantly Islamophobic" Steyn articles the Canadian Islamic Congress took to the "human rights" commissions was my review of a situation comedy - the taxpayer-funded Canadian Muslim sitcom "Little Mosque On The Prairie". I reviewed it for *Maclean's*, and it wasn't exactly a non-stop laugh-riot. Which would be an unexceptional observation, especially with regard to taxpayer-funded CBC sitcoms. But the Canadian Islamic Congress alleged that finding Muslims insufficiently funny is deeply Islamophobic. Perhaps I should call several Iranian scholars as expert witnesses. You may recall that, in one of his many pronouncements, the Ayatollah Khomeini declared – definitively, one would have thought – that "there are no jokes in Islam." But apparently the Canadian Islamic Congress disagrees: Their position is that not finding Muslims funny is no laughing matter. And in this case the joke's on me.

While I was being hauled up for "flagrant Islamophobia", Brigitte Bardot found herself dragged into court on a similar charge in France. The former sex kitten is a big animal rights activist and was prosecuted and convicted by the French state for expressing her objections to Muslim slaughtering practices. In the course of a radio report on various of these "free speech" cases, the correspondent attempted to link Mlle Bardot's travails with mine and explained to his listeners: "Basically, Brigitte Bardot is the Mark Steyn of France." Well, I know she's getting a bit long in the tooth, but I thought that was uncalled for. If you'd held a competition 30 years ago to construct a combination of words the English language would never have any use for, "Brigitte Bardot is the Mark Steyn of France" would be pretty close to a shoo-in for first prize.

Brigitte Bardot and I are small pieces of a very big picture. In the years since 9/11, the most prominent Muslim lobby groups have devoted much of their energy to attempts to suppress open debate, whether it's the media pressure applied by the low-membership but lavishly Saudi-funded Council on American-Islamic Relations (an unindicted co-conspirator in an FBI terrorism-funding investigation), or at the international level the Organization of the Islamic Conference's subversion of the UN "Human Rights" Council. In the deranged Dominion, it was the grandly named Islamic Supreme Council of Canada which took my friends at *The Western Standard* to the Alberta "Human Rights" Commission for republishing the Danish "Mohammed" cartoons. In fact, if you want a snapshot of what's happening in our world, consider this: For reprinting those pictures, Ezra Levant was hauled before a government tribunal in Canada and spent two years and a six-figure sum defending himself, while in London the masked men who objected to the cartoons by marching through the streets with signs reading "Behead The Enemies Of Islam" (and who promised to rain down both a new 9/11 and a new Holocaust on Europe) were protected by a phalanx of London policemen. Multicultural societies are so invested in "tolerance" that they'll tolerate the explicitly intolerant (and avowedly unicultural) before they'll tolerate anyone pointing out that intolerance.

It's been that way for two decades now, ever since 1989, when large numbers of British Muslims marched through English cities openly calling for Salman Rushdie to be killed. A reader of mine recalled that he'd asked a policeman on the streets of Bradford during one such demonstration why the various "Muslim community leaders" weren't being arrested for incitement to murder. The policeman told him to "fuck off, or I'll arrest *you*." Salman Rushdie was infuriated when the then Archbishop of Canterbury lapsed into root-cause mode. "I well understand the devout Muslims' reaction, wounded by what they hold most dear and would themselves die for," said His Grace.

Rushdie replied tersely: "There is only one person around here who is in any danger of dying."

That's the way it always goes. For all the talk about rampant "Islamophobia", it's usually only the other party who is "in any danger of dying." And the response of the state to explicit Islamic intimidation is to find ways to punish those citizens foolish enough to point out that intimidation. The Council on American-Islamic Relations understands that, and the Islamic Supreme Council of Canada understands that, and so does the Supreme Islamic Council of New South Wales down in Australia, and the Supreme Islamic Council of Pocatello and all the rest of them. (I love these names. My favorite is a group I get press releases from occasionally – the Supreme Islamic Council of Ireland. They're one of the more moderate lobby groups, but the notion of a "Supreme Islamic Council of Ireland" still gives me a chuckle. Makes you wonder what the Catholics and Protestants bothered fighting over all those years. Any future sectarian strife on the island seems likely to be between Sunni and Shia.)

How did we get to this state of affairs? I was reminded the other day of an observation by the American writer Heywood Broun:

> *Everybody favors free speech in the slack moments when no axes are being ground.*

I think that gets it exactly backwards. It was precisely at the moment when no axes were being ground that the west decided it could afford to forego free speech. There was a moment 30 or so years ago when it appeared as if all the great questions had been settled: There would be no more Third Reichs, no more Fascist regimes, no more anti-Semitism; advanced social democracies were heading inevitably down a one-way sunlit avenue into the peaceable kingdom of multiculturalism. And so it seemed to a certain mindset entirely reasonable to introduce speech codes and thought crimes essentially as a kind of mopping up operation. Canada's "human rights" tribunals were originally created to deal with employment and housing discrimination, but Canadians aren't terribly hateful and there wasn't a lot of that, so they advanced to prosecuting so-called "hate speech". It was an illiberal notion harnessed supposedly in the cause of liberalism: A handful of neo-Nazi losers in rented rooms posting white supremacist messages on unread websites? Hold-out groups of homophobic fundamentalist Christians flaunting the more robust passages of Leviticus? Hey, relax, we'll hunt down the basement losers and ensure they'll trouble you no further. Just a few recalcitrant knuckledraggers who decline to get with the program. Don't give 'em a thought. Nothing to see here, folks.

Canada is not under any threat from Nazis. If any "white supremacist" were really a "supremacist", he wouldn't be living in his mom's basement. The real "supremacists" are the moral poseurs fighting, as moral poseurs often do, phantoms. The Nazis are gone. We won that one, a long time ago now. Nevertheless, the human rights establishment started shutting up neo-Nazis who don't like Jews, and fundamentalist Christians who disapprove of gay marriage and whiled away the idle moments in between by chastising a few kooks who think the Royal Family are giant space lizards. (Seriously. See page 235.) As I said, just a bit of mopping up en route to the great multicultural utopia.

And at that point Islamic lobby groups figured out, hey, if liberals are so eager to police speech, why not let them? After all, Canada and much of Europe have statutes prohibiting Holocaust denial, and everybody seems to think that's entirely reasonable, notwithstanding the befuddlement of many eminent Muslim intellectuals. "Nobody can say even one word about the number in the alleged Holocaust," says Sheikh Yusuf al-Qaradawi, the favorite Islamic "scholar" of many Euroleftists, and a key associate of the big new mosque in Boston. "Even if he is writing an MA or PhD thesis, and discussing it scientifically. Such claims are not acceptable." And a savvy imam knows an opening when he sees one. "The Jews are protected by laws," notes Mr Qaradawi. "We want laws protecting the holy places, the prophets, and Allah's messengers."

In other words, he wants to use the constraints on free speech imposed by Europe and Canada to protect Jews in order to put much of Islam beyond political debate.

The free world is shuffling into a psychological bondage whose chains are mostly of our own making. The British "historian" David Irving wound up in an Austrian jail because of his Holocaust denial. It's not unreasonable for Muslims to conclude that, if gays and Jews and other approved identities are to be protected groups who can't be offended, why shouldn't they be also?

They have a point. How many roads of inquiry are we prepared to block off in order to be "sensitive"? And, once we've done so, will there be anything left to talk about other than Paris Hilton and Jamie Lynn Spears? Holocaust denial should be ridiculous and contemptible. But not illegal.

If the objection is that hate speech laws would have prevented the rise of Nazism, well, pre-Nazi Germany had such laws. Indeed, as we'll see, the Weimar Republic was a veritable proto-Trudeaupia of Canadian speech restrictions, and a fat lot of good it did.

If the objection is a subtler one - that the Holocaust is a uniquely terrible stain on humanity that cannot be compared with other crimes – that's all the more reason to talk about it openly. Instead, we live in a world where David Irving sits in a cell for querying the numbers of the last Holocaust while the President of Iran plans the next Holocaust and gets invited to speak at Columbia.

The more we hedge ourselves in with "hate speech" regulations, the less we're able to hold any genuinely inquiring discussion on the challenges we face. And once that's the case, as the angry young men in the streets have figured out, you might as well just threaten to burn and kill to get your way. You won't have to do a lot of burning and killing – just give the impression, in a not particularly subtle way, that you're an excitable type, and it's best not to provoke you. That's why the state justifies its need to crack down on Islamophobia by fretting over the entirely mythical wave of anti-Muslim violence - at a time when Danish cartoonists and Dutch parliamentarians and even California professors are in hiding, and French synagogues and schools and kosher butchers are being bombed and torched. In the wake of the bloody kidnappings, torture and mass murder in Bombay at the end of 2008, Mohamed Elmasry, the founder of the Canadian Islamic Congress and the man who launched the three lawsuits against *Maclean's*, produced a perfect if inadvertent parody of the indestructible Islamic victim complex. Here's the opening sentence of his analysis:

> *The recent terrorist attacks in Mumbai, India highlight the dangerously vulnerable situation of India's Muslims...*

Ah, right. So that's what all those Hindu, Christian and Jewish corpses highlight: the vulnerability of Muslims.

The price of liberty is eternal vigilance. And what the Council on American-Islamic Relations, the Canadian Islamic Congress and similar groups in Britain and Europe are trying to do is criminalize vigilance. They want to use the legal system and other routes to circumscribe debate on one of the great central questions of the age - the relationship between Islam and the west - and to enforce silence on the most basic reality of that relationship: the remorseless Islamization of much of the western world as part of what the United Nations calls the fastest population transformation in history.

I'm often accused of being a demographic alarmist, so I'll quote instead one bald line from *Le Figaro* in March 2008:

> *La capital européenne sera musulmane dans vingt ans.*

That's French for "Nothing to see here, folks."

If you're a young European adult, you'll be reaching middle age in a society that's half Islamic and half cowed infidels, and you'll be ending your days somewhere beyond that intermediate stage.

Are we allowed to talk about that? Modern social-democratic governments preside over multicultural societies which have less and less glue holding them together, and they're very at ease with the idea of the state as the mediator between different interest groups. Most of these governments haven't a clue what to do about their turbulent surging Muslim populations, but they have unbounded faith in their own powers, and so it seems entirely natural to manage the problem by regulating freedom in the interests of social harmony.

For example, in *America Alone*, I mention Iqbal Sacranie, a Muslim of such exemplary "moderation" he's been knighted by the Queen. Sir Iqbal, the head of the Muslim Council of Britain, was on the BBC and expressed the view that homosexuality was "immoral", "not acceptable", "spreads disease" and "damaged the very foundations of society". A gay group complained and Sir Iqbal was investigated by Scotland Yard's "community safety unit" which deals with "hate crimes" and "homophobia".

Independently but simultaneously, the magazine of GALHA (the Gay And Lesbian Humanist Association) called Islam a "barmy doctrine" growing "like a canker" and deeply "homophobic". In return, the London Race Hate Crime Forum asked Scotland Yard to investigate GALHA for "Islamophobia".

Got that? If a Muslim says that Islam is opposed to homosexuality, he can be investigated for homophobia; but if a gay says that Islam is opposed to homosexuality, he can be investigated for Islamophobia.

Personally I'm phobiaphobic. The reason I'm a phobiaphobe is that I have a great fear that all these mostly fictional "phobias" encourage the shrinking of the public square and the expansion of the state as the sole legitimate arbiter of acceptable discourse. And because a lot of these phobia-prone identity groups are not equally motivated, the one that wins will be the one willing to apply the most muscle. A while back, Her Majesty's Government in London passed a law requiring elementary schools to teach kindergartners and other youngsters all about the joys of same-sex marriage. You know the kind of books – *Heather Has Two Mommies*; or *King & King*, in which a handsome prince goes looking for a bride, meets three lovely princesses but eventually marries one of the princesses' brothers and they reign happily over their magic fairy kingdom together. When evangelical

Christians object to these books, they're told you uptight squares need to get with the beat. But when the Muslim parents at the grade school in Bristol, England complained, the city council caved in nothing flat and yanked them from the school. It's an interesting lesson not just in the internal contradictions of multiculturalism but in which side is likely to win. If it's a choice between *Heather Has Two Mommies* or *Heather Has Two Imams*, bet on *Heather Has Two Imams* – or *Heather Has Four Mommies And A Big Bearded Daddy Who Wants To Marry Her Off To A Cousin Back In Pakistan*.

That's the way it goes. If you point out that EU prohibitions on "xenophobia" or the proposed British law restricting comment on religion would be unconstitutional in America, the more thoughtful Europeans will respond ruefully that things like the First Amendment presuppose a social consensus that across the Atlantic doesn't exist: It's all very well to say Danish cartoonists should be able to draw what they like, but not if it means people are getting killed and your cities are burning. Yet, oddly enough, the state's urge to coerce self-restraint only applies to one party. If the true believers at the Grand Mosque of Stockholm are enjoined to sally forth and kill "the brothers of pigs and apes" – ie, Jews – well, that's just part of their rich, vibrant cultural tradition. But, if I quote what's being said in the mosque, I'm the one committing a hate crime. Crumbs, I might even do it accidentally. The Archbishop of Canterbury says he wants new laws to punish "thoughtless and, even if unintentionally, cruel styles of speaking". The ever more illiberal liberal state is advancing from "thought crime" to "thoughtless thought crime".

My supposedly Islamophobic book, *America Alone*, isn't really about Islam, it's about us. And the single most important line in it isn't by me, it's a famous and profound observation by the historian Arnold Toynbee:

Civilizations die from suicide, not murder.

One manifestation of that suicidal urge is the willingness of government ministers, judges, police agencies, social workers and other officers of the state to make common cause with an ideology explicitly committed to overturning the liberal utopia they claim to be working for. Up north, the Ontario Federation of Labour decided to support the Canadian Islamic Congress' case. As Terry Downey of the OFL primly explained, "There is proper conduct that everyone has to follow" – and she and her union clearly feel my article is way beyond the bounds of that "proper conduct". Don't ask me why. I don't pretend to understand the peculiar psychological impulses that would lead the OFL to throw its lot in with Dr Elmasry, the openly, cheerfully, judeophobic homophobic misogynist head of the CIC - except that there seems to be some kinky kind of competition on the western left to be, metaphorically speaking, Islam's lead prison bitch.

Oh, dear. Is that "offensive" to the executive committee of the Ontario Federation of Labour? Very probably so. I may well have another "human rights" suit on my hands. Heigh-ho. Might as well be hung for a sheep (see page 269) as a lamb.

Or we could all grow up and recognize the dangers in forcing more and more legitimate debate into the shadows. As the columnist David Warren summed up Canada's "human rights" laws, the punishment is not the verdict, but the process - the months of time-consuming distractions and legal bills that make it easier for editors to shrug, "You know, maybe we don't need a report on creeping sharia, after all. How about we do 'The Lindsay Lohan Guide To Celebrity Carjacking' one more time?"

And, if you do get hauled up before the kangaroo court, bear in mind that no complaint brought to the Canadian "Human Rights" Tribunal under Section 13 has been settled in favor of the defendant. A court where the rulings only go one way is the very definition of a show trial. These institutions should have been a source of shame to Canadians for many years.

Instead, the Canadian Islamic Congress and Muslim lobby groups throughout the west are now using the pieties of political correctness to enforce a universal submission to Islam's self-evaluation. And their multiculti enablers seem happy to string along: Australian publishers decline novels on certain, ah, sensitive subjects; British editors insist forthcoming books are vacuumed of anything likely to attract the eye of wealthy Saudis who happen to have a flat in Mayfair. These are the books we will never read, the plays we will never see, the movies that will never be made.

I said when this legal battle started that I wasn't interested in the verdict - except insofar as an acquittal would be more likely to legitimize the "human rights" commissions' attempt to regulate political speech, and thus contribute to the shriveling of liberty in Canada. I'm interested only in getting the HRCs out of this business entirely, in repealing Section 13 of the Canadian Human Rights Code and its provincial equivalents, and in helping restore freedom of expression to those parts of the western world where it has been ever more circumscribed by the PC-Islamist alliance. To reprise Sir Edward Grey, when it comes to free speech on one of the critical issues of the age, the lamps are going out all over the world - one distributor, one publisher, one silenced novelist, one cartoonist in hiding, one sued radio host, one murdered film director at a time. It's time to stop it and to reverse it, and to relight the lights of liberty.

I

THE CASE AGAINST MACLEAN'S:

A FLAGRANTLY
ISLAMOPHOBIC READER

There is proper conduct that everyone has to follow.
TERRY DOWNEY
of the Ontario Federation of Labour
announcing their support of the Canadian Islamic Congress suits

On December 4th 2007, the Canadian Islamic Congress announced that it had filed three separate "human rights" complaints over an excerpt from my book, America Alone. *Simultaneously, it published a report called* Maclean's Magazine: A Case Study Of Media-Propagated Islamophobia *by five students from Canada's supposed leading law school, Osgoode Hall. The "case study" cited 19 "Islamophobic" articles from* Maclean's. *I was responsible for the highest number, although it was a close-run thing: There were eight Steyn columns, seven by my eminent colleague Barbara Amiel, nipping at my Islamophobic heels. Linda Frum and Steve Maich contributed one apiece, and a pair of staff news reports made up the rest.*

So here are my thoughts on the various examples of Maclean's *Islamophobia – plus the Steyn columns that the CIC and their "human rights" stooges sought to ban from the Dominion of Canada:*

EXHIBIT #1
The future belongs to Islam

T HE PRINCIPAL exhibit in the Canadian Islamic Congress case against me and *Maclean's* was the cover story of October 23rd 2006. It was not my regular column for the magazine but an excerpt from my then new book, *America Alone: The End Of The World As We Know It*. As is customary when a new tome launches down the slipway, portions therefrom are published hither and yon – in my case, in *The New York Post* and *National Review*, *The Times* of London and *The Australian*, and various Continental publications.

Unfortunately, Regnery, my publishers in Washington, also licensed an excerpt to *Maclean's*, Canada's oldest news magazine. I say "unfortunately" not because the cover story wasn't a big hit: It certainly was, generating more reader mail than any other story that year. What was unfortunate was that, in their innocence, my publishers were unaware that the Canadian state no longer believes in freedom of speech. And so, unlike the US, British, Aussie and European publications, in Canada the biggest-selling news weekly published an excerpt from a Canadian Number One bestseller and found itself embroiled in three law suits.

The extract in question was billed on the cover as "Why The Future Belongs To Islam". Inside it bore the more representative headline "The New World Order": The piece touched on a lot more than Islam, including such non-Muslim-related issues as the unaffordability of the welfare state, the lack of obstetricians in Japan, and the likelihood of transhuman experimentation. We're not reprinting the excerpt here because it's available in hardback and paperback in *America Alone*, and it's still posted at the *Maclean's* website for anybody who wants to read what I actually wrote. Not a lot of my critics do, as we'll discover. Sadly, taking Dr Mohamed Elmasry and the Canadian Islamic Congress' word for it led many a pundit astray. If you plough your way through the CIC's long list of enumerated grievances, you'll find that Number 28 objects to the following "assertion" from my piece:

> The number of Muslims in Europe is expanding like 'mosquitoes'.

That's certainly a shocking statement. Here's the American commentator Jim Henley:

> The excerpt from Mark Steyn's America Alone *that ran in* Maclean's *last year is far more blatantly racist than I figured it would be when I began reading it. I knew Steyn was a bigot, with a 1920s obsession with demographic decline. (cf Tom Buchanan in* Gatsby, *who can't stop talking about* Rise Of The Colored Empires, *'by this man Goddard'.) But I imagined Steyn was more adroit in his use of code words and deniability feints. No! 'Just look at the development within Europe, where the number of Muslims is expanding like mosquitoes' is merely the most spectacular example of - not code words. I'm not completely shocked that Steyn would write with such frank bigotry, or that Regnery would publish it. I'm somewhat surprised that an establishment organ like* Maclean's *would run it.*
>
> *Nor am I surprised actual existing Muslim Canadians would take offense at the article. The article can't touch me, an Anglo American, in the same way it can hit the emotions of a Canadian Muslim - it can't feel as personal to me as it can to them... Mark Steyn is a racist douchebag in addition to being a ridiculous figure...*

Etc. The words that so offend him are, indeed "frank bigotry". However, had Mr Henley actually read my racist diatribe, he would have seen that the bigotry is not mine but that of a bigshot Scandinavian Muslim:

'We're the ones who will change you,' the Norwegian imam Mullah Krekar told the Oslo newspaper Dagbladet *in 2006. 'Just look at the development within Europe, where the number of Muslims is expanding like mosquitoes. Every Western woman in the EU is producing an average of 1.4 children. Every Muslim woman in the same countries is producing 3.5 children.' As he summed it up: 'Our way of thinking will prove more powerful than yours.'*

Hello, Mr Henley? Anybody home in there? Those are quotation marks, because they're someone else's words - not the blatant racism of the racist douchebag Steyn but of a prominent imam. It's tempting to say to Jim Henley, "Douchebag, douche thyself", and leave it at that. However, I'm curious to know, in light of his carelessness, what is it precisely about this statement that makes it "blatantly racist"? That a Euro-Muslim imam uttered the words? Or that an "Anglo American" (if I can be said to count as such) was culturally insensitive enough to reveal the mullah's words to a wider audience? If the problem is the "frank bigotry" of the statement itself, he (and "actual existing Muslim Canadians") should take it up with Mullah Krekar. Or is the real problem "Anglo Americans" boorish enough to quote statements made routinely by prominent Muslims around the western world? Are Mullah Krekar's words themselves Islamophobic? Or do they only become so when a non-Muslim quotes them? As my year in "human rights" hell proceeded, the answer to that question became all too obvious.

The complainants want a world in which an imam is free to make what statements he wants, but if an infidel quotes him, it's a "hate crime". It's striking to examine the Canadian Islamic Congress' complaints and see how many of their objections are to facts, statistics, quotations – not to their accuracy but merely to the citing thereof. But, of course, they picked the correct forum: before Canada's "human rights" commissions, truth is no defense. If I'm charged with holding up a liquor store, I enjoy the right to the presumption of innocence and to defend myself in court. But when it comes to the crime of "Islamophobia" all the centuries-old safeguards of English Common Law go out the window.

In the *Maclean's* excerpt from my book, I wrote:

> *In a few years, as millions of Muslim teenagers are entering their voting booths, some European countries will not be living formally under sharia, but - as much as parts of Nigeria, they will have reached an accommodation with their radicalized Islamic compatriots, who like many intolerant types are expert at exploiting the 'tolerance' of pluralist societies.*

Abe Greenwald of *Commentary* responded:

> *So, is that 'flagrant Islamophobia' or a tragically prescient summation of the predicament in which Steyn now finds himself (sooner than 'in a few years' I may add)?*

Indeed. The Islamo-PC alliance attempting to criminalize my book excerpt is the best proof of its thesis.

Am I an "Islamophobe"? If it helps, my colleague at *The Washington Times*, Diana West, thinks I'm a bit of a pusillanimous nancy boy because of the periodic glimpse in my prose of the word "Islamist". She dislikes the obfuscatory suffix of "Islamism". She regards it as a linguistic dodge that attempts to draw a false distinction between Islam in general and a, er, few bad apples.

It's true I do use what she regards as the weasel word "Islamism", but I generally reserve it for a particular strand of hyper-Islam – say, a speech by Osama bin Laden. Islam itself is a profound challenge to any free society, for reasons I explain in *America Alone*, and it's true that in many ways Islam and Islamism function as a good cop/bad cop routine in the pressures they exert on western nations. Unlike Miss West, I find it useful to have a word that distinguishes depraved death-cultists from the generality of Muslims leaning on wimp western governments to advance creeping sharia, Islamic banking, de facto polygamy, etc. They are the phenomena that interest me most, and they're rooted in the very heart of Islam. No suffix.

That makes it difficult to discuss in an age of multiculti relativism. But discuss it we must.

Not if the Canadian Islamic Congress gets its way. Six months after publication, they decided belatedly that they didn't care for the excerpt from my book, and their objections to it formed the basis of the *Case Study Of Media-Propagated Islamophobia* they submitted to the various "human rights" commissions. The authors were five Osgoode Hall law students: Khurrum Awan, Muneeza Sheikh and Naseem Mithoowani (of whom more later), and Ali Ahmed and Daniel Simard (of whom surprisingly little later). Here's what they had to say:

> *Adopting a fear mongering tone, this article focuses on the influx of Muslim immigrants into Europe and North America. It explicitly and implicitly states that this influx poses a threat to the fabric of Western society, to democracy, and to human rights due to the religious identity and beliefs of Muslims in general. Another significant theme contained in the article is that there is allegedly an ongoing war between Muslims and Non-Muslims, that Muslims are part of a global conspiracy to take over Western societies, and that Muslims in the West need to be viewed through this lens as the enemy.*

Several of the CIC's objections I don't particularly disagree with:

> *2. A 'substantial number' of Muslims living in the West share the basic goals of terrorists; one of these objectives is the imposition of an oppressive branch of Shariah Law on Western societies.*

I did say that. Because it's true. In *America Alone*, I cite one poll showing 60 per cent of British Muslims want to live under sharia – in the United Kingdom. If you find that a bit unsettling, don't worry: another poll says the percentage favoring the introduction of "hardline" sharia is a mere 40 per cent. But, either way, that's a big chunk of British Muslims who share the principal goal of Osama bin Laden. The difference is that for the most part they don't want to fly planes into skyscrapers to achieve it: A disagreement about means rather than the end.

3. Muslims looking to commit terrorist acts have a support network within mosques in general, that encourage them to commit such acts.

I'll stand by that, too. Whenever they turn up in court and we get to hear their stories, where invariably were these young western Muslim terrorists "radicalized"? At the local mosque. The objection of Dr Elmasry's sock puppets is not that these assertions are false but that I shouldn't be making them because they offend their tender sensibilities.

However, when they get specific, their "case study" turns plain wacky:

16. Muslims are attempting to colonize the West in a manner similar to that in which the "white man" colonized "Indian territory", implying that Muslims could potentially do to Westerners what the "white man" did to the Aboriginal peoples.

Is that really what I said? For a start the "Indian Territory" comparison is not mine, but the impeccably mainstream analyst Robert Kaplan's. Here's the passage in full:

In Thomas P M Barnett's book Blueprint For Action, *Robert D Kaplan, a very shrewd observer of global affairs, is quoted referring to the lawless fringes of the map as 'Indian territory'. It's a droll joke but a misleading one. The difference between the old Indian territory and the new is this: no one had to worry about the Sioux riding down Fifth Avenue. Today, with a few hundred bucks on his ATM card, the fellow from the badlands can be in the heart of the metropolis within hours.*

Here's another difference: in the old days, the white man settled the Indian territory. Now the followers of the badland's radical imams settle the metropolis.

And another difference: technology. In the old days, the Injuns had bows and arrows and the cavalry had rifles. In today's Indian territory, countries that can't feed their own people have nuclear weapons.

But beyond that the very phrase 'Indian territory' presumes that inevitably these badlands will be brought within the bounds of the ordered world. In fact, a lot of today's 'Indian territory' was relatively ordered a generation or two back -- West Africa, Pakistan, Bosnia. Though Eastern Europe and Latin America and parts of Asia are freer now than they were in the Seventies, other swaths of the map have spiraled backwards. Which is more likely? That the parts of the world under pressure will turn into post-Communist Poland or post-Communist Yugoslavia? In Europe, the demographic pressures favor the latter.

It requires a fairly fantastic interpretation to get that to mean what Elmo's Sock Puppets claim in Assertion #16. But the geniuses of Osgoode Hall Law School are not done yet:

31. Japan will inevitably be taken over by Muslims

Really? Here again is the relevant passage:

So what will happen? There are a couple of scenarios…

Actually, let's just leave it there. For after all if there are "a couple of scenarios", how can either of them be "inevitable"? And, as it happens, the Japanese section is nothing to do with Muslims: it's about, er, the Japanese. As I put it, "Japan offers the chance to observe the demographic death spiral in its purest form. It's a country with no immigration, no significant minorities and no desire for any: just the Japanese, aging and dwindling." The boneheadedness of Assertion #31 alone should have been enough even for the PC drones at the "human rights" commissions to toss out this half-baked report. It's a "case study" not of *Maclean's* Islamophobia but of the basic cognitive skills of students at what purports to be one of Canada's most elite institutions.

Once it became clear that my "hate crime" was nothing more than grotesque misrepresentation facilitated by the multicultural cringers of the PC establishment, I started getting a lot of letters along these lines:

What I don't understand is why you are even bothering to acknowledge Canada's human rights commission. You live in New Hampshire, right? So why don't you just ignore them? No court in America is going to extradite you over this stupid Islamic Congress case.

Well, maybe not - although for a while it looked as if that Saudi sheik might have some success enforcing his English legal judgment against Rachel Ehrenfeld in a US court. But my reader was right in a broader sense: I live in the hills, I have an inexpensive lifestyle, I could afford to write off my Canadian business interests - and my British ones, or European ones, or Australian ones, or wherever the next of these legal assaults arises. But I'm not prepared to give up on free expression in one of the oldest settled democracies on the planet, simply because defending it is a pain in the neck and consumes way too much time and money.

And there's another reason. The Sock Puppets' fraudulent misrepresentations were subsequently recycled throughout the Canadian media with the usual carelessness. I found myself obliged to point out time and again that that line about Muslims "breeding like mosquitoes" was not mine but a direct quotation from Mullah Krekar. Four months after Jim Henley was forced to issue a correction, Naseem Mithoowani (in person, one of the most charming of the Socks) was interviewed on America's National Public Radio and still somehow managed to attribute the mosquito crack to me rather than Mullah Krekar. If she's that bugged by it, why not take it up with her coreligionist?

The man who interviewed Mullah Krekar was a journalist called Carsten Thomassen. On January 14th 2008, he was in Kabul covering the Norwegian Foreign Minister's tour of Afghanistan. That

28

day, he was in the lobby of the Serena Hotel waiting to meet with the minister, Jonas Gahr Støre, when two members of the Taliban killed the exterior guards, forced their way inside and opened fire. Carsten Thomassen died of his injuries at a Nato field hospital. The Prime Minister Jens Stoltenberg called the terrorist murders an attack not only on Norway but on freedom of speech.

I didn't know Carsten Thomassen, except as a skilled reporter who extracted devastating quotes from Mullah Krekar and others. But we owe it to his memory to insist on the truth about that mosquito line - not just because his murder reminds us of the difference between real "hate" and the pseudo-victims of the Canadian "human rights" circus, but because to allow Dr Emasry and his Osgoode Hall sock puppets to bully the media into going along with their misrepresentations is to collude in a lie. And no society that does that can be truly free. Mr Thomassen gave his life. The least I can do is stand up to a twerp like Elmasry and his enablers in the Canadian "human rights" racket.

Aside from my book excerpt, the Sock Puppets' "case study" cited a bunch of other "flagrantly Islamophobic" *Maclean's* columns, including reviews of novels and sitcoms. So here they come – the original articles, in all their Islamophobic glory, followed by the Socks' forensic analysis of their offensiveness. Enjoy!

EXHIBIT #2

Is it already too late for Europe?

Maclean's, April 5th 2006

I'VE HAD A RECURRING experience in the last few months. I'll be reading some geopolitical tract like *Sands Of Empire: Missionary Zeal, American Foreign Policy, and the Hazards Of Global Ambition* by Robert W Merry, and two-thirds of the way in I'll stumble across:

> *With the onset of the Iraq War and European opposition, many Americans embraced a severe anti-European attitude. 'To the list of polities destined to slip down the Eurinal of history,' wrote Mark Steyn in the* Jewish World Review.

Or I'll be slogging through *Beyond Paradise and Power: Europe, America and the Future of a Troubled Partnership*, edited by Tod Lindberg, and find that Timothy Garton Ash's essay on "The New Anti-Europeanism In America" begins thus:

> *In the year the United States went to war against Iraq, readers saw numerous articles in the American press on anti-Americanism in Europe. But what about anti-Europeanism in the United States? Consider the following:*
> > *'To the list of polities destined to slip down the Eurinal of history, we must add the European Union and France's Fifth Republic. The only question is how messy their disintegration will be.' (Mark Steyn,* Jewish World Review, *May 1, 2002)*

If the best evidence of the pandemic of "anti-Europeanism in the United States" is a Canadian columnist writing for a Canadian newspaper (*Jewish World Review* is a plucky New York website that

30

happened to reprint a piece of mine from *The National Post*), that would seem to be self-refuting. A European who wanders along to his local bookstore to sate his anti-Americanism will find a groaning smorgasbord of tracts catering to every taste, including the French bestseller that claims the plane that hit the Pentagon on 9/11 never existed. An American who strolls into Barnes & Noble to sate his anti-Europeanism will have to make do with a two-sentence quote by an obscure Canadian on page 243 of some book sternly warning of the rampant anti-Europeanism all around.

Until now. Two books have just hit the shelves - *While Europe Slept: How Radical Islam Is Destroying The West From Within* by Bruce Bawer, and *Menace In Europe: Why The Continent's Crisis Is America's, Too* by Claire Berlinski. In media-speak, two of anything is just one short of a trend, and Clive Davis doesn't care for this one. Davis is a perceptive commentator for *The Times* of London and, in reviewing Bawer and Berlinski for the *Washington Times*, he sniffed: "What worries me about books like this is that they risk reducing Europe to a caricature in much the same way as *Stupid White Men* turns America into one big Wal-Mart with drive-by shootings."

That's unfair, and does a disservice to both authors. For many Europeans - and Canadians - the *Stupid White Men* school of anti-Americanism is a form of consolation: the Great Moron may be economically, militarily and culturally dominant but we can still jeer at what a bozo he is. Bawer and Berlinski, both genuine American Europhiles, have a serious purpose: in his titular evocation of Winston Churchill's book on pre-war European appeasement, *While England Slept*, Bruce Bawer makes plain that he wants to wake Europe up - and, if it's too late for that, then at least to wake up America. Neither is a xenophobic yahoo: Miss Berlinski "divides her time" - as the book jackets say - between Paris and Istanbul; she has a doctorate in international relations from Oxford. Mr Bawer is a homosexual who moved to the Continent because he was weary of the theocratic oppressiveness of redneck America and wanted to live his life in the gay utopia of the Netherlands. Alas, when he got there he found the gay scene had gone belly up and, theocratic oppressor-wise, Pat Robertson has nothing on some of the livelier Amsterdam madrassahs. Both books are somewhat overwrought – Miss Berlinski dwells on her own relationship with some Muslim lad who later figured in Zadie Smith's hit novel *White Teeth*, and Bruce Bawer is reluctant to give up on the idea that a bisexual pothead hedonist utopia is a viable concept rather than, as it's proving in the Netherlands, a mere novelty interlude; his book might have been better called *While Europe Slept Around*.

Nonetheless, if Clive Davis thinks this is anti-Euro rotten fruit-pelting, that's more of a reflection on the complacency of the Continent's own commentariat. The difference between "anti-Americanism" and "anti-Europeanism" is obvious. In, say, 2025, America will be much as it is today - big, powerful, albeit (to sophisticated Continentals) absurdly vulgar and provincial. But in 20 years' time Europe will be an economically moribund demographic basket case: 17 Continental nations have what's known as "lowest-low" fertility - below 1.3 live births per woman - from which no population has ever recovered.

All those heavyweight scholars who immortalized between hard covers my cheap Eurinal-of-history aside did so because it was so self-evidently risible. Well, it looks a lot less so in 2006 than it did in 2002. The trap the French political class is caught in is summed up by the twin pincers of the fall and spring riot seasons. The fall 2005 rioters were "youths" (ie, Muslims from the suburbs), supposedly alienated by lack of economic opportunity. The spring 2006 rioters are "youths" (ie, pampered Sorbonne deadbeats), protesting a new law that would enable employers to terminate the contracts of employees under the age of 26 in their first jobs, after two years.

To which the response of most North Americans is: you mean, you can't right now? No, you can't. If you hire a 20-year-old and take a dislike to his work three months in, tough: chances are you're stuck with him till mid-century. In France's immobilized economy, it's all but impossible to get fired. Which is why it's all but impossible to get hired. Especially if you belong to that first category of "youths" from the Muslim ghettoes, where unemployment is around 40 to 50 per cent. The second group of "youths" - the Sorbonne set - protesting the proposed new, more flexible labour law ought to be able to understand that it's both necessary to the nation and, indeed, in their own self-interest: they are after all the nation's elite. Yet they're like lemmings striking over the right to a higher cliff.

When most of us on this side of the Atlantic think of "welfare queens", our mind's eye conjures some teenage crack whore with three kids by different men in a housing project. But France illustrates how absolute welfare corrupts absolutely. These Sorbonne welfare queens are Marie Antoinettes: Unemployment rates for immigrants? Let 'em eat cake, as long as our pampered existence is undisturbed.

The only question about Europe is whether it's going to be (a) catastrophically bad or (b) apocalyptically bad, as in head for the hills, here come the Four Horsemen: Death (the self-extinction of European races too self-absorbed to breed), Famine (the withering of unaffordable social programs), War (civil strife as the disaffected decide to move beyond mere Citroën-torching), and Conquest (the inevitable victory of the Muslim successor population already in place). I'd say option (b) looks the better bet for a few if not all Continental nations (united they'll fall, but divided, a handful might stand a chance).

However, if, like Clive Davis, you find Bawer and Berlinski too shrill, try Charles Murray's new book, *In Our Hands*. This is a fairly technical economic plan to replace the US welfare system, but, in the course of it, he observes that in the rush to the waterfall the European canoe is well ahead of America's. Murray stops crunching the numbers and makes the point that, even if it were affordable, the European social democratic state would still be fatal. "Give people plenty and security, and they will fall into spiritual torpor," he writes. "When life becomes an extended picnic, with nothing of importance to do, ideas of greatness become an irritant." If Bawer's book is a wake-up call, Murray reminds us that Western Europe long ago threw away the alarm clock and decided to sleep in.

And, if even Murray's too much, go back to the granddaddy of them all – Gibbon's *Decline and Fall of the Roman Empire*. Recounting the Muslim march on France 1,300 years ago, Gibbon writes:

> *The decline of the French monarchy invited the attack of these insatiate fanatics. The descendants of Clovis had lost the inheritance of his martial and ferocious spirit; and their misfortune or demerit has affixed the epithet of lazy to the last kings of the Merovingian race. They ascended the throne without power, and sunk into the grave without a name. . . . The vineyards of Gascony and the city of Bordeaux were possessed by the sovereign of Damascus and Samarcand; and the south of France, from the mouth of the Garonne to that of the Rhone, assumed the manners and religion of Arabia.*

Hmm.

ISLAMOPHOBIA ALERT

According to Khurrum Awan, Muneeza Skeikh, Naseem Mithoowani, Ali Ahmed and Daniel Simard, the authors of *Maclean's Magazine: A Case Study Of Media-Propagated Islamophobia*, the above is "Islamophobic" because of the following assertions:

1. Intolerance and homophobia against gays has grown in the Netherlands due to Muslims.

2. There will be a Muslim "conquest" in Europe as a result of the local Muslim population already in place

3. Due to the growing number of Muslims in Europe there will be a Muslim conquest of Europe and France. This conquest will be similar to that of the "Muslim march" on France 1300 years ago.

THE ISLAMOPHOBE RESPONDS:

Well, let's just take that first point, as Numbers 2 and 3 can only be known in the fullness of time. In the introduction to the paperback edition of *America Alone*, I returned to the subject of 'homophobia' in the Netherlands:

> *Gay-bashing is on the rise in the most famously 'tolerant' cities in Europe. Chris Crain, editor of the gay newspaper* The Washington Blade, *was beaten up by a gang of Muslim youth while visiting Amsterdam in 2005. As* Der Spiegel *reported, 'With the number of homophobic attacks rising in the Dutch metropolis, Amsterdam officials are commissioning a study to determine why Moroccan men are targeting the city's gays.'*
>
> *Gee, whiz. That's a toughie. Wonder what the reason could be. But don't worry, the brains trust at the University of Amsterdam is on top of things:*

> > Half of the crimes were committed by men of Moroccan origin and researchers believe they felt stigmatized by society and responded by attacking people they felt were lower on the social ladder. Another working theory is that the attackers may be struggling with their own sexual identity.

> *Bingo! Telling young Moroccan men they're closeted gays seems certain to lessen tensions in the city! While you're at it, a lot of those Turks seem a bit light on their loafers, don't you think?*

One can debate the speed of transformation, but that that transformation is underway is indisputable.

EXHIBIT #3

What should I do, Imam?

Maclean's, February 23rd 2006

The second half of the Super Bowl began right after midday prayers. The fans in Khomeini Stadium had performed their ablutions by rote, awkwardly prostrating themselves, heels splayed, foreheads not even touching the ground. . .

AT THE SPEED history's moving right now, you gotta get your futuristic novels in fast, and Robert Ferrigno's is the first in the potentially extensive genre of Islamotopian fiction. In *Prayers For The Assassin*, the fun starts on the inside cover: a map of the Islamic Republic of America in the year 2040. The nation extends over most of the north and west of the Lower 48. Chicago, Detroit and the East Coast cities are ruined and abandoned, Mount Rushmore is rubble, and Seattle is the new capital. Catholics remain as a subordinate class to their Muslim rulers. The evangelicals - the "peckerwoods" - are hunkered down in a breakaway state called "the Bible Belt" (the old Confederacy), where they still have the Second Amendment and the original Coca-Cola formula: up north, they have to make do with Jihad Cola, which sucks big time. South Florida is an "independent unaligned" area, the Mormon Territories have held out, and the Nevada Free State remains a den of gambling, alcohol and fornication. And in the most intriguing detail on the map, there's a dotted line heading through Washington State to British Columbia marked "Rakkim's route to Canada" - the new underground railroad along which he smuggles Jews, gays and other problematic identity groups to freedom across the 49th parallel. I can suspend almost all disbelief at the drop of a hat, but the notion of our already semi-dhimmified Dominion as a beacon of liberty is certainly among the harder conceits to swallow.

36

Every successful novelist has to convey the sense that his characters' lives continue when they're not on the page: An author has to know what grade school his middle-aged businessman went to even if it's never mentioned in the book. In an invented world, that goes double. And in a "what if?" scenario, where you're overlaying an unfamiliar pattern on the known map, it goes at least triple. Saying "Imagine the US under a Muslim regime" is the easy bit, creating the "State Security" apparatus and Mullah Oxley's "Black Robes" - a Saudi-style religious police - is only marginally more difficult. It's being able to conceive the look of a cul-de-sac in a suburban subdivision – what's the same, what's different - that determines whether the proposition works or not. Ferrigno has some obvious touches - the USS Ronald Reagan is now the Osama bin Laden - and some inspired ones - the Super Bowl cheerleaders are all male - but it's the rich layers of detail that bring the world to life. In one scene, a character's in the back of a cab and the driver's listening to the radio: instead of Dr Laura and Dr Phil, it's a popular advice show called "What Should I Do, Imam?" It doesn't have any direct bearing on the plot but it reinforces the sense of a fully conceived landscape. There's no scene set in 2028, but if you asked Ferrigno what Character A was doing that year he'd be able to tell you. If you said "What's Dublin or Brussels like in this world?" he'd have a rough idea.

The Islamic Republic came into being 25 years earlier in the wake of simultaneous nuclear explosions in New York, Washington and Mecca: "5-19-2015 NEVER FORGET." A simple Arabic edition of the Koran found undamaged in the dust of DC now has pride of place at the House of Martyrs War Museum. On the other hand, the peckerwoods retrieved from the wreckage the statue of Jefferson, whose scorched marble now graces the Bible Belt capital of Atlanta. But what really happened on that May 19th? Was it really a planet-wide "Zionist Betrayal"? Ferrigno's story hinges on the dark secret at the heart of the state, which various parties have kept from the people all these years. Car-chase-wise, it's not dissimilar to *Fatherland*, Robert Harris' what-if-Hitler-won-the-war novel, in which a 1960s Third Reich is determined to keep its own conspiracy hidden. And in the sense that both plots involve the Jews, *plus ça change* - in life as in art.

The local colour is more compelling than either the plot or the characters: there's a guy - maverick ex-fedayeen - and a girl - plucky, and dangerous with a chopstick - and a sinister old villain with the usual psycho subordinates. Standard fare, but in a curious way the routine American thriller elements lend the freaky landscape a verisimilitude it might not otherwise have had. Writing into the future, a novelist has to figure out what will have been invented in 35 years' time. Projecting from, say, 1890 to 1925 takes some skill: who'd foresee that telephones and automobiles would be everyday items and that nations would have things called "air forces"? By comparison, from 1970 to 2005, the look of our world has barely altered: the changes are significant but visually marginal - email and computers. Technologically, Ferrigno's 2040 seems little different from today, but he has a persuasive explanation for it: Nothing works unless it's foreign-made. American inventiveness has shrivelled and the country's already mired in the entrepreneurial arthritis that afflicts most of the Muslim world. As one character says:

> *Marian and I used to discuss the fact that the nation is coasting on the intellectual capital amassed by the previous regime, and we're running low on reserves. Islam dominated Western intellectual thought for three hundred years, a period when Muslims were most open to the contributions of other faiths.* This *is the caliphate that should be restored, not some military-political autocracy.*

In a Muslim America, there are not just fundamentalists but moderates and "moderns", and, though the Islamic Republic is a land in decline, it's not a totalitarian dystopia. Ferrigno is too artful to give us an "Islamophobic" rant. If you're familiar with his earlier work, you'll know he's an efficient writer of lurid Californian crime novels full of porno stars, junkies and a decadent elite: in other words, everyday life in the Golden State. At one level, the Islamic future is a corrective to that present. "You were too young to remember what the country was like before, but let me tell you, it was *grim*," a Catholic cop tells the young Muslim hero. "Man against man, black against white, and God against all - that was the joke, but I sure never got a laugh out of it... Your people are big on the punishment part of crime and punishment, and they don't take to blasphemy. I like that. The old government actually paid a man to drop a crucifix into a jar of piss and take a picture of it. Don't give me that look, I'm *serious*. He got paid money to take the picture, and people lined up around the block to look at it. So I'm not exactly pining for the good old days..."

It's not an unprecedented arc: Hitler followed Weimar - or, for fans of *Cabaret*, prison camps followed transvestites in cutaway buttocks. There's an extremely fine line between "boldly transgressive" and spiritually barren, and it's foolish of secular western establishments to assume their own populations are immune to the strong-horse pitch. There's a reason that Islam is the fastest-growing religion in Europe and North America, while, say, the Anglicans are joining Broadway up a chi-chi gay dead end. In Europe, it's demography that's ushering in the Islamification of a continent. In America, Ferrigno posits conversion:

> *Jill Stanton's proclamation of faith while accepting her second Academy Award would have been enough to interest tens of millions of Americans in the truth of Islam, but she had also chosen that moment in the international spotlight to announce her betrothal to Assan Rachman, power forward and MVP of the world champion Los Angeles Lakers. Celebrity conversions cascaded in the weeks after that Oscars night...*

Ayatollah Khomeini's designation of "the Great Satan" at least acknowledges that America is a seducer - which makes it considerably more sophisticated an insult than that of Canadians who sneer at the US as the Great Moron. What gives *Prayers For The Assassin* an unsettling compelling power is the premise behind that fictional Oscar speech. As that cop says, "Muslims were the only people with a clear plan and a helping hand." If it's a choice between the defeatism and self-loathing of the Piss Christified West and a stern unyielding eternal Allah, maybe it's Islam that will prove the great seducer.

ISLAMOPHOBIA ALERT

According to Khurrum Awan, Muneeza Skeikh, Naseem Mithoowani, Ali Ahmed and Daniel Simard, the authors of *Maclean's Magazine: A Case Study Of Media-Propagated Islamophobia*, the above is "Islamophobic" because of the following "assertions and implications":

> 1. American will be an Islamic Republic by the year 2040 – there will be a Muslim / Islamist takeover

> 2. As a result of the Muslim takeover, there will be a break for prayers during the Super Bowl, the stadium will have a stereotypical Muslim name, and the fans will be forced to watch the game in a Muslim prayer posture

> 3. Due to the Muslim takeover, the US will have split into different countries and states. Much of the country will be destroyed, there will be a Christian state, there will be a Muslim state in which will be filled with ideas of Jihad, and Jews and other minorities will have to be smuggled into Canada to escape from the Muslims who will be out to eliminate them

> 4. As a result of the Muslim takeover there will an oppressive religious police enforcing Islamic/Muslim norms on the population, important US icons [such as the USS Ronald Reagan] will be renamed after Osama bin Laden, no females will be allowed to be cheerleaders, and popular American radio and television talk show hosts will have been replaced by Muslim imams

> 5. The Muslim takeover of American will occur in a violent way through a nuclear attack on the US. A copy of the Quran that will survive the nuclear attack will be placed in a War Museum hat will be built by the Muslims. On the whole

this Muslim takeover will be like that of Hitler's and the Third Reich's takeovers Europe; Jews will be accused of various false conspiracies and will be massacred by the Muslims

6. Muslims and Islam are taking over Europe and North America; Europe is becoming "Islamified".

7. As a result of the Muslim takeover, the star basketball player for an iconic American basketball team will be a Muslim. Further, a popular American actress, while accepting an Academy award will announce her conversion to Islam and announce her marriage to the Muslim star basketball player for the Los Angeles Lakers. Her conversion and announcement will inspire tens of Millions of Americans to do the same furthering the Muslim takeover.

8. A Muslim takeover is quite feasible – Islam will prove to be the "great seducer" and will takeover the West. The West needs to return to its Christian roots in order to resist the Islam/Muslim takeover.

THE ISLAMOPHOBE RESPONDS:

Er, no. I didn't "assert" that any of the above will happen. They are aspects of the plot of Robert Ferrigno's *Prayers For The Assassin*. A novel. A work of fiction. A creative art form. My column is a review of the novel. It is customary in reviewing novels to cite aspects of the plot, and usually without litigious Muslims taking you to court.

Or at least one had always assumed it was. Mr Ferrigno's book is a "what if?" novel: What if America became Muslim? It's an established genre: As I mentioned in the column, my columnar confrere on *The Daily Telegraph*, Robert Harris, wrote a novel on the premise "What if Hitler had won the war?" And no over-sensitive Germans took him to court over it.

Khurrum Awan, Muneeza Skeikh, Naseem Mithoowani, Ali Ahmed and Daniel Simard, the authors of this report, submitted it to the various "human rights" commissions on the grounds that *Maclean's* exposed them to "hatred and contempt". I certainly don't hate them, but I do hold them in contempt. They don't have the excuse, as many of the firebreathing imams of the west do, of being illiterate, at least in English and about anything other than the Koran. Yet Canada's allegedly finest law school is turning out lawyers who believe that describing the plot of a novel should be actionable. I wonder how, say, Margaret Atwood feels about that. A few years back, she wrote *The Handmaid's Tale*, her own dystopian theocratic fantasy about an America renamed the Republic of Gilead and under the thumb of a Falwell-Schlaflyesque Christian tyranny. What's to stop a Christian group taking a doting Atwood reviewer - or maybe the author herself - to a Canadian "human rights" kangaroo court? C'mon, you leftie novelists, what do you think there'll be left for you to write about once the plot of a work of fiction becomes a recognized "hate crime"?

EXHIBIT #4

Celebrate tolerance or you're dead

Maclean's, February 5th 2006

OVER IN SWEDEN, they've been investigating the Grand Mosque of Stockholm. Apparently, it's the one-stop shop for all your jihad needs: you can buy audio cassettes at the mosque encouraging you to become a martyr and sally forth to kill "the brothers of pigs and apes" – ie, Jews. So somebody filed a racial-incitement complaint and the coppers started looking into it, and then Sweden's Chancellor of Justice, Goran Lambertz, stepped in. And Mr Lambertz decided to close down the investigation on the grounds that, even though the porcine-sibling stuff is "highly degrading", this kind of chit-chat "should be judged differently - and therefore be regarded as permissible - because they were used by one side in an ongoing and far-reaching conflict where calls to arms and insults are part of the everyday climate in the rhetoric that surrounds this conflict."

In other words, if you threaten to kill people often enough, it will be seen as part of your vibrant cultural tradition - and, by definition, we're all cool with that. Celebrate diversity, etc. Our tolerant multicultural society is so tolerant and multicultural we'll tolerate your intolerant uniculturalism. Your antipathy to diversity is just another form of diversity for us to celebrate.

Diversity-wise, Europe is a very curious place - and I mean that even by Canadian standards. In her latest book, *The Force Of Reason*, the fearless Oriana Fallaci, Italy's most-read and most-sued journalist, recounts some of her recent legal difficulties with the Continental diversity coercers. The Federal Office of Justice in Berne asked the Italian government to extradite her over her last book, *The Rage and*

The Pride, so she could be charged under Article 261b of the Swiss Criminal Code. As she points out, Article 261b was promulgated in order to permit Muslims "to win any ideological or private lawsuit by invoking religious racism and racial discrimination. 'He-didn't-chase-me-because-I'm-a-thief-but-because-I'm-a-Muslim.'" She's also been sued in France, where suits against writers are routine now. She has had cases brought against her in her native Italy and, because of the European Arrest Warrant, which includes charges of "xenophobia" as grounds for extradition from one EU nation to another, most of the Continent is now unsafe for her to set foot in. What's impressive is the range of organized opposition: the Islamic Centre of Berne, the Somali Association of Geneva, the SOS Racism of Lausanne, and a group of Muslim immigrants in Neuchâtel, just to name a random sampling of her Swiss plaintiffs. After the London bombings and the French riots, the commentariat lined up to regret that European Muslims are insufficiently "assimilated". But, in fact, at least in their mastery of legalisms and victimology, they're superbly assimilated. One might say the same of the imam who took my chums at *The Western Standard* to the Alberta Human Rights Commission over their publication of the Danish cartoons.

Racked by cancer, Oriana Fallaci spends most of her time in one of the few jurisdictions in the western world where she is not in legal jeopardy - New York City, whence she pens magnificent screeds in the hope of rousing Europe to save itself. Good luck with that. She writes in Italian, of course, but she translates them into what she calls "the oddities of Fallaci's English", and the result is a bravura improvised aria, impassioned and somewhat unpredictable. It's full of facts, starting with the fall of Constantinople in 1453, when Mehmet II celebrated with beheading and sodomizing, and some lucky lads found themselves on the receiving end of both. This section is a lively read in an age when most westerners, consciously or otherwise, adopt the blithe incuriosity of Jimmy Kennedy's marvellous couplet in his 1950s pop hit "Istanbul (Not Constantinople)":

Why did Constantinople get the works?
That's nobody's business but the Turks.

Signora Fallaci then moves on to the livelier examples of contemporary Islam - for example, Ayatollah Khomeini's "Blue Book" and its helpful advice on romantic matters: "If a man marries a minor who has reached the age of nine and if during the defloration he immediately breaks the hymen, he cannot enjoy her any longer." I'll say. I know it always ruins my evening. Also: "A man who has had sexual relations with an animal, such as a sheep, may not eat its meat. He would commit sin." Indeed. A quiet cigarette afterwards as you listen to your favourite Johnny Mathis LP and then a promise to call her next week and swing by the pasture is by far the best way. It may also be a sin to roast your nine-year-old wife, but the Ayatollah's not clear on that.

Kinky as this is, it has nothing on Fallaci's next circle of cultural diversity - the weirdly masochistic pleasure European leaders get out of talking themselves down and talking Islam up. Beginning with the German foreign minister Hans-Dietrich Genscher at the 1983 Hamburg Symposium for the Euro-Arab Dialogue, Signora Fallaci rounds up a quarter-century's worth of westerners who've insisted that everything you know was invented by Islam: paper, medicine, sherbet, artichokes, on and on and on…

Always clever, the Muslims. Always at the top. Always ingenious.
In philosophy, in mathematics, in gastronomy, in literature, in
architecture, in medicine, in music, in law, in hydraulics, in
cooking. And always stupid, we westerners. Always inadequate,
always inferior. Therefore obliged to thank some son of Allah who
preceded us. Who enlightened us. Who acted as a schoolteacher
guiding dim-witted pupils.

This, it seems to me, is the most valuable contribution of Oriana Fallaci's work. I enjoy the don't-eat-your-sexual-partner stuff as much as the next infidel, but the challenge presented by Islam is not that the cities of the western world will be filling up with sheep-shaggers. If I had to choose, I'd rather Mohammed Atta was downriver in Egypt hitting on the livestock than flying through the windows of Manhattan skyscrapers. But he's not. And one reason why westernized Muslims seem so confident is that Europeans like Herr Genscher, in positing a choice between a generalized "Islam" and "the west", have inadvertently promoted a globalized pan-Islamism that's become a self-fulfilling prophecy. After all, Germany has Turks, France has Algerians, Britain has Pakistanis, the Netherlands has Indonesians. Even though they're all Muslims, the differences between them have been, historically, very significant: Sunni vs. Shia, Arab Islam vs. the more moderate form prevailing in Southeast Asia.

Once upon a time we used to understand this. I've noticed in the last few years that, if you pull any old minor 19th-century memoir off the shelf, the *en passant* observations about Islam seem more informed than most of the allegedly expert commentary that appeared in the year after 9/11. For example, in *Our Crisis: Or Three Months at Patna During the Insurrection of 1857*, William Tayler wrote:

> *With the Soonnees the Wahabees are on terms of tolerable agreement, though differing on certain points, but from the Sheahs, they differ radically, and their hatred, like all religious hatred, is bitter and intolerant. But the most striking characteristic of the Wahabee sect, and that which principally concerns this narrative, is the entire subservience which they yield to the Peer, or spiritual guide.*

Mr Tayler, a minor civil servant in Bengal, was a genuine "multiculturalist". That's to say, although he regarded his own culture as superior, he was engaged enough by the ways of others to study the differences between them. By contrast, contemporary multiculturalism absolves one from knowing anything about other cultures as long as one feels warm and fluffy toward them.

In 1946, Colonel William Eddy, the first US minister to Saudi Arabia, was told by the country's founder, Ibn Saud: "We will use your iron, but you will leave our faith alone." William Tayler might have questioned whether that was such a great deal. The House of Saud used the Americans' "iron" to enrich themselves and export the hardest, most unyielding form of Islam to the Balkans and Indonesia and Britain and North America.

This resurgent Islam - promoted by a malign alliance between Europe and the Saudis - is a much better example of globalization than McDonald's. In Bangladesh and Bosnia, it's put indigenous localized Islams out of business and imposed a one-size-fits-all Wahhab-Mart version cooked up by some guy at head office in Riyadh. One way to reverse its gains would be with a kind of antitrust approach designed to restore all the less threatening mom'n'pop Islams run out of town by the Saudis' Burqa King version of globalization. If a 21st-century William Tayler is unlikely, perhaps Naomi Klein could step into the breach.

ISLAMOPHOBIA ALERT

According to Khurrum Awan, Muneeza Skeikh, Naseem Mithoowani, Ali Ahmed and Daniel Simard, the authors of *Macleans Magazine: A Case Study Of Media-Propagated Islamophobia*, the above is "Islamophobic" because of the following assertions:

1. Mosques are a "one-stop shop" for Muslims looking to wage a "Jihad" against the West.

2. Mosques generally and commonly promote the killing of Jews.

3. Muslims commonly threaten to kill innocents; violence and threats have come to be recognized as part of the Muslim "cultural tradition" and are therefore accepted by Western society under the guise of diversity.

4. Oriana Fallaci is really a fearless and heroic figure who is being harassed by law enforcement for no good reason.

5. Oriana Fallaci is wanted in several European countries for the promotion of hatred and racism against Muslims only because Muslims have ganged up on her and are exploiting the legal system to their advantage.

6. Laws have been made in Europe in order to permit Muslims to win lawsuits by invoking bogus claims of religious and racial discrimination.

7. Muslims routinely launch meritless lawsuits against writers.

THE ISLAMOPHOBE RESPONDS:
From *The Globe And Mail,* April 15th 2008:

Dear Sir,

In his letter, Imam Delic of the Canadian Islamic Congress says that, in my Maclean's *columns, I 'allege' that 'Muslims believe in drinking their enemies' blood' and that 'contemporary Islam condones sex with minors and animals'.*

Er, no. It was not I who 'alleged' that. The latter 'allegation' was made in the 1980s by the late Ayatollah Khomeini, a quite famous Muslim in his day, and the former 'allegation' was made by Sheikh Omar Brooks, a British Muslim, in a well reported debate at Trinity College, Dublin, the oldest debating society in the world.

Imam Delic says these articles were 'scurrilous'. If by 'scurrilous' he means 'the crime of accurately quoting prominent Muslims', then I plead guilty – though I confess I am surprised to discover this is apparently a crime in Canada. But if the imam disputes these and other characterizations, he should surely take them up with the Islamic scholars who made them rather than attempting to eliminate the middle man.

Incidentally, perhaps I might take this opportunity to extend an invitation to Imam Delic and his boss, Dr Mohamed

Elmasry, to be my guests at this year's World Press Freedom Awards in Ottawa on May 2nd.

Yrs, etc,

MARK STEYN

The sheep-shaggery was to become a persistent motif of my year in the vise-like grip of the thought police. Despite the above, the tireless "human rights" apparatchik Pearl Eliadis, pushing back against what she saw as a threat to the entire racket, revived the matter of ovine fornication in a long snoozeroo of a piece in *Maisonneuve* called "The Controversy Entrepreneurs" - a not-quite-good-enough concept she spent many months attempting to plant in the zeitgeist, presumably in hopes of landing a book deal. "The Controversy Entrepreneur" is meant to be me, frantically milking my notoriety, although dear old Pearl seems to be the one who can't let go of the udders. Anyway, here's an excerpt:

> *In December, Awan, Mithoowani and Sheikh - a fourth complainant has since dropped out - filed human rights complaints against* Maclean's *with the Ontario Human Rights Commission (OHRC). The complaints singled out Steyn's article 'The Future Belongs to Islam', which predicts a Muslim global takeover, and* Maclean's *refusal to provide space for a rebuttal, as discriminatory. (Steyn clarified that he was not trying to say that 'the cities of the Western world will be filling up with sheep-shaggers.')*

The sheep-shagging bit sounded a bit odd to the blogger Scaramouche, who went looking for the source. It's not a "clarification" of "The Future Belongs To Islam" or anything to do with that piece at all, but, as Scaramouche discovered, comes from the entirely separate column above:

> *So it appears that it was that late, great holy rollah, Khomeini, who brought up the subject of sheep-shtupping and whether or not, having had one's way with lambikins, it was appropriate to then ingest him/her for lunch. The idea was not, as Pearl Eliadis*

would have you believe, something that suddenly popped into Steyn's mind, 'flagrantly Islamophobic' though she and the Sockies may consider that mind to be. Steyn was merely riffing (and goofing) on the Ayatollah. In which case, maybe the Socky triad should consider hauling the late Ayatollah's mouldering carcass in front of the HRCs, since, clearly, he's the one who had the "dangerous" ideas.

I'd go a little further. Pearl Eliadis' idea of a "diverse" "multicultural" society is one in which it's okay for ayatollahs to riff on sheep-shagging but not okay for others - and she and her fellow "human rights" hacks will be the arbiters of which persons are permitted to raise the subject. Sorry, but that's the death of liberty.

Ayatollah Khomeini was the single most influential Muslim of the last four decades. He was a murderous thug, but at another level he was a ridiculous figure, as any man who issues rulings on when it's appropriate to eat one's ovine concubine must surely be to any civilized society. I reserve the right to make what gags I want to about the Ayatollah, and I reject the jurisdiction of a self-important third-rate plonker like Pearl Eliadis over the jokes of a free people.

One of the pathetic aspects of Canada's "human rights" regime is its prostration before identity politics. At the eventual trial in Vancouver in June 2008, the "expert witness" called by the absent Dr Elmasry's mouthpiece was a Muslim professor flown in from Philadelphia. He testified that he didn't think the Muslim youths rioting in France were motivated by Islam because that wasn't the impression he'd got from reading the papers - presumably *The Philadelphia Inquirer*, *The Philadelphia Daily News*, maybe *The New York Times* or *The Washington Post*.

I've been to the Muslim ghettoes of Paris. I know well what role institutional Islam plays in the local power structure. He's never set foot in those places. In real courtrooms, repeating what he'd read in the papers or someone had told him would be "hearsay", not "expert testimony". But, under the ersatz justice of Canada's "human rights" commissions, because he's a Muslim he's the "expert" on the French riots, and because I'm not a Muslim I can't be, and shouldn't be commenting on it. Just like the Ayatollah can do the sheep shtick, but I can't.

Canadian post-Christian secularists might like to note that ultimately this kind of intellectual apartheid spells the death of rationalism and objective inquiry. And buffoons like Pearl Eliadis are entirely on board with that.

Oh, and Dr Elmasry and Imam Delic declined to respond to my invitation to the Press Freedom Awards, although I'm sure they would have enjoyed the occasion. Happily, the event was covered by *The Arab-American News*:

Steyn Honored

The Canadian Committee for World Press Freedom announced its Tenth Annual Press Freedom Awards on May 2... Runner-up was Mark Steyn, who was nominated by Maclean's *for his article in their magazine, 'The Future Belongs to Islam.' The Canadian Islamic Congress brought charges against* Maclean's *in various human rights commissions across Canada, claiming that the article constitutes a hate crime. The second place acknowledgement by the Committee serves to illustrate the self-defeating nature of the complaint, which has given* Maclean's, *the article, and Steyn publicity which they ill deserve.*

For more on the "sheep shagging" aspects of the above, please see page 269.

EXHIBIT #5

Feeding the hand that bites them

Maclean's, May 17th 2006

FOUR YEARS ago, *The Economist* ran a cover story on the winner of the Brazilian election, the socialist leader Luiz Inácio Lula da Silva. It was an event of great hemispherical significance. Hence the headline: "The Meaning Of Lula."

The following week, a Canadian reader, Asif Niazi, wrote to the magazine:

> *Sir,*
> *'The meaning of Lula' in Urdu is penis.*

No doubt. It would not surprise me to learn that the meaning of Chávez in Arabic is penis. An awful lot of geopolitics gets lost in translation, especially when you're not keeping up. Since 9/11, Latin America has dropped off the radar, but you don't have to know the lingo to figure out it clearly doesn't mean what it did five years ago at the Summit of the Americas in Quebec City. In April 2001 I spent a pleasant weekend on the Grand-Allée inhaling the heady perfume of SQ tear gas and dodging lumps of concrete lobbed over the security fence by the anti-glob mob. The fence itself was covered in protest bras hung there by anti-Bush feminist groups. "VIVA" said the left cup. "CASTRO" said the right. (Cup-wise, I mean stage left.) On another, "MA MERE" (left) "IS NOT FOR SALE" (right). 48D, if you're wondering how they got four words on. That's one big earth mother. I'm not much for manning the barricades and urging revolution, but it's not without its appeal when you're stuck inside the perimeter making chit-chat with the deputy trade minister of Costa Rica.

That was the point: hemispheric normality. As the Bush Administration liked to note, the Americas were now a shining sea of democracy, save for the aging and irrelevant Fidel, who was the only head of government not invited to the summit. But, other than that, no more *generalissimos* in the presidential palace; they were republics, but no longer bananas. When George W Bush arrived, he was greeted by Jean Chrétien. "*Bienvenue.* That means 'welcome'," said the Prime Minister, being a bit of a lula. But what did Bush care? He was looking south: that was the future, and they were his big amigos.

Then September 11th happened. And the amigos weren't quite so friendly, or at any rate helpful, and Bush found himself holed up with the usual pasty white blokes like Tony Blair and John Howard, back in the Anglosphere with not an enchilada in sight. And everyone was so busy boning up on sharia and Wahhabis and Kurds and Pashtuns that very few of us noticed that Latin America was slipping back to its old ways.

Frank Gaffney's new book *War Footing* is subtitled *Ten Steps America Must Take To Prevail In The War For The Free World,* and includes, as one might expect, suggestions for the home front, the Middle East, the transnational agencies. But it's some of the other chapters that give you pause when it comes to the bigger picture - for example, he urges Washington to "counteract the re-emergence of totalitarianism in Latin America". That doesn't sound like the fellows Condi and Colin were cooing over in Quebec. But, as Gaffney writes, "Many Latin American countries are imploding rather than developing. The region's most influential leaders are thugs. It is a magnet for Islamist terrorists and a breeding ground for hostile political movements... The key leader is Chávez, the billionaire dictator of Venezuela who has declared a Latino jihad against the United States."

Even Castro's bounced back. Did you see that story in *Forbes* about the world's richest rulers? Lot of familiar names on there: Saudi King Abdullah, the Sultan of Brunei, Prince Albert of Monaco... But Fidel came in seventh, pipping our own dear Queen. How'd he get so rich? It can't all be Canadian tourist dollars, can it? Well, no. Castro is Chávez's revolutionary mentor and the new kid on the block's been happy to pump cash infusions into the old boy's impoverished basket case. "Venezuela," writes Gaffney, "has more energy resources than Iraq and supplies one-fifth of the oil sold in America." In 1999, when Chávez came to power, oil was under ten bucks a barrel. Now it's pushing US$70. And, just like the Saudis, Chávez is using his windfall in all kinds of malign ways, not merely propping up the elderly Cuban dictator but funding would-be "Chávismo" movements in Peru, Bolivia, El Salvador, Paraguay, Ecuador.

And Chávismo fans are found way beyond the hemisphere. Señor Chávez will be in London this week as a guest of the mayor, Ken Livingstone. The Venezuelan President is on record saying Bush was a "madman" who should be "strapped down" and Blair was an "ally of Hitler" who should "go to hell". What else does a Brit leftie need to know before rolling out the red carpet? Last year, the MP George Galloway was in Syria to see Baby Assad and gave a pep talk to Araby's only remaining Baathist regime:

> *What your lives would be if from the Atlantic to the Gulf we had one Arab union - all this land, 300 million people, all this oil and gas and water, occupied by a people who speak the same language, follow the same religions, listen to the same Umm Kulthum. The Arabs would be a superpower in the world... Hundreds of thousands are ready to fight the Americans in the Middle East, and in Latin America there is revolution everywhere. Fidel Castro is feeling young again. Brazil, Argentina, Uruguay, Bolivia, Ecuador, Chile are all electing left-wing governments which are challenging American domination. And in Venezuela, the hero Hugo Chávez has stood against them over and over and over again.*

At first glance, an Islamo-Chávismo alliance sounds like the bus-and-truck version of the Hitler-Stalin pact. But it's foolish to underestimate the damage it could do. As Gaffney points out,

American taxpayers are in the onerous position of funding both sides in this war. The price of oil is US$50 per barrel higher than it was on 9/11. "Looking at it another way," writes Gaffney, "Saudi Arabia - which currently exports about 10 mbd - receives an extra half billion dollars every day." Where does it go? It goes on Saudi Arabia's *real* principal export: ideology - the radical imams and madrassahs the Saudis fund in Pakistan, Central Asia, Africa, the Balkans, Indonesia, the tri-border region of Latin America, not to mention Oregon and Ontario. But, not content with funding the enemy in this great clash of civilizations, American taxpayers are also bankrolling various third parties, like Venezuela. And there's nothing like increasing oil wealth to drive powerful despots down ever crazier paths (I'm thinking of Chávez and King Abdullah rather than Ralph Klein, but the general rule holds).

What to do? Gaffney proposes Americans boycott Citgo gas stations (owned by the Venezuelan government) and switch over to FFVs (flexible fuel vehicles). He's right. The telegram has been replaced by the e-mail and the Victrola has yielded to the iPod, but, aside from losing the rumble seat and adding a few cupholders, the automobile is essentially unchanged from a century ago. Yet as long as industry "reform" is intended to force Americans into smaller, less comfortable, less safe vehicles, it's hard to see anyone taking it seriously. (As a world-class demography bore, by the way, I don't think it's coincidence that the only western country with healthy birth rates is also the one that drives around in the biggest vehicles: the nanny state can't mandate bulky child seats and then require a young family to drive around in a Fiat Uno.)

After 9/11, Bush told the world: you're either with us or with the terrorists. But an America that for no reason other than its lack of will continues to finance its enemies' ideology has clearly checked the "both of the above" box. It's hardly surprising then that the other players are concluding that, if forced to make a choice, they're with the terrorists. I get a surprising amount of mail from Americans who say, aw, we're too big a bunch of pussies to kick Islamobutt but fortunately the Russkies and the ChiComs have got their own Muslim wackjobs and they won't be as squeamish as us wimps when it comes to sorting them out once and for all. Dream on. Muslim populations in the Caucasus and western China pose some long-term issues for Moscow and Beijing but, in the meantime, both figure the jihad's America's problem and it's in their interest to keep it that way. Hence, Russo-Chinese support for every troublemaker on the planet, from Iran's kooky president to Chávismo in America's backyard. The meaning of Chávez in just about any language is "opportunity".

ISLAMOPHOBIA ALERT

According to Khurrum Awan, Muneeza Skeikh, Naseem Mithoowani, Ali Ahmed and Daniel Simard, the authors of *Maclean's Magazine: A Case Study Of Media-Propagated Islamophobia*, the above is "Islamophobic" because of the following assertions:

1. South America is filling up with Muslim terrorists; there is a "Latino Jihad" underway against the United States.

2. There exists an alliance between Muslims and Hugo Chavez which is analogous to the alliance between Hitler and Stalin, and which can cause much damage to Western world.

3. Saudi Arabia is funding radical and extremist Islamic schools in Ontario, meaning that extremism and radicalism is prevalent in Ontario.

4. There is a clash between Islam and the West; American taxpayers are funding third parties to this clash such as Venezuela.

5. American [sic] are not being as vigorous in the process of kicking "Islamobutt" as they should; the Russians and Chinese also have problems with Muslims, but they will not be too concerned about human rights in "sorting them out once and for all".

THE ISLAMOPHOBE RESPONDS:

On the matter of whether "extremism and radicalism is prevalent in Ontario", I wonder whether Mr Awan & Co would regard this as "radical:

PERSON 3: *What happens, what happens at the Parliament?*

PERSON 1: *We go and kill everybody.*

PERSON 3: *And then what?*

INFORMANT: *And then read about it...*

PERSON 1: *We get victory.*

That's not in the Sunni Triangle, that's in Toronto: Young Muslims who've spent virtually their entire lives in the Province of Ontario. That's a police transcript of the conversations of an Islamist cell subsequently arrested for plotting to behead the Prime Minister. The wife of one, a graduate of Meadowvale Secondary School in Mississauga, wanted her husband to sign a prenuptial agreement requiring the marriage to be dissolved if he failed to commit big-time jihad. That is one serious prenup, but is it "extreme"?

How about this? On the long trail of jihadism stretching back to the rapid growth of the Ontario Muslim community in the Nineties, we find Mahmoud Jaballah, who was banned from unsupervised communications with the outside world after he was discovered to have relayed messages for al-Qaeda before the 1998 African embassy bombings. Is that "extreme"? Apparently not. His bail conditions were somewhat carelessly breached in 2008, when a City of Toronto program for needy families installed a new high-speed Internet connection in his home.

That's always handy. In September 2007, three Muslims were arrested in Germany and accused of plotting to blow up the Ramstein Air Base and Frankfurt Airport. Later that same day, Salman Hossain, a Canadian – actually, make that "Canadian" – student in Mississauga, Ontario, went on the Internet and posted the following:

I hope the German brothers were gonna blow up US-German bases in their country. We should do that here in Canada as well. Kill as many western soldiers as well so that they think twice before entering foreign countries on behalf of their Jew masters... Canadian soldiers in Canadian soil who are training to go to Afghanistan or Iraq are legitimate targets to be killed...

When do I get to shoot a few Jews down for attempting to blow up dozens of mosques in America right after 9-11... why fucking target the Americans when the Jews are better?

An "extreme" reaction to the sad news of the thwarted carnage? Not at all. *The National Post* reports that Mr Hossain does this on a regular basis. As he likes to say, "A merry 9-11, and I wish y'all many more merry 9-11s." He is treasonous and incites murder against Canadian troops in Afghanistan. Yet, as he crows on the website, "You can't charge me for possessing a thought." Which would appear to be true. In Canada, you can charge me and Ezra Levant and *Maclean's* for "possessing a thought", but the "human rights" commissions are totally cool with his urge to "shoot a few Jews". The Canadian Jewish Congress and "human rights" crusader Richard Warman, both so zealous in rooting out the last white supremacist in Moose Jaw, are entirely relaxed about Mr Hossain's multiple postings about "the filthy Jews". Ezra and I are "radical and extremist", but not the wannabe Jew-shooter champing at the bit.

In a way, I agree with the CIC's objections: How can the views of Messrs Hossain and Jaballah be described as "radical" or "extremist" when, in the former case, they're accepted by the Ontario "human rights" regime, and, in the latter, disseminated at the expense of Ontario taxpayers?

EXHIBIT #6

The little mosque that couldn't

Maclean's, February 5th 2007

THE OTHER day I was giving a speech in Washington and, in the questions afterwards, the subject of "Little Mosque On The Prairie" came up.

"Muslim is the new gay," I said. Which got a laugh. "That's off the record," I added. "I want a sporting chance of getting home alive." And I went on to explain that back in the Nineties sitcoms and movies began introducing gay characters who were the most likeable and got all the best lines, and that Muslims were likely to be the lucky beneficiaries of a similar dispensation. And, just as the sitcom gays were curiously desexed gays (butter wouldn't melt in their mouths, never mind anywhere else), so the Muslims, I reckoned, would prove to be curiously deIslamized Muslims. In both cases, the intent is the same: to make Islam, like homosexuality, something only uptight squares are uncool with.

At the time I hadn't seen so much as a trailer for "Little Mosque". But it seemed a reasonable enough assumption that nine times out of ten the joke would be on the "irrational" prejudices and drearily provincial ignorance of the Saskatchewan hicks. And sure enough, if you settled down to watch the first episode, it opened up with some stringy stump-toothed redneck stumbling on a bunch of Muslims praying and racing for the telephone:

"Is this the Terrorist Attack Hotline?" he pants. "You want me to *hold?*"

Well, of course, the local Anglican vicar tries to explain that he's just rented the parish hall to a harmless group of local Mohammedans. "This is simply a pilot project," he says reassuringly.

"Pilot?" gasps the redneck. "They're training pilots?" And off he goes to the talk-radio blowhard who is, naturally, a right-wing hatemonger.

Meanwhile, the mosque's dishy new imam is waiting to board his flight and yakking into his cell phone about how taking the gig in Mercy, Saskatchewan is going to be career suicide. Another passenger overhears that last word, and the cops pull the guy out of line and give him the third degree: "You lived for over a year in Afghanistan?"

"I was volunteering for a development agency," says the metrosexual cappuccino-swilling imam, who's very droll about his predicament: If my story doesn't hold up, he cracks, "you can deport me to Syria."

"Hey," warns the bozo flatfoot sternly, "you do *not* get to choose which country we deport you to."

Fair enough. Never mind that, in the real Canada, the talk-radio guy would be off the air and hounded into oblivion by the Saskatchewan Humans Rights Commission; and that, instead of looking like Rick Mercer after 20 minutes on a sunbed and being wry and self-deprecating and Toronto-born, your typical western imam is fiercely bearded, trained in Saudi Arabia and such linguistic dexterity as he has is confined to Arabic; and that airline officials who bounce suspicious Muslims from the flight wind up making public apologies and undergoing sensitivity training; and that, in the event they do bust up a terrorist plot, the Mounties inevitably issue statements saying this in no way reflects on any particular community in our glorious Canadian mosaic, particularly any community beginning with "Is-" and ending with "-lam"; and that the most prominent Canadians "volunteering" for good works in Afghanistan were the Khadr family, whose pa was sprung from the slammer in Pakistan by Prime Minister Chrétien in order that he could resume his "charity work" and, for his pains, he had to suffer vicious Islamophobic headlines like "Caught In

A Muddle: An Arrested Aid Worker Appeals For Chrétien's Help" (*Maclean's*).

Never mind all that. There is after all no more heartwarming tradition in Canadian popular culture – well, okay, unpopular culture: it's the CBC, after all – than the pleasant frisson induced by the routine portrayal of rural Canadians as halfwit rednecks. One would characterize it as Canadophobic were it not for the fact that the CBC's enthusiasm for portraying us as a nation of knuckle-dragging sister-shaggers reinforces our smug conviction that we're the most progressive people on the planet: we celebrate diversity through the ruthless homogeneity of CBC programming; we're so boundlessly tolerant we tolerate an endless parade of dreary sitcoms and dramas about how intolerant we are. In that sense, the relentlessly cardboard stereotypes are a way of flattering the audience. In the second episode of "Little Mosque", for example, the non-Muslim gals of Mercy, Sask stage a protest against the mosque: every single infidel woman in the march is large and plain and simple-minded. The only white folks who aren't condescended to are the convert wife of the Muslim patriarch and the impeccably ecumenical Anglican minister (although his church, unlike the mosque, is dying).

But in this cross-cultural gagfest what of the jokes on the other side? Well, these are the cuddliest Muslims you've ever met. They're not just moderate Muslims, they're moderately funny! Not screamingly funny like, say, Omar Brooks, the British Muslim comic whose boffo Islamostand-up routine was reported in *The Times* of London last year:

> *At one point he announces dramatically that the September 11 attacks on the World Trade Center 'changed many people's lives'. After a pause, he brings the house down by adding: 'Especially those inside.'*

He didn't bring the house down literally. He leaves that to Mohammed Atta. By contrast, "Little Mosque"'s creator, Zarqa Nawaz, opts for "Ozzie And Harriet" in a chador. The nearest thing to an Islamist firebreathing mullah in the cast warns sternly about how

Canadian society lures Muslims into decadent ways: "*Wine* gums. *Rye* bread. *Liquor*-ish. Western traps designed to seduce Muslims to drink alcohol… The enemy," he warns, "is in the kitchen."

At which point the Muslim women eavesdropping outside joke to each other that, if the enemy's in the kitchen, perhaps he could do the washing up. Boy, I loved that gag when Samantha did it to Darren on the second season of "Bewitched", and it's just as funny in a hijab. This is the point, of course: the Muslims on the show are scaled down, from a global security threat to warm low-key domesticity, to all the same generation-gap and battle-of-the-sexes japes as every other hi-honey-I'm-home sitcom. Miss Nawaz is certainly capable of a sharp line – "'Good-looking terrorist'? Isn't that an oxymoron?" (surely more like a redundancy, considering the number of western women who find Osama dishy). But for the most part she holds off: for a cross-cultural comedy, it's striking that both groups operate to white stereotypes – it's just that the Muslims have been handed the blandly benign stereotypes of "Life With Father". The synopses of upcoming episodes – "Yasir's overbearing mother wants him to try something new – a second wife", "Rayyan and her mother end up on opposite sides of the fence over co-ed swimming" – suggest the familiar issue-of-the-week format of long forgotten, worthily controversial sitcoms like "Maude", the ones that won all the awards and are never in reruns. But here controversies are painless: when gender-segregating barriers are proposed for the mosque, the savvy quasi-feminist women have no problem running rings round the menfolk; the stern dad determined to put his adolescent daughter into her veil crumples without a fight. "Next week confusion abounds when Rayyan has a pronounced bulge in her belly and her brother arranges an honour killing. But it turns out she's just hiding the latest huge edition of *The Oxford Anthology of Islamofeminist Writing*!"

I would love to see a really great Muslim sitcom. After all, one of the worst forms of discrimination is to exclude someone from the joke. Gags are one of the great pillars of a common culture, which is why bicultural societies tend toward the humourless: see Belgium.

(Before you call in a hate crime to the Council on Belgo-Canadian Relations, I should point out I'm semi-Flemish.) You don't have to look hard to find comedy in the Muslim world. In a debate at Trinity College, Dublin recently, the aforementioned Omar Brooks said that Mohammed's message to non-believers was: "I come to slaughter all of you." He meant it, but come on, you'd have to have a heart of stone not to weep with laughter. Warming to his theme, he said, "We are the Muslims. We drink the blood of the enemy, and we can face them anywhere."

He won't be getting a call from "Little Mosque" any time soon. But, on the other hand, he is a genuine practicing Muslim, which is more than can be said for any of the cast of the CBC's sitcom. The Muslim members of Canadian Equity decided to sit this thing out, and so every warm fluffy moderate Muslim on the show is played by a Protestant or Catholic, Italian or Indian. As comedy of bicultural manners goes, it's like a surreal latterday PC version of the old vaudeville act "The Hebrew And The Coon", where the Hebrew was the genuine article and the Coon was played by Al Jolson. So today Muslim funnymen are happy to stand up in public and threaten to drink your blood but won't risk doing anodyne CBC sitcoms. Which is also pretty hilarious when you think about it.

As for my throwaway crack that "Muslim is the new gay", well, Washington isn't like Swift Current. In DC's sleepy backwater, on a slow news day with not much going on, a Beltway reporter picked up on my line and sought a reaction from a local Islamo-bigshot, Hady Amr. Predictably enough Mr Amr denounced my observation as "inappropriate":

"'American Muslims are taking their rightful place at the political table,' Amr said, 'and America needs to come to terms with that in terms of its rhetoric.'"

Oh, dear. You try to pay a compliment and it gets taken as a beheading offence. Zarqa Nawaz has done her best but for most of her coreligionists Islam remains no laughing matter.

ISLAMOPHOBIA ALERT

According to Khurrum Awan, Muneeza Skeikh, Naseem Mithoowani, Ali Ahmed and Daniel Simard, the authors of *Maclean's Magazine: A Case Study Of Media-Propagated Islamophobia*, the above is "Islamophobic" because of the following assertions:

1. Even a small joke ("Muslim is the new gay") related to Islam and or Muslims results in your life being put in danger.

2. The sitcom, "Little Mosque on the Prairie" is part of a campaign to hide the "truth" that Muslims and Islam: that they are radical, violent, and extremist. The intention of the show is to make Islam, just like homosexuality, normal and acceptable.

3. The sitcom attempts to crack jokes about "irrational" prejudices about Muslims. But in reality, these prejudices are perfectly rational and not prejudices at all.

4. In Canada today, you cannot say anything about Muslims without being put into "oblivion".

5. The ordinary Imam in the West has a "fierce" beard, is trained in Saudi Arabia, and is fluent only in Arabic.

6. Muslims are obtaining undue and unwarranted cultural sensitivity from law enforcement (ridiculing of any kind of sensitivity towards the Muslim community)

7. The only kind of activity Muslim Canadians are engaging in, in Afghanistan, is terrorist activity

8. Churches in Canada are emptying out while mosques are filling up.

9. Moderate Muslims are a rarity; Moderate Muslims who are actually funny are an even greater rarity.

10. Muslim comics generally crack jokes belittling terrorist events like those of 9/11.

11. Muslim comics are aligned with the 9/11 hijackers.

12. The show attempts to "scale down" the Muslims from "a global security threat" to warm "lowkey domesticity" ---

64

the show is trying to deceive the Canadian public away from the "fact" that Muslims are a global security threat and into believing that Muslims are just like the average person next door.

13. The real Muslims are "no laughing matter": they believe that they have to kill non-Muslims and drink their blood everywhere.

14. The actors playing the moderate Muslims on the show are not really Muslims. This fact indicates that there are no moderate Muslims.

15. Actual Muslims comics talk about drinking blood and killing non-Muslims, but are not prepared to play moderate Muslims on CBC.

THE ISLAMOPHOBE RESPONDS:

Shortly after the above analysis was made public, the creator of the taxpayer-funded "Little Mosque On The Prairie" criticized the American sitcom "Seinfeld" for "failing to deal with the contentious issue of Jewish settlements in Palestinian territory". Were they still on the air, I doubt "Seinfeld"'s writers would have risen to the bait and done a show about Jewish settlements. However, they might have done a show about being accused of not doing a show about Jewish settlements. After all, it's pretty funny when a famous "show about nothing" gets accused of not dealing with geopolitical issues.

By contrast, "Little Mosque On The Prairie" purports to be about geopolitical – or, at any rate, cross-cultural – issues, and turns out to be about nothing – or, at any rate, nothing more than wafer-thin propagandization. And, for pointing that out, my review became the subject of three law suits. Whereas Zarqa Nawaz has yet to file a "human rights" complaint about "Seinfeld".

A couple of years back, I started having some sport with a fellow called Oscar van den Boogaard. He's a novelist over in Europe, and, while I'm not the most assiduous reader of Continental fiction, my eye was caught by an interview he gave to the Belgian newspaper

De Standaard. Reflecting on Europe's accelerating Islamification, he concluded that the jig was up for the Eutopia he loved, but what could he do? "I am not a warrior, but who is?" he shrugged. "I have never learned to fight for my freedom. I was only good at enjoying it."

This seemed such a poignant epitaph for the Continent that I started quoting it hither and yon. That involved explaining that Mr van den Boogaard is a Dutch gay humanist, which is, as I like to say, pretty much the trifecta of Eurocool. A cheap joke, but it got a laugh. And before you know it Mr van den Boogaard was playing the same function in my act that Elizabeth Taylor does in Joan Rivers'. (I haven't seen Miss Rivers since, oh, 1973, so this may have changed.)

Anyway, what with this Internet thingy that the young people are crazy about, it was inevitable that at some point the Dutch novelist wallah would be Googling himself and discover he was now a household name in Cedar Rapids, or wherever I'd last used him as the butt of my Eurowimp mockery. And so it came to pass. In 2008, in the newspaper *De Morgen*, Mr van den Boogaard noted that he had recently attracted the attention of "*de Canadese oerconservatieve commentator* Mark Steyn" who had derided him as "*een Nederlandse homoseksuele humanist*", which is "*de heilige drievuldigheid van Eurocool*". And he attempted to put my soundbite in context. The column wound up as a sentimental, writerly and contrived meditation on his dad's lifelong service to the Dutch Army, but it ended with what he regarded as the best hope of saving his beloved Netherlands: "*De islam moet eindelijk om zichzelf leren te lichen.*"

"Islam must learn to laugh at itself."

Good luck betting the future on that. When the British Columbia "Human Rights" Tribunal convened in a Vancouver courthouse to try my "flagrant Islamophobia", it devoted the best part of a day to Khurrum Awan's critique of my jokes and "tone". As we see in the above complaint, my throwaway line that "Muslim is the new gay" had not been received terribly well. Subsequently, I tried to explain that I meant it as a compliment, but that only appears to have made things worse. Both the quip and the clarification went down about as well as that University of Amsterdam study into the recent increase in gay bashing by Dutch Muslims, which concluded that "the attackers may be struggling with their own sexual identity". Amazingly enough, suggesting that these Muslim chappies are most likely a bit light on their loafers doesn't seem to have done anything to ease inter-communal relations in Europe's "most tolerant city".

Which is by way of saying that, if Minheer van den Boogaard is banking on the old Islamic funny bone to preserve his Eutopia, it's a bit of a long shot. More to the point, he's looking at the problem the wrong way round. It's not about "them", it's about him – or, if you prefer, us: much of the western world has a big hole where its sense of identity ought to be. As Ruth Gledhill, the Religious Correspondent of *The Times* of London, put it: "It feels as if the soul of Britain is dying." She was discussing a new report projecting that by 2050 Christian churchgoers in the United Kingdom will be outnumbered three to one by Muslims. But the hole-in-the-soul line applies just as well to another new report, on the "evolution" of the European family: The marriage rate fell by 24 per cent between 1980 and 2006. One in five pregnancies ends in abortion. One million fewer babies were born in the EU last year than in 1980. Europe has six million more over-65s than under-14s. Two out of three households have no children...

The first comment on the *Times* story was from "Mark" (no relation), who wrote:

> *I may be mistaken, but I believe that Muslims tend to have larger families. If that is the case, wouldn't it make more sense to encourage/accept more Muslim immigrants?*

Why, yes, it would – if you don't mind ending your days in a Muslim society.

You can't beat something with nothing – which in the end is what those grim Euro-statistics represent. Islam reckons it's one almighty something, and that's all it has to be up against the contemporary west. It's very odd to live in a world where a sitcom review is a "hate crime". Happily, once the new speech codes are in force, we won't have to worry about jokes anymore, and every sitcom will be a show about nothing funny. Islam doesn't need to laugh at itself because it's too busy laughing at us.

EXHIBIT #7

The real women's issue

Maclean's, January 9th 2006

WHAT PATRIARCHAL dragons are left for feminists to slay? Well, according to Rachel Smolkin in *The Pittsburgh Post-Gazette*, "Women make up only 1.3 per cent of plumbers, pipe fitters and steamfitters…"

Golly. Maybe laying pipe is something that particularly appeals to boys, and maybe girls would rather be the hotshot lawyers who sue the contractor for not hiring enough female plumbers: in America, after all, 60 per cent of college graduates are now women. If it's hard to get a female pipe-fitter, it's because they're all at law school.

Both sets of statistics come from Kate O'Beirne's rollicking polemic *Women Who Make the World Worse*, and, whether or not you agree with the title, it's hard to argue that feminism hasn't triumphed in pretty much every battle in every sphere of modern life. The western feminist left are like those Japanese guys in the jungle who don't know the war is over. Ms Smolkin doesn't know the war is over and she won. It's not just that 60 per cent of graduates are female but that the 40 per cent who aren't exist in a thoroughly feminized culture.

Thus, every December 6th, our own unmanned Dominion lowers its flags to half-mast and tries to saddle Canadian manhood in general with the blame for the Montreal massacre - the 14 women murdered by Marc Lepine, born Gamil Gharbi, the son of an Algerian Muslim wife-beater, though you wouldn't know that from the press coverage. Yet the defining image of contemporary Canadian maleness is not M Lepine/Gharbi but the professors and the men in that classroom, who, ordered to leave by the lone gunman, meekly did so, and abandoned their female classmates to their fate - an act of abdication that would have been unthinkable in almost any other culture throughout human history. The "men" stood outside in the

corridor and, even as they heard the first shots, they did nothing. And, when it was over and Gharbi walked out of the room and past them, they still did nothing. Whatever its other defects, Canadian manhood does not suffer from an excess of testosterone.

Your average western feminist lobby group doesn't see it that way, naturally. "The feminism I think of is the one that embodies inclusivity, multiculturalism and the ability to change the world through the humanity that women do bring," twitters Stephanie Davis, executive director of Atlanta's Women's Foundation. "If there were women in power in representative numbers - 52 per cent - I think that the World Trade Center would still be standing."

That's a familiar line. If only your average Security Council meeting looked like a college graduating class, or that room at the École Polytechnique after the men had departed, there would be peace on earth. As an argument, it overlooks the fact that large parts of the world are already, in political terms, as thoroughly feminized as they can get. Robert Kagan's book, *Of Paradise And Power*, explicitly frames transatlantic relations as a gender relationship: "Americans are from Mars, Europeans are from Venus." And, though we live in the Martian part of town, Canada long ago had the hormone treatments and a couple of snips and crossed over to the Venusian side of the street.

Unfortunately, those societies that most enthusiastically aligned themselves with feminist priorities are also the ones that are - what's the word? - doomed. If abortion is, as Kate O'Beirne calls it, feminism's "holy grail", there are more than a few countries that must wish they'd never stumbled upon it. In the Seventies, the average Russian woman apparently exercised her "right to choose" no less than seven times. Today, abortions outnumber live births. As a result, Russia is at the start of a demographic death spiral unprecedented in a relatively advanced society not at war. While its womenfolk have a life expectancy comparable to their Canadian counterparts, the sickly Russian male expires in his fifties. So far, in this first large-scale experiment on the dispensability of men, it appears that, in the broader societal sense, fish do indeed need bicycles.

70

That's a Gloria Steinem line, of course. These days Gloria is - what? 83? 112? - and still looks fabulously hot, but, like *The Feminism of Doria Gray*, it's her ideology that's gotten all wrinkled and saggy. In their peculiarly reductive definition of "women's issues", older Western feminists sound squaresville and younger ones sound kooky. Just before the 2004 U.S. elections, Cameron Diaz appeared on the Oprah Winfrey show to explain what was at stake: "Women have so much to lose. I mean, we could lose the right to our bodies . . . If you think that rape should be legal, then don't vote. But if you think that you have a right to your body," she advised Oprah's viewers, "then you should vote."

The question is not whether Cameron's lost all rights to her body, but whether she's lost her mind. After presenting the 2004 Presidential election as a referendum on the right to rape, Miss Diaz might be interested to know that men enjoy that right under Islamic legal codes around the world - and, given that more countries live under Sharia than did 50 years ago, that means more women have "lost the right to their bodies". Under the Taliban, women were prevented by law from ever feeling sunlight on their faces. Following the country's liberation by right-wing patriarchs like Bush and Blair, there are now, as Linda Frum noted here the other week, more females in electoral politics in Afghanistan than in Canada.

In other words, isn't the war on terror the real "women's issue"? As Ahmad al-Baqer, an MP from one of the more progressive Muslim nations (Kuwait), breezily put it, nixing a proposal to give broads the right to vote, "God said in the holy Koran that men are better than women. Why can't we settle for that?" Why indeed? From the Associated Press:

> Multan, Pakistan - *Nazir Ahmed appears calm and unrepentant as he recounts how he slit the throats of his three young daughters and their 25-year-old stepsister to salvage his family's 'honor'* . . .

Alas for Mr. Ahmed's daughters, that's all a long way away for Susan Sarandon, Gloria Steinem and the other sisters whose contribution to the liberation of Afghanistan was to oppose it. But the "honour killings" are getting closer. In London last summer, the police announced they were re-opening investigations into 120 deaths among British Muslim girls that they'd hitherto declined to look at too closely on grounds of "cultural sensitivity". There's a small flurry - enough almost to form a new category for the Governor-General's Awards - in books itemizing the violence to women, gay men and other approved groups in the new EUtopia: Claire Berlinski's *Menace In Europe* and Bruce Bawer's *While Europe Slept* are a staggering accumulation of riveting vignettes, like the non-Muslim girls in *les banlieues* of France opting to wear veils and other Islamic coverings to lessen the likelihood of being abused and assaulted in the streets.

Which issue will impact more women's lives? The lack of female pipefitters? Or the combination of factors at play in those French - and Belgian, and Scandinavian, and maybe even Canadian - suburbs? Yet western feminists sing the ancient songs of long-won revolutions as relentlessly as drunks on St Patrick's Day: "Have fewer children, later in life," advises Joan Peters. That's the strategy that demographically's delivering western Europe into the hands of a culture far more patriarchal than a 1950s sitcom dad.

"Keep your Bush off my bush!" chanted the ladies on Washington's Mall a year ago at the Million-Abortionist March or whatever it was called. If any of those women still exercise their "reproductive rights", they might want to ponder the likelihood of any girl born today being able to prance around demonstrations in the Eurabian Paris or Brussels of 2030 or 2040 yelling "Hands off my bush!" C'mon, gals! Anyone can beat up post-feminist neutered western males. Why not pick on a target worth the effort?

ISLAMOPHOBIA ALERT

According to Khurrum Awan, Muneeza Skeikh, Naseem Mithoowani, Ali Ahmed and Daniel Simard, the authors of *Maclean's Magazine: A Case Study Of Media-Propagated Islamophobia*, the above is "Islamophobic" because of the following assertions:

1. Muslims believe that Men are better than Women

2. Muslims believe that honour killing of women is acceptable.

3. Many European Muslims are now engaging in honour killings.

4. Non-Muslim girls and women are forced to wear veils and other "Islamic coverings" in France to save themselves from being abused and assaulted in the streets by Muslims.

5. The growing Muslim populations in France, Belgium, and Scandinavia have resulted in a severe threat to women's rights. In particular there is a growing chance of women being killed in the name of honour or of them being assaulted / abused.

6. Feminists and feminism are "delivering" Western Europe into the hands of the Muslims and their culture.

7. As a result of the growing Muslim population in the West, women will be unable to participate in protests by the year 2030.

8. By 2030 Europe will have become "Eurabia".

9. Feminists need to be "picking" on Muslims and their culture as opposed to "picking" on "postfeminist neutered Western males".

THE ISLAMOPHOBE RESPONDS:

Apropos point #5, the relationship between Islam and "women's rights" is certainly a topic worthy of exploration, even if distressingly few western feminists seem attracted to it.

Let's start with the basic premise that developed societies are now absurdly deferential toward Islam. We heard a lot in the wake of 9/11 about various headscarved women and bearded men being pulled out of the airport security line: They were guilty of nothing other than "Flying While Muslim". Okay, but how about being pulled over for DWP – Driving While Polygamous? That's what happened to Mohammed Anwar, who was stopped by Glasgow police for doing 64mph in a 30mph zone. In normal circumstances, that would be enough for automatic disqualification from driving. But at Airdrie Sheriff Court Mr Anwar explained that he needed his car because he has one wife in Motherwell and another in Glasgow and sleeps with them on alternate nights. Sheriff John C Morris ruled he could keep his license. Make it one for my baby, one for my other baby, and one more for the road.

Is a de facto acceptance of polygamy in the interests of women? Clash-of-civilizations types often say that Islam wants to return us to the 7th century, etc, but in fact Muslim networks are very effective at picking and choosing which bits of the modern world suit its purposes. Take arranged marriages. No need to schlep all the way back to upcountry Pakistani villages to pick up your child bride any more, when the marriage ceremony is just a phone call away. From *The Toronto Sun*:

> *Long-distance telephone marriages can be dialled up under sharia law and then used to sponsor loved ones into Canada, Muslim leaders say.*
>
> *Two Muslim leaders have told* The Toronto Sun *telephone marriages are permissible under Islamic law and require two witnesses and imams here and abroad to conduct the vows, which may have the bride in Pakistan and the groom in Toronto...*

THE REAL WOMEN'S ISSUE

The vow takes less than five minutes and a dowry is exchanged to seal the ceremony, Ali said.

Dial 1-800-1st-COUSIN and leave off the "IN" for Inshallah.

There are now forced cousin marriages in Muslim communities throughout the developed world: In 80 per cent of New York Pakistani families, the parents determine whom and when you marry; the rate of cousin marriage among British Pakistanis (57 per cent) and the recognition by Canadian immigration authorities of arranged marriages performed over the telephone are noted elsewhere in this book. There are "FGM resource coordinators" – as in "Female genital mutilation" - in Australian hospitals. In the Netherlands, Muslims account for the vast majority of those taken in to battered women's shelters. Yet western feminists are increasingly at ease with a two-tier sisterhood, in which upscale liberal women twitter about the lack of female pipe-fitters while the women of the fastest growing population group in the western world are forced into clitoridectomies, forced into burqas, forced into marriage, forced into psychiatric wards, forced into hiding – and, if all else fails, forced off the apartment balcony by their brothers and fathers to fall to their deaths, as has happened to a startling number of young Muslim girls in Sweden.

The state isn't much help in such cases. A Muslim advisor to the British Home Office recommended to Baroness Scotland that she scuttled planned legislation against honour killing on the grounds that that these culturally sensitive issues would be better handled informally. Two things strike the casual observer:

i) Western nations now need laws against honour killing

ii) ...but they're too controversial to pass.

The girls can go to the authorities, but there are now many stories of young women under police protection having the addresses of their safe houses leaked to their parents by Muslim officers. Many simply disappear. According to Yasmin Whittaker-Khan, every year 3,000 British schoolgirls vanish: "One day they are in their classroom, the next they are gone" - abducted by their parents and shipped to an arranged spouse somewhere else. According to a report by Kevin Brennan, the minister for child safety, in the heavily Muslim city of Bradford and in 14 similar communities hundreds of girls have simply dropped off the school register, and it's not clear whether the police even investigate. As Ms Whittaker-Khan says, "The police and teachers are often reluctant to intervene for fear of being seen as racist."

But it gets better. If you're a charity that specializes in helping Muslim girls from being forced into marriage, the relevant municipal body in London will withdraw funding because you're insufficiently "inclusive", as happened to Ms Whittaker-Khan's charity. She is, by the way, a British Muslim woman whose mother was the victim of an honour killing.

So apropos point #2, here's what I think a body calling itself the "Canadian Islamic Congress" ought to be concerning itself with. In December 2007, a few days after the Canadian Islamic Congress launched their complaint against *Maclean's*, Aqsa Parvez, a 16-year old schoolgirl in the Toronto suburbs was strangled to death allegedly by her father, Muhammad Parvez, with the help of her brother, Waqas Parvez, for the crime of refusing to wear a hijab. The *Washington Post* headline?

Canadian Teen Dies; Father Charged

Which at least is blandly indisputable. Faced with an honour killing in Ontario, much of the rest of the coverage added insult to fatal injury. Mohamed Elmasry, President of the Canadian Islamic Congress, said:

I don't want the public to think that this is really an Islamic issue or an immigrant issue... It is a teenager issue.

Kids today, right? It's like *Bye Bye Birdie - The Director's Cut*. Yet much of the media rushed to echo him. Canada's Number One news anchor went to weirdly contorted lengths to avoid the word "strangle":

Her neck was compressed, to the point she couldn't breathe.

And a strangely insistent editorial in the Montreal *Gazette* declared:

> *Muhammed Parvez might have been fighting a losing battle trying to make Aqsa wear a hijab, but that hardly sets him apart. Few are the fathers, of any faith or none, who have not clashed with their adolescent daughters over something...*

Hmm. Choking from the stranglehold of political correctness, a Canadian reader sent me the following observation:

> *If the allegation is true, his unquestioning obedience to a culturally enforced dress code overrode the natural love of a father for his daughter to the extent that he strangled her to death to enforce it. Again, if the allegation is true, it is difficult to imagine an act more diametrically opposed to Western values; more filled with hatred and contempt; or an act more damningly illustrative of violence arising from systemic discrimination against women.*

The key word here is "systemic". "Honour killings" were something we assumed took place on the fringes of the map - the Pakistani tribal lands, Yemen, Jordan. They now happen in the heart of western cities, and western feminist groups are silent, and western media rush to excuse it as just one of those things, couldda happened to anybody, and the Canadian Islamic Congress regards a Canadian honour killing as a "teenager issue" that distracts from their complaint against me for suggesting that (some) Muslims find honour killing "acceptable". The day after Aqsa's strangling, the lunchtime call-in poll on Toronto's CITY-TV posed the following question:

> *Do you think society discriminates against women who wear a hijab?*

Gotcha. It's our fault.

The underlying message the press coverage communicated was horrible and heartless: the murder of Aqsa Parvez is an acceptable price to pay for cultural diversity. The best column I read on the murder came not from the mushy relativists at the Montreal *Gazette* and their brethren across Canada, but from a Pakistani newspaper. "A year ago, Muhammad took a passenger to Applewood Heights Secondary School. Perchance, he spotted Aqsa without her headscarf. Since that day, a year ago, Aqsa had been showing up at school with bruised arms," began Farrukh Saleem in *The Daily Times*. He continued:

> *Honor killing is our export to Canada... Here's a fact: Aqsa has been murdered. For us, denial is not an option. According to the United Nations Population Fund more than 5,000 women worldwide fall victim to honor killing. Denial is not an option.*
>
> *According to the UN's Special Rapporteur "honour killings had been reported in Egypt, the Islamic Republic of Iran, Jordan, Lebanon, Morocco, Pakistan, the Syrian Arab Republic, Turkey and Yemen". Egypt is 90 percent Muslim, Iran 98 percent, Jordan 92 percent, Lebanon 60 percent, Morocco 99 percent, Pakistan 97 percent, the Syrian Arab Republic 90 percent and Turkey 99 percent. Of the 192 member-states of the United Nations almost all honor killings take place in nine overwhelmingly Muslim countries. Denial is not an option.*
>
> *More recently, honor killings have taken place in France, Germany, the United Kingdom and Canada...*

Dr Saleem concludes:

> *Who will take the honour out of these killings? Who will expose the horror from under the hijab? Who will protect women from the laws of men?*

Well, don't look to Dr Mohamed Elmasry and the Canadian Islamic Congress, or their enablers in western feminist groups. In staying silent, the latter endorse "second-class sisterhood" for Muslim women. In December 2008, on the first anniversary of her murder, Joe Warmington of *The Toronto Sun* paid a visit to Meadowvale Cemetery in Brampton and found Aqsa Parvez buried (presumably by the members of her family) in an unmarked grave – no name, no marker, just a number: section 17, plot 774.

But I remember Aqsa Parvez, and I stand by what I wrote.

EXHIBIT #8

The church dance that snowballed

Maclean's, September 21st 2006

GULBUDDIN Hekmatyar, later a Prime Minister of Afghanistan and an opponent of the Taliban, and later still an ally of the Taliban, and more recently Iran's Mister Big in the Hindu Kush, made his name in the Eighties, when there were so many Afghan refugees in Peshawar that the Pakistani intelligence service, the ISI, decided to streamline operations and make the human tide sign up with one of six designated émigré groups in order to be eligible for aid. Hekmatyar headed one of the two biggest, with some 800,000 people under his banner. He also has the distinction of being the commander of Osama's first foray into the field. In 1985, bin Laden and 60 other Arabs were holed up in Peshawar doing nothing terribly useful until they got the call to head across the Afghan border and join up with Hekmatyar's men to battle the Soviets near Jihad Wal. So off they rode, with a single local guide. They arrived at Hekmatyar's camp at 10 in the evening only to find the Soviets had retreated and there was no battle to fight.

"Your presence is no longer needed," Hekmatyar told Osama's boys. "So go back." So the neophyte warriors shot a few tin cans off fence posts, handed in their weapons and caught the bus back to Peshawar: mujahedeen tourists who'd missed the show.

This poignant vignette occurs in Lawrence Wright's masterful work *The Looming Tower: Al-Qaeda and the Road To 9/11*. I picked the book up a couple of weeks ago without much enthusiasm, mainly because of a growing suspicion these last five years that a "human interest" view of current events is bound to be misleading. Osama himself seems merely an extreme embodiment of larger globalized trends he's barely aware of. The praise *The New York Times* heaped on Wright for his portrayal of John O'Neill, the "driven, demon-ridden FBI agent who worked so frantically to stop Osama bin Laden, only to perish in the attack on the World Trade Center", suggested one of those artificially novelistic accounts too obviously aimed at getting a sale to Miramax. And most of the Wahhabist fellows over on the other side are too irrational for the psychological demands of fiction: it would surely be as unsatisfying as reading a detective novel where every character's insane.

But I was wrong. The human comedy in *The Looming Tower* is very illuminating. Bin Laden, for example, emerges not as the fearless jihadist and scourge of the Soviets but as a laggard and faintheart with a tendency to call in sick before battle and, if pressed into service, to pass out during it due to his blood pressure. The "nap" he took during the battle of the Lion's Den in 1987 is spoken of by awed al-Qaeda types as evidence of his cool under fire, but it seems more likely he just fainted. In Afghanistan, the local lads were hard and brave, the Arab volunteers they dismissed as "useless".

Had the Americans funded the mujahedeen directly, the Afghan resistance of the 1980s might have remained a conventional war of liberation against the Soviet invaders. But Zbigniew Brzezinski, facing the Congressional oversight of post-Watergate Washington, chose instead to run the operation through third parties and plumped for the Saudis' Prince Turki and the ISI. And next thing you know, a more or less straightforward nationalist resistance had become jihad central. The deeply sinister Prince Turki (full disclosure: he's not big on me, either – "The arrogance of Mark Steyn knows no bounds") used bin Laden's money to attract to Afghanistan a bunch of freaks and misfits from the Arab world and beyond, and their natural tendency to self-glorification did the rest: from the Soviet point of view, the Lion's Den was an inconsequential tactical retreat; to Osama's boys, living in the heightened pseudo-religiosity of jihadism, it was an exhilarating victory, a moment when (as Wright puts it) "reality knelt before faith".

THE CHURCH DANCE THAT SNOWBALLED

When the Soviet empire fell apart a few years later, the bin Laden crowd genuinely believed it was they who had inflicted the fatal blow with their famous triumph at this rinky-dink no-account nickel'n'dime skirmish the Commies had barely noticed. So their thoughts naturally turned to what they might do for an encore. And, having taken down one superpower, they figured the next move was pretty obvious.

Wright's book is a marvellously vivid recreation of a kind of sustained unreality. My talk-radio pal Hugh Hewitt calls it a "genealogy of jihad", and I think that's a very good way of putting it: *The Looming Tower* is a family tree, the chain connecting some weirdsmobile in Cairo with another in Riyadh and then Islamabad and then Hamburg and London and pretty much everywhere. One thing it demolishes is the lazy leftist trope that the "root cause" is poverty. The penniless yak herds aren't the problem. The very first words of the very first chapter are:

In a first-class stateroom on a cruise ship bound for New York...

It's 1948 and inside the first-class stateroom is Sayyid Qutb, the first of a grand parade of privileged middle-class westernized Muslims for whom a mis-wired encounter with the modern world is enough to make them hot for jihad. There's a sad inevitability when al-Qaeda's head honchos are ready to give up on 9/11 because they haven't any Muslim westerners who can pull it off, and just at that moment a Hamburg engineering student called Mohammed Atta shows up. In the jihad, somebody always shows up, somebody middle-class and prosperous and educated and perfectly assimilated except for an urge to self-detonate on the London Underground.

It's tempting to think history might have turned out a little differently had that drunken floozy on the ship not come on to Sayyid late one night or the nurse in George Washington University Hospital not been showing quite so much cleavage. But reading of Qutb's sojourn in America in the late 1940s you begin to wonder whether the girl really did come on to him or if the nurse truly disclosed to him the particulars of what she sought in a lover. His disgust at the lasciviousness of America is vaguely reminiscent of the old joke about the spinster who complains that the young man across the street strips naked in full view every night: when the cop says he can't see anything, she explains you have to climb up on the wardrobe and crane your neck up over the skylight. If you're looking for it as assiduously as Qutb was, you'll find it everywhere.

The title of Wright's book comes from the Koran's fourth sura, the one Osama quoted in a speech on the eve of 9/11:

> *Wherever you are, death will find you,*
> *Even in the looming tower.*

In an Islamist grievance culture, the tower doesn't have to be that tall to loom. The tragedy in Wright's book is that across little more than half a century a loser cult has metastasized, eventually to swallow almost all the moderate, syncretic forms of Islam. What was so awful about Sayyid Qutb's experience in America that led him to regard modernity as an abomination? Well, he went to a dance in Greeley, Colorado:

> *The room convulsed with the feverish music from the gramophone. Dancing naked legs filled the hall, arms draped around the waists, chests met chests, lips met lips ...*

In 1949, Greeley, Colorado, was dry. The dance was a church social. The feverish music was Frank Loesser's charm song "Baby, It's Cold Outside". But it was enough to start a chain that led from Qutb to Zawahiri in Egypt to bin Laden in Saudi Arabia to the mullahs in Iran to the incendiary "Yorkshiremen" on the London Underground in July last year. And it's a useful reminder of how much we could give up and still be found decadent and disgusting by the Islamists. A world without "Baby, It's Cold Outside" will be very cold indeed.

ISLAMOPHOBIA ALERT

According to Khurrum Awan, Muneeza Skeikh, Naseem Mithoowani, Ali Ahmed and Daniel Simard, the authors of *Maclean's Magazine: A Case Study Of Media-Propagated Islamophobia*, the above is "Islamophobic" because of the following assertions:

1. The root causes of terrorism are Islam and Muslims in general: a Muslim's encounter with a basic manifestation of Western civilization is sufficient to fill them with hatred and cause them to become terrorists ("hot for jihad"). Further, such Muslims are not an isolated case: there is a "grand parade" of them.

2. It is very easy to find a Muslim university student from a prosperous and educated background ready and willing to engage in an act of terrorism against the West.

3. Western Muslims actively look for what they perceive as acts of immorality. Therefore they are bound to find imagined signs of immorality and then to resort to terrorism

4. The events of 9/11 were directly inspired by the Quran.

5. There exists a "culture" of grievance in Islam and in Muslims; Muslims do not need much provocation or ignition to resort to acts of terrorism

6. A violent and extremist brand of Islam / Muslims has "metasized" [sic] and "swallowed" up all the moderate forms of Islam and of Muslims. Therefore, there are barely any moderate Muslims or moderate forms of Islam.

7. Muslims despise Western culture: looking at dances and music fills them with rage / hatred which drives them to commit acts of terrorism.

8. Basic manifestations of Western culture, such as a church social event, causes Muslims to develop a world-wide terrorist network.

THE ISLAMOPHOBE RESPONDS:
Most of these points are argumentative, which is reason enough why they shouldn't be the subject of legal hearings. But Assertion #2 – that it is "very easy to find a Muslim university student from a prosperous and educated background ready and willing to engage in an act of terrorism" – is worth mulling over. How easy is it?

In the course of the 2008 Presidential campaign, Senator John McCain, with his usual glibness, maintained that in the fight against radical Islam "scholarships will be far more important than smart bombs."

Really? Even as a theoretical proposition, trusting the average North American college education to woo young Muslims to the virtues of the Great Satan would be something of a long shot, even if one does not draw as one's mentor Sami el-Arian or Ward Churchill, or – lest we forget – Mohamed Elmasry, head of the Canadian Islamic Congress and engineering prof at the University of Waterloo in Ontario. But one doesn't have to be theoretical about it: There's plenty of evidence out there that the most extreme "extremists" are those who've been most exposed to the west - and western education:

Who was the cell leader of the 9/11 slaughter?

- Hamburg University urban planning student Mohammed Atta.

Who led the plot to behead Wall Street Journal reporter Daniel Pearl?

- London School of Economics graduate Omar Sheikh.

Who was Jemaah Islamiah's "Demolition Man", the most wanted terrorist bomber in south-east Asia, and the murderer of many western tourists in Bali?

- Adelaide mechanical engineering student Azahari bin Husin.

Who was arrested in South Carolina in a car packed with explosives?

> ~ University of South Florida graduate student Ahmed Abdellatif Sherif Mohamed.

Who killed dozens of commuters in the July 7th London Tube bombings?

> ~ Leeds Metropolitan University business management graduate (and Hillside Primary School "learning mentor") Mohammad Sidique Khan.

Who murdered the Dutch film director Theo van Gogh?

> ~ Nyenrode College student Mohammed Bouyeri.

Who is the head of al-Qaeda?

> ~ Former Oxford summer school student and punter of the River Thames Osama bin Laden.

To repeat the point made above: It's not about Pushtun goatherds living in caves. It's about the appeal of jihad to well-educated, middle-class, westernized Muslims. If only John McCain were right, and we could hand out college scholarships to young Saudi males and get them hooked on Starbucks and car-chase movies. But right now western education is second only to western welfare systems as a facilitator of jihad.

EXHIBITS #9-19

"Depicting Saudi Arabia in a negative light"

Steynposts, January 13th 2008

THE REMAINING exhibits in Messrs Awan, Ahmed and Simard's and the Misses Skeikh and Mithoowani's "case study" of *Maclean's* Hall of Shame include several columns by my colleague Barbara Amiel. Barbara has been battling Canada's "human rights" commissions since their inception, and is more than capable of seeing off this assault, and the ones that will follow. However, the concluding "hate crime" in the Canadian Islamic Congress isn't a column or polemic at all, but a straightforward piece of reportage called "I Begged To Confess". Written by Steve Maich, it tells the story of the repeated rape and torture of a Canadian citizen, William Sampson, in a Saudi jail. As with much of the other material, it's in the context of a new book – a memoir by Mr Sampson about his experience. Here's what the Osgoode Hall geniuses say:

> *This article is written for the purpose of promoting a book that depicts Saudi Arabia and Muslims in a negative light.*

And "depicting Saudi Arabia in a negative light" is now a crime in Canada?

Well, it will be if the five authors of this report get this way. As a crude display of political muscle, what they're doing at least has a kind of logic. Harder to understand is the reaction of chaps like Garry J Wise, a Toronto lawyer who's taken an interest in the CIC's "human rights" complaints and has been quoted on the story in *The Washington Times*. His shtick is very consistent: Mister Moderate, dean of the let's-strike-a-sensible-balance brigade; nothing to see here, nothing to worry about, folks. "My impression," he writes, "remains that the complaints against him [Steyn] are dubious, politically motivated and extremely unlikely to succeed." This thing'll work its way through the system, and at some stage toward the end of this year or maybe next year, the Canadian, British Columbia and Ontario "Human Rights" Commissions will all decide that *Maclean's* and I should be "acquitted", and that will demonstrate that the system "works".

That may make sense from a lawyer's viewpoint. But it's not how the world operates. As evidence of how the process is ultimately "fair", Mr Wise cited a 2002 case from Saskatchewan, in which the HRC ordered both *The Saskatoon Star Phoenix* and Hugh Owens to pay $1,500 to each of three complainants who had objected to the *Star Phoenix*'s publication of an advertisement by Mr Owens. The advertisement quoted some of the sterner Biblical passages on homosexuality. Actually, it didn't "quote" them. It merely listed the relevant chapter and verse:

Romans 1:26
Leviticus 18:22 and 20:13
I Corinthians 6:9

Nonetheless, that was enough for the HRC, which relieved the parties of nine thousand bucks for "exposing homosexuals to hatred or ridicule".

However, as Mr Wise pointed out, four years later the Saskatchewan Court of Appeals overturned the verdict, and he evidently regards this as a satisfactory outcome demonstrating the robustness of freedom of expression in Canada. He's right, in an extremely narrow legal sense. But in real terms what's the consequence of Mr Owens' four-year struggle? I would invite Mr Wise to attempt to place the very same advertisement as Mr Owens with *The Saskatoon Star Phoenix* today. They won't take it. They've learned their lesson. So, regardless of the appeal, the practical consequence of the Owens case has been the narrowing of the bounds of public discourse in Canada.

I would expect the same consequence from an "acquittal" in these cases, which is why neither *Maclean's* nor I want one. Yet Mr Wise thinks we should be proud of a system which takes four years to determine whether a Canadian citizen and a major provincial newspaper are permitted to cite passages from the world's all-time bestselling book. What's offensive is not the accusations of Dr Elmasry and his sock puppets, but the willingness of Canada's pseudo-courts to take them seriously. To modify Pierre Trudeau, "The state has no business in the bedrooms of the nation. Unless you're tucked up reading a copy of *Maclean's*."

It is especially important for the press to remain free to "depict Saudi Arabia in a negative light" because the Saudi subversion of western institutions is ongoing and insidious. For example, in 2004 Britain's Serious Fraud Office launched an investigation into allegations that the arms manufacturer BAE paid huge bribes to Saudi princes. In December 2006, Prince Bandar, the head of the Saudi national security council, flew to London to see Tony Blair, and shortly thereafter the Prime Minister leaned on the SFO to shut down the fraud investigation.

What happened? *The Guardian* takes up the story:

> *Saudi Arabia's rulers threatened to make it easier for terrorists to attack London unless corruption investigations into their arms deals were halted, according to court documents revealed yesterday.*
>
> *Previously secret files describe how investigators were told they faced 'another 7/7' and the loss of 'British lives on British streets' if they pressed on with their inquiries…*

That's quite a threat from one friendly government to another. BAE was under investigation for, among other bribes, a secret payment of one billion pounds made to Prince Bandar while he was the long *long*-serving Saudi ambassador to the US and a big Washington insider, a pal of the Bushes and Colin Powell and everybody else who mattered. When a company is willing to pay a billion quid - two billion dollars -

in bribes to an individual, it's difficult to know what humdrum restraints such as the law can do. The Saudis, who are the chief exporters of an ideology pledged to our destruction, have pretty much bought up everyone in the western world they need to. The right to be able to publish stories that "depict Saudi Arabia in a negative light" is fundamental to preserving our freedom.

William Sampson did not enjoy his stay as a guest of Prince Bandar's family. As Steve Maich wrote in *Maclean's*:

Much of the book consists of a meticulous reconstruction of marathon beatings interrupted only by Muslim calls to prayer, and meal breaks. Sampson says he was chained up, standing, to his cell door, and prevented from sleeping for days, which led to terrifying hallucinations of giant spiders crawling throughout his cell. He was hung upside down from a metal bar while interrogators whipped the soles of his feet with a bamboo cane or pounded his legs, back, and genitals with an axe handle. Sometimes, he was hog-tied, whipped and kicked. Others, he was punched in the kidneys, and had his testicles squeezed until he wailed in agony... Sampson claims he was dragged to an interrogation room where two Saudi 'investigators' raped him. When he lost control of his bowels after the assault, his attackers shoved his face into the mess and severely beat him yet again.

The Canadian Islamic Congress thinks that printing the above is a "hate crime".

William Sampson is a Canadian citizen, yet, when he was seized, tortured and sentenced to be beheaded, his government entirely failed him. The only reason he's walking around today is because the United Kingdom intervened on behalf of his fellow (British) hostages and Mr Sampson was released on their coat-tails, so to speak. He was sprung by Her Majesty's Government in London, not in Ottawa. Yet the Canadian state that abandoned Bill Sampson to Saudi torturers is now prepared to drag into "court" the magazine that told the truth about his ordeal - on the grounds that five law students object to casting Saudi Arabia in a "negative light".

How about casting Canada in a "negative light"? That's exactly what the kangaroo courts' deference to this totalitarian "case study" does.

II

SOME THOUGHT
CRIMES THEY MISSED

And you know what, if you're not going to allow us to do that, there will be consequences. You will be taken to the human rights commission, you will be taken to the press council, and you know what? If you manage to get rid of the human rights code provisions (on hate speech), we will then take you to the civil courts system. And you know what? Some judge out there might just think that perhaps it's time to have a tort of group defamation, and you might be liable for a few million dollars.

HEAD SOCK PUPPET KHURRUM AWAN
from a speech on "human rights"
Canadian Arab Federation, June 2008

And you know what? The Canadian Islamic Congress dossier on my criminal opinions barely skimmed the surface of my "Islamophobia". I've been writing about the intersection of Islam and the west ever since I joined Maclean's. *Here are some additional hate crimes the thought police might like to take into consideration:*

ADDITIONAL INDICTMENT #1
A terrorist bomb

Maclean's, July 25th 2006

ONE OF THE very very minor aftershocks of 9/11 was how bad the "good writing" was. I don't quite know why you'd commission a novelist to say something about the Twin Towers, but *The New Yorker* made John Updike an offer he couldn't refuse and he sat down and got to it. And, even by the standards of the other contributors that week, it was painfully enervated: presumably, he thought going in for the old primal righteous anger routine would have been embarrassing. As it was, the elaborate avoidance thereof was even more cringe-making, a lot of fussy prettified self-regarding subordinate clauses condescending to their subjects:

> *Smoke speckled with bits of paper curled into the cloudless sky, and strange inky rivulets ran down the giant structure's vertically corrugated surface. It fell straight down like an elevator, with a tinkling shiver and a groan of concussion distinct across the mile of air. An empty spot had appeared, as if by electronic command...*

Etc. Oh, for a monosyllabic tabloid hack! The ghastly false tinkle of all those shivers and groans and curling rivulets, stillborn as they hit the page. We're told that the movies are no longer "real", but on that Tuesday morning a lot of the camcorder footage looked like slightly grittier versions of *Godzilla* and *Independence Day*: the moment of the tower's collapse, with the crowds pounding down the sidewalk like film extras trying to outrun the fireball; or the startled "What the fuh..." of a street-level New Yorker, as high above him in the slit of sky between the buildings the second plane sailed across the blue and through the south tower. The laboured detachment of Updike's prose "as if by electronic command" - reminded me of England's recent poet laureates sloughing off birthday odes to minor royal duchesses.

Perhaps sensing that he hadn't exactly risen to the occasion, Updike has now given us the Big Novel on terrorists, so Big indeed that its title is simply *Terrorist*. The eponymous terrorist - or "terrorist" - is Ahmad, a high school student in a decrepit New Jersey town called New Prospect, who gets mixed up in a plot to blow up the Lincoln Tunnel. And Updike gets stuck into his protagonist from the opening sentence:

> Devils, *Ahmad thinks.* These devils seek to take away my God. *All day long, at Central High School, girls sway and sneer and expose their soft bodies and alluring hair. Their bare bellies, adorned with shining navel studs and low-down purple tattoos, ask,* What else is there to see?

What else, indeed? It's doubtful anyone could write "the" novel about Islam today - it is a faith, after all, that can seduce everyone from Ontario welfare deadbeats like Steven Chand to the Prince of Wales himself. Yet it seems to me Updike has gone awry from the very first word. If Muslims were simply über-devout loners, this whole clash-of-civilizations rigmarole would be a lot easier. But the London Tube bombers were perfectly assimilated: they ate fish'n'chips, loved cricket, sported hideous Brit leisure wear. Updike's absurdly alienated misfit is a lot less shocking than the pre-detonation video that aired recently on Al Jazeera of July 7th jihadist Shehzad Tanweer: he's spouting all the usual suicide-bomber claptrap, but in a Yorkshire accent. "Eeh-oop, Allahu akbar!" Imagine threatening "Death to the Great Satan!" in Cockney or Brooklynese. Or Canadian: "Death to the Great Satan, eh?" That's far creepier and novelistic than Updike's opening: it's someone who appears perfectly normal until he gets in the subway car and self-detonates. As for the revulsion at navel studs, compare Ahmad with Assem Hammoud, recently arrested in a real-life plot to blow up another New York tunnel - the Holland. Mr Hammoud said he had been ordered by Osama bin Laden to "live the life of a playboy... live a life of fun and indulgence." That way he would avoid detection. Pretty cunning, huh? Just to show how seriously he took his assignment, there was a picture of Assem with three hot babes (all burka-less) on a "mission" in Canada. "I was proud," declared Mr Hammoud, "to carry out my orders" - even though they required him to booze it up and bed beautiful infidels all week long. But it's okay, because he was nailing chicks for Allah. So he gamely put on a brave show of partying like it's 1999, even though as a devout Muslim he'd obviously much rather party like it's 799.

Like Shehzad Tanweer, Assem Hammoud seems a more vividly novelistic character than Ahmad. In fact, as that opening paragraph suggests, Ahmad is little more than an Updike-esque aesthetic distaste for contemporary America filtered through some rather unconvincing Koranic prissiness. Here's another example: Joryleen, a black gal who enjoys coming on to Ahmad, tries to get him to ease up on his "purity". "What about all them virgins on the other side? What happens to purity when those young-men martyrs get there, all full of spunk?"

"My teacher at the mosque," explains Ahmad, "thinks that the dark-eyed virgins are symbolic of a bliss one cannot imagine without concrete images. It is typical of the sex-obsessed west that it has seized upon that image, and ridicules Islam because of it."*

Oh, phooey. In the will he left behind after 9/11, Mohammed Atta wrote:

He who washes my body around my genitals should wear gloves so that I am not touched there.

He'd gone to the trouble of shaving off his pubic hair the day before the mission, and the principal preoccupation of his last will and testament was that the old frank-and-beans (if he'll forgive such a porcine formulation) should make it to paradise without being contaminated by infidels and whores.

So pretty much any Islamist terrorist, big or small, is a more interesting co-mingling of east and west than Updike's Jersey boy.

How'd that happen? The author certainly did his research, jamming it in at every opportunity. Ahmad's imam, for example, draws the lad's attention to a "rather amusing controversy over the scholarly dicta of a German specialist in ancient Middle Eastern tongues, one Christoph Luxenberg". A couple of years back, if you recall, Professor Luxenberg suggested that the 72 black-eyed virgins business was a mistranslation and that it was actually 72 "white raisins" of "crystal clarity". "I fear," says Shaikh Rashid, "this particular revision would make Paradise significantly less attractive for many young men."

Westernized Muslims are not without their drolleries. My old friend Ghazi Algosaibi, the Saudi Minister of Labour, may well be the funniest cabinet minister in the world. After some public skirmishing over my plans for the destruction of the House of Saud, he sent me a copy of his novel with the cutest inscription:

To Mark. Ambivalently, Ghazi.

And yet I'll wager there's not a mosque in North America where the imams rouse their young charges to destroy the enemies of Allah by engaging in wry disquisitions on metaphor, symbolism and literary interpretation. "Christoph Luxenberg" is a pseudonym: the author was advised not to publish his scholarly work *The Syro-Aramaic Reading Of The Koran* under his own name on the grounds that Muslims offended by the 72-raisin passage might decide to kill him. What Updike is doing here is imposing the default literary voice of English letters - amused irony - on a world in which it is largely absent and, in its rare occurrences, life-threatening. Islam is very literal: that's one of the problems.

That said, Ahmad is a marvel of three-dimensional realization next to the novel's Jews and Irish (pale green eyes, freckles, red hair, pale skin) and blacks (with names like Tylenol Jones), all tied together neatly and geometrically: the Jewish guidance counsellor's lardbutt wife's sister is a secretary at the Department of Homeland Security who blabs incessantly. And Updike gets Ahmad a gig delivering furniture solely for the purpose of being able to conceal the dough for the terrorist operation inside an ottoman. An Ottoman! Geddit? You can't help feeling that real cells would find less clunky conveyances for cash disbursement and, if they were forced into using furniture, would be more likely to deploy a La-Z-Boy recliner. But an ottoman is the kind of pointedly elegant visual image you need a big-time novelist for.

By the time we reach the end, and the Manhattan crowd scenes with each denizen "impaled live upon the pin of consciousness", the author seems to be recycling discarded metaphors from his 9/11 dispatch. Two years ago, a first-time novelist, Lorraine Adams, wrote a book called *Harbor* about Algerian illegal immigrants in Boston (and, briefly, Montreal). Like Updike, Miss Adams tells the story from the Muslim fellow's point of view, and sympathetically. But, unlike him, she brings to life a weird particular world in which innocent acts - frequent visits to a storage locker - can attract all the wrong kind of attention. In its artifice of self-delusion, Updike's book is enough to make one despair of the novelist's art: this is one of the most numbingly inadequate attempts to engage a major subject I've ever read. Or, as he'd say, its strange inky rivulets fall straight down like an elevator.

* Raisin questions

If you think it's the "sex-obsessed west" that's hung up on the 72 virgins, consider this sales pitch by the leading Saudi cleric Omar al-Sweilem. Obviously, when the alternative is a Saturday night out in Riyadh, many young lads are tempted by the idea of strapping on the old plastics explosives and self-detonating their way to the virgin jackpot. But how hot are our 72 cuties likely to be? Imam al-Sweilem, while stopping short of offering a

"Your body parts back if not fully satisfied" guarantee, is nevertheless very reassuring on the general quality control:

> Harith Ibn Al-Muhasibi told us what would happen when we meet the black-eyed virgin with her black hair and white face - praised be He who created night and day.
>
> What hair! What a chest! What a mouth! What cheeks! What a figure! What breasts! What thighs! What legs! What whiteness! What softness! Without any creams - no Nivea, no Vaseline. No nothing..!
>
> When they get hold of you, they will push you onto your back, on the musk cushions. They will push you onto your back, Jamal! Allah Akbar! I wish this on all people present here... Another one would press her cheek against yours, yet another would press her chest against yours, and the others would await their turn. There is no god but Allah.

Hoo-boy, it's heaven as an Eliot Spitzer-class bordello, like an eternal reservation in Room 817 at the Mayflower - but with a complimentary mini-bar:

> He told us that one black-eyed virgin would give you a glass of wine. Wine in Paradise is a reward for your good deeds. The wine of this world is destructive, but not the wine of the world to come.

Hold the raisins.

ADDITIONAL INDICTMENT #2
Skank battles

Maclean's, February 8th 2007

THE ENEMY At Home: The Cultural Left And Its Responsibility For 9/11 is the geopolitical *If I Did It*. As you may recall, that was the title of the artful tome by OJ Simpson no sooner announced than yanked from the warehouses and pulped by its publisher. But its general thrust was: OJ isn't saying he did do it but if he had done it he'd have done it like this. Likewise, Dinesh D'Souza's new book: he's not saying he wants a gig as the jihad's marketing consultant but, if he were, this is pretty much the critique of America he'd have offered to buck up the lads in the cave on September 10th 2001.

It's impressive stuff. Why do they hate us? Hey, that's easy. D'Souza has rounded up a ton of denunciations of the Great Satan's appetite for "fornication, homosexuality, intoxicants, gambling, and trading with interest" (to cite Osama bin Laden himself). Quote after quote about America's godless sodomites jostle on the page like eye-catching young lads in a San Francisco bathhouse on a Saturday night in 1978: Human rights for homosexuals? "What human? What rights?" scoffs a columnist for the Egyptian newspaper *Al Akhbar*. After a couple of pages of such zingers, D'Souza usually feels obliged to distance himself:

However uncharitable these sentiments...

And occasionally one can almost hear his editor at Doubleday urging the author to make the distancing a little less perfunctory:

However uncharitable these sentiments – and I find them appallingly so...

Much better! Distance-wise, that's a good foot and a half. D'Souza's publisher has taken out advertisements at US conservative magazines under the slogan "Let The Debate Begin", but debate-wise his conservative confrères seem to have stampeded for the cone of silence. So let me tiptoe in. D'Souza lays his argument out on page one:

"The cultural left and its allies in Congress, the media, Hollywood, the nonprofit sector, and the universities are the primary cause of the volcano of anger toward America that is erupting from the Islamic world... Without the cultural left, 9/11 would not have happened." American conservatives should understand that "moderate Muslims" around the world are their natural allies in resisting "the enemy at home".

Er, okay. Before we get to that, let's acknowledge what D'Souza gets right. He's correct to bemoan what he calls the "ethnocentrism" of much western analysis of Islam. Take Patty Murray, Washington State's senator (Democratic), and her bizarre assertion that Osama bin Laden's popularity is due to EU-Canadian-sized social-welfare programs:

He's been out in these countries for decades, building schools, building roads, building infrastructure, building daycare facilities, building health-care facilities, and the people are extremely grateful.

This is not just, as they say in Britain, bollocks on stilts but bollocks on such dizzying stilts as to put Senator Murray's head way up in cloud-cuckoo land. Al-Qaeda has never built a single "daycare facility", and they never will. Why? Because they believe Islam, like most traditional societies (including ours, until a generation or two back) already has a perfectly good "daycare facility": the home. For a mother to leave her children to be raised by strangers while she goes to work at the convenience store would not strike most Muslims as societal progress. Maybe they're wrong, maybe they're right. But we ought at least to see the difference. Especially if we're one of only a hundred out of 300 million people who get to be a US senator.

Patty Murray was a relatively lonely cheerleader for Osama bin Laden's daycare program. But D'Souza identifies a much more widespread and dangerous form of "ethnocentrism" in the photographs from Abu Ghraib. For hysterical liberal ninnies, this was (and remains) a shocking exposé of torture. The question for western commentators was very simple: How far up the chain of command did authorization for these revolting techniques go? Faced with a guy being led around on a dog collar with female panties on his head and a banana sticking out his butt, the anti-war crowd wanted to know whether the Attorney-General had issued a memo on the use of tropical fruits in interrogation techniques and whether there was a smoking-gun invoice at the Pentagon revealing massive bulk purchases from Victoria's Secret. The larkier conservative commentators scoffed: Anyone who'd spent ten minutes in an Iraqi – or Syrian or Egyptian or Saudi or Yemeni – prison would not regard the Abu Ghraib scenes as torture.

We scoffers were only half-right. In the Arab world, the "shocking exposé of torture" was shocking not because it was torture but because it exposed something worse. "Most Muslims did not view it as a torture story at all," writes D'Souza. "Abu Ghraib was one of Saddam Hussein's most notorious prisons. Tens of thousands of people were held there and many were subject to indescribable beatings and abuse. Twice a week, there were hangings outside the prison. This is what Muslims mean by torture, not the lights-on, lights-off version that American liberals are so indignant about... The main focus of Islamic disgust was what Muslims perceived as extreme sexual perversion." Saddam's guards pulling out your fingernails is torture. But a nobody like Lynndie England, a female soldier and adulteress, boozed up and knocked up and posing naked for photographs with paralytic casual acquaintances and making men masturbate in front of her and e-mailing the photographs all over the Internet... To Muslims, all that represented something far darker than a psycho dictator:

"It was just for fun," reported Paul Arthur, the military investigator who interviewed Private England. "They didn't think it was a big deal." To the Muslim world, that's the point: a society whose army recruits drunken pregnant adulterous fornicating exhibitionist women, and it's no big deal.

When the Ayatollah Khomeini dubbed America "the Great Satan", he was making a far more perceptive critique than Canadians and Europeans who dismiss the US as the Great Moron. Satan is a seducer, and so is America. And, when Muslims see Lynndie England, they don't like where that leads.

I agree, up to a point. Remember a year or two back when Janet Jackson's nipple put in an appearance at the Super Bowl? Everyone was affronted, and the Federal Communications Commission launched an investigation. But it wasn't the nipple. I like nipples. Bring 'em on. The more the merrier. What struck me about the Super Bowl "entertainment" was how hollow and joyless and mechanical it was in the 20 minutes leading up to the offending nipple. It was sleazy and trashy when it was still fully clothed. I'm with that *Maclean's* cover story on our skanky tweens: the sensibility of much of our pop culture is loathsome and degrading. D'Souza makes a shrewd observation about pornography: Every society has it, but you used to have to pull your hat down and turn your collar up and skulk off to the seedy part of town. Now it's provided as a service in your hotel room by every major chain. That's a small sign of a big shift.

Where I part company is in his belief that this will make any difference to the war on terror. In what feels like a slightly dishonest passage, the author devotes considerable space to the writings of Sayyid Qutb, the intellectual progenitor of what passes for modern Islamist "thought". "Qutb became fiercely anti-American after living in the United States," writes D'Souza without once mentioning where or when this occurred: New York in the disco era? San Francisco in the summer of love? No. It was 1949 – the year when America's lascivious debauched popular culture produced Doris Day, "Rudolph The Red-Nosed Reindeer" and *South Pacific*. And the throbbing pulsating nerve center of this sewer of sin was Greeley, Colorado, where Sayyid Qutb went to a dance: "The room convulsed with the feverish music from the gramophone. Dancing naked legs filled the hall, arms draped around the waists, chests met chests, lips met lips…"

As I wrote in *Maclean's* a couple of months back: "In 1949, Greeley, Colorado, was dry. The dance was a church social. The feverish music was Frank Loesser's charm song 'Baby, It's Cold Outside'…" Esther Williams and Ricardo Montalban introduced it in the film *Neptune's Daughter*.

Look, if it would persuade 'em to hang up the old suicide-bomber belts, I'd lay off the Tupac CDs and Charlie Sheen sitcoms and Britney Spears navel piercings. But you'll have to prise "Baby, It's Cold Outside" from my cold dead hands and my dancing naked legs. As I said back then, "A world without 'Baby, It's Cold Outside' will be very cold indeed."

From a sophisticated writer, the central proposition of this book is absurd - that western conservatives should make common cause with "moderate Muslims". That would be merely the inversion of the freakshow alliance between the godless left and the jihadists embodied by the participation in one of the big "anti-war" rallies of a group called "Queers For Palestine". "Moderate" Islam is preferable to jihadism, has many admirable qualities and many less so. But attempting to align our social values with theirs would be the right's strain of appeasement and just as doomed. The reality is that Islam sees our decadence not as a threat but as an opportunity. For the west to reverse the gains of the cultural left would not endear us to Islam but it would make us better suited to resisting its depradations. However, the rationale ought to be that cultural decadence is bad for us in absolute terms, not because it makes Muslims despise us. We should reject Britney because she's rubbish not as a geopolitical peace offering.

ADDITIONAL INDICTMENT #3

The silence of the artistic lambs

Maclean's, November 22nd 2007

HERE IS PART of the opening chapter of Daniel Silva's new novel *The Secret Servant*: Professor Solomon Rosner, a Dutch Jew and author of a study on "the Islamic conquest of the West", is making his way down the Staalstraat in Amsterdam, dawdling in the window of his favourite pastry shop, when he feels a tug at his sleeve:

> *He saw the gun only in the abstract. In the narrow street the shots reverberated like cannon fire. He collapsed onto the cobblestones and watched helplessly as his killer drew a long knife from the inside of his coveralls. The slaughter was ritual, just as the imams had decreed it should be. No one intervened - hardly surprising, thought Rosner, for intervention would have been intolerant - and no one thought to comfort him as he lay dying. Only the bells spoke to him.*

They ring from the tower of the Zuiderkirk church, long since converted into a government housing office:

> *'A church without faithful,' they seemed to be saying, 'in a city without God.'*

Obviously, Professor Rosner is an invented character playing his role in an invented plot. But, equally obviously, his death on the streets of a Dutch city echoes the murder in similar circumstances of a real Dutchman for the same provocation as the fictional professor: giving offence to Islam. Theo van Gogh made a movie called

Submission, an eye-catching take on Islam's treatment of women that caught the eye of men whose critiques of motion pictures go rather further than two thumbs up or down. So, in the *soi-disant* most tolerant country in Europe, a filmmaker was killed for making a film - and at the next Academy Awards, the poseur dissenters of Hollywood were too busy congratulating themselves on their bravery in standing up to the Bushitler even to name-check their poor dead colleague in the weepy Oscar montage of the year's deceased. In contrast to Hollywood's self-absorbed "artists", Daniel Silva has noted what is happening in Europe and thinks it worth making art from - reshaping, distilling, enlarging, to capture a moment. Professor Rosner's murderer is a man called Muhammad Hamza, a house painter from north Amsterdam. As one intelligence chief explains:

> *The Amsterdam police found a videotape inside Hamza's apartment after his arrest. It was shot the morning of Rosner's murder. On it Hamza calmly says that today would be the day he killed his Jew.*

That line echoes the headlines, too. Almost four years ago, a 23-year old Parisian disc jockey called Sebastien Selam was heading off to work when he was jumped in the parking garage by his Muslim neighbour Adel. Selam's throat was slit twice, his face was ripped off with a fork, and his eyes were gouged out. And then Adel climbed the stairs of the apartment house dripping blood and yelling, "I have killed my Jew. I will go to heaven."

Western Europe is undergoing a remarkable transformation, and it's hardly surprising that Daniel Silva should want to novelize it. In my own more prosaic way, I published a book a year ago on the same theme which the executive honchos at *Maclean's* were pleased to excerpt in these pages as a cover story called "The Future Belongs To Islam". The title is not overstated: given the demographic wind behind Islam, insofar as Germany and France and Britain and the Low Countries and Scandinavia have a future, it will be principally determined by the mediation between a resurgent Islam and a declining ethnic European population, and also by the mediation between so-called "radical Islam" and so-called "moderate Muslims". As the late Mr van Gogh and the late Mr Selam might tell you if they could, the cross-cultural exchange doesn't always go as well as it might. But, even when it's not homicidal, it's still arresting, and transformative. Let me give you a small example, from last week's London *Evening Standard*:

Women Get 'Virginity Fix' NHS Operations In Muslim-Driven Trend.

Sex, Islam and government health care, all in one convenient headline! According to one expert cited in the story, Muslim girls are "modern and they have adventures like other Europeans". Which sounds good, doesn't it? Soon they'll be so assimilated they'll be indistinguishable from any old homegrown Britneyfied teen slattern. Alas, as the expert continues, "But on the other hand, fundamentalism is spreading and these girls are getting sent back to their countries of origin to marry. And they will be rejected if it is found out that they are not virgins."

Solution? Free "hymen replacement". And, needless to say, all the politicians interviewed by the reporter see it mainly as a question of whether it's appropriate for this procedure to be provided by Britain's National Health Service. "What nobody would understand is if taxpayers' money is being used to fund operations of this kind," says Tory health spokesman Mike Penning. "I don't think it should be available on the NHS," agrees Labour MP Ann Cryer.

Heigh-ho. Best to see "hymen reconstruction" as purely a matter of budgetary overstretch. Long-term, incremental, remorseless, profound cultural change is the hardest for democratic legislators to address, especially when it requires them to march into areas where your average squeamish politician would rather not tiptoe. Yet the silence of the artistic lambs is more puzzling. The English novelist Martin Amis has found himself drawn to the subject and, for his pains, has been all but disowned by the London literary set. (Full disclosure:

Mr Amis agrees with the premise of my book but thinks I'm a crap writer. Or, as he put it, Steyn's "thoughts and themes are sane and serious - but he writes like a maniac.") But, even if you disagree with Amis, wouldn't you at least agree that something big and transformative is underway? Graham Greene, for one, would surely have had something to say. As he wrote in *The Lawless Roads*:

The border means more than a customs house, a passport officer, a man with a gun. Over there everything is going to be different; life is never going to be quite the same again after your passport has been stamped and you find yourself speechless among the money-changers. The man seeking scenery imagines strange woods and unheard-of mountains; the romantic believes that the women over the border will be more beautiful and complaisant than those at home; the unhappy man imagines at least a different hell...

All true, when you see the border post ahead of you down the road, or when the customs inspector demands "Your papers, *mein herr*." But what if instead the border comes to you? Not explicitly, but in a kind of demographic equivalent to the overlaid area codes of a North American metropolis. Amsterdam is the city of legalized pot and prostitution and a gay hedonist paradise. But it's also a Muslim city, overlaid on the pothead playground. At what point does the nice Dutch gay couple realize they've crossed a border? That, without getting their passports stamped or changing their currency, they're now strangers in a strange land. That's something Greene would have been fascinated to write about.

So why don't his successors? Well, for one answer we can turn to a recent panel convened at the Queen Elizabeth Hall in London to discuss the topic "Is All Modern Art Left Wing?" The formal discussion was dreary and predictable but things turned livelier when it was opened to the floor, and the question of double standards was raised: "Courageous" artists seemed happy to mock Christianity but curiously reluctant to hurl equivalent jibes at Islam. Grayson Perry, the

Turner Prize-winning transvestite artist who looks very fetching in his little Disney-princess frocks, reveals that he self-censors when it comes to Muslims because "I don't want my throat cut."

But that doesn't entirely explain it, does it? Earlier this year, Channel 4 in London broadcast a documentary called "Undercover Mosque" in which various imams up and down the land were caught on tape urging men to beat their wives and toss homosexuals off cliffs. Viewers reported some of the statements to the local constabulary. The West Midlands Police then decided to investigate not the fire-breathing clerics but the TV producers. As the coppers saw it, insofar as any "hate crime" had been perpetrated, it lay not in the urgings and injunctions of the imams but in a TV production so culturally insensitive as to reveal the imams' views to the general public. As *The Spectator*'s James Forsyth put it, "The reaction of West Midlands Police revealed a mindset that views the exposure of a problem as more of a problem than the problem itself."

Exactly. Did you see the latest remake of *Invasion Of The Body Snatchers*? It sank without trace a couple of months back and not just because it had Nicole Kidman in the lead. The new version relocates the story from small-town America to Washington, and sees it as a metaphor for power: cue endless references to Iraq and glimpses of Bush on the TV screens. Yet *Body Snatchers* isn't about power so much as conformity*. That's what the West Midlands Police were attempting to enforce with Channel 4, and what the Rotterdam police managed to enforce rather more successfully when they destroyed a mural created to express disgust at Theo van Gogh's murder. Chris Ripke's painting showed an angel and bore the words "Thou Shalt Not Kill". But his studio is next to a mosque, and the imam complained that the mural was "racist", so the cops showed up, destroyed it, arrested the TV crew filming it, and wiped their tape. A "tolerant" society cannot tolerate any assaults on its most cherished myths.

Professor Rosner, Daniel Silva's fictional murder victim, would have understood. At the scene of his ritual slaughter there are no protesters, just piles of tulips and the banner "ONE AMSTERDAM,

ONE PEOPLE" - one mass delusion. It's not just that you'll get your throat cut, but that you'll get it cut and they'll still string the same sappy happy-face multiculti banner over the crime scene.

*An afterthought on The Invasion Of The Body Snatchers

With hindsight, I think the makers of the latest version started out wanting to make an anti-Bush allegory - hence all those endless background news bulletins about Iraq - and then couldn't figure out how to make it fit the Body Snatchers *narrative. The nearest thing to a coherent message was the Russian guy's observation toward the end that a world without war would be a world in which we're no longer human. And, message-wise, I'll bet that was an accidental one.*

Nonetheless, it's interesting. Since my difficulties with the "human rights" thought police began, I've been struck by how many Canadians (and Europeans) sincerely believe that a better world can be built by giving the state the exclusive power to "ban hate" and enforce niceness. Such a world will by definition be totalitarian. I'm not proposing that the next remake of Invasion Of The Body Snatchers *should be an allegory for the Canadian "Human Rights" Commission, not unless Hollywood really wants to lose a ton of dough. But nevertheless that fits the story's theme better than whatever Nicole Kidman was running through the streets perspiring over. In its successful manifestations, the* Body Snatchers *narrative is not about Bush but about sedating the populace into bland conformity for ostensibly "nice" reasons. A human society is a messy one: a lot of people will be "partisan" and "mean-spirited", others will be hateful and bigoted, a few will bomb and kill and maim. You hope that most folks will stay down the low-key end of that spectrum, and that those who don't will be resisted. But that is the price of remaining human, and the alternative - a state-mandated niceness - is fascistic.*

ADDITIONAL INDICTMENT #4

Your lyin' eyes

Perhaps the most conspicuous absence from the Canadian Islamic Congress dossier on Maclean's *"flagrant Islamophobia" is a column of mine from June 2006. At first glance it would appear to meet all the criteria used to establish the Islamophobia of the preceding exhibits. Like "The Future Belongs To Islam", it could easily be said that this piece...*

> ...focuses on the influx of Muslim immigrants into Europe and North America... Another significant theme contained in the article is that there is allegedly an ongoing war between Muslims and Non-Muslims, that Muslims are part of a global conspiracy to take over Western societies, and that Muslims in the West need to be viewed through this lens as the enemy.

Like "Feeding The Hand That Bites Them", it surely suggests that...

> Extremism and radicalism is prevalent in Ontario.

Like "The Little Mosque That Couldn't", it explicitly states that...

> Muslims are obtaining undue and unwarranted cultural sensitivity from law enforcement.

Like "The Church Dance That Snowballed", it states that...

> There exists a 'culture' of grievance in Islam and in Muslims.

So it would appear to be no different from all the other "hate crimes" the CIC took to the "human rights" commissions. And yet this column was strangely absent from the otherwise comprehensive "case study". Why should such a flagrantly flagrant piece of Islamophobia get off so lightly?

Perhaps because, unlike the "The Future Belongs To Islam", this column deals not with Europe or other distant climes but with a jihadist plot smack in the middle of Canada — and that to complain about Maclean's *publishing it would have been a near parodic demonstration of the "victim complex" and the "moral inversion" that the piece itself addresses. So here is the hate crime that got away, as published in Maclean's on June 13th 2006:*

WITHIN A FEW hours of those arrests from the - what was the phrase? – "broad strata" of Canadian society, I had a little flurry of emails from radio and TV producers inviting me to toss in my two bits. But my two bits on Toronto is pretty much the same as my two bits on London and Madrid and Bali, and that's quite a mound of quarters piled up over the past five years. What's to say? The best summation is a line I first quoted in 2002, when a French oil tanker was attacked off the coast of Yemen. Back then, you'll recall, the French foreign minister was deploring American *"simplisme"* on a daily basis, and President Chirac was the principal obstructionist of the neocon-Zionist-Halliburton plan to remake the Middle East. If you were to pick only one western nation not to blow up the oil tankers of, France would surely be it.

But they got blown up anyway. And afterwards a spokesman for the Islamic Army of Aden said, "We would have preferred to hit a US frigate, but no problem because they are all infidels."

No problem. They are all infidels. In the scheme of things, launching a plot to behead the Prime Minister of Canada would not seem to be an obvious priority. No doubt they would have preferred to behead the President of the United States. But no problem. We are all infidels.

The multicultural society posits that each of its citizens can hold a complementary portfolio of identities: one can simultaneously be Canadian and Jamaican and gay and Anglican and all these identities can exist within your corporeal form in perfect harmony. But, for most western Muslims, Islam is their primary identity, and for a significant number thereof, it's a primary identity that exists in opposition to all others. That's merely stating the obvious. But, of course, to state the obvious is unacceptable these days, so our leaders prefer to state the absurd. I believe the old definition of a nanosecond was the gap between a New York traffic light changing to green and the first honk of a driver behind you. Today, the definition of a nanosecond is the gap between a western terrorist incident and the press release of a Muslim lobby group warning of an impending outbreak of Islamophobia. After the London tube bombings, Angus Jung sent the Aussie pundit Tim Blair a note-perfect parody of the typical newspaper headline:

> British Muslims Fear Repercussions Over Tomorrow's Train bombing.

An adjective here and there, and that would serve just as well for much of the coverage by *The Toronto Star* and the CBC, where a stone through a mosque window is a bigger threat to the social fabric than a bombing thrice the size of the Oklahoma City explosion. "Minority-rights doctrine," writes Melanie Phillips in her new book *Londonistan*, "has produced a moral inversion, in which those doing wrong are excused if they belong to a 'victim' group, while those at the receiving end of their behaviour are blamed simply because they belong to the 'oppressive' majority." If you want to appreciate the forces at play among western Muslims in societies hollowed out by multiculturalism, *Londonistan* is an indispensable read. "It is impossible to overstate the importance - not just to Britain but to the global struggle against Islamist extremism - of properly understanding and publicly challenging this moral, intellectual and philosophical inversion, which translates aggressor into victim and vice versa."

That's true - although I wonder for how long even our decayed establishments can keep up the act. After the London bombings, the first reaction of Brian Paddick, the Deputy Assistant Commissioner of the Metropolitan Police, was to declare that "Islam and terrorism don't go together." After the Toronto arrests, the CSIS Assistant Director of Operations, Luc Portelance, announced that "it is important to know that this operation in no way reflects negatively on any specific community, or ethnocultural group in Canada." Who ya gonna believe? The RCMP diversity outreach press officer or your lyin' eyes?

112

In the old days, these chaps would have been looking for the modus operandi, patterns of behaviour. But now every little incident on the planet is apparently strictly specific unto itself: all jihad is local. The Islamic Army of Aden PR guy seems by comparison to have a relatively clear-sighted grasp of reality.

Melanie Phillips makes a point that applies to Britain, Canada and beyond: "With few exceptions, politicians, Whitehall officials, senior police and intelligence officers and academic experts have failed to grasp that the problem to be confronted is not just the assembly of bombs and poison factories but what is going on inside people's heads that drives them to such acts." These are not Pushtun yak herders straight off the boat blowing up trains and buses. They're young men, most of whom were born and all of whom were bred in London, Toronto and other western cities. And offered the nullity of a contemporary multicultural identity they looked elsewhere - and found the jihad. If we try to fight it as isolated outbreaks - a suicide attack here, a beheading there - we will never win. You have to take on the ideology and the networks that sustain it and throttle them. Instead Toronto's mayor expresses bafflement that young lads should turn to terrorism in a city with "very good social services". A reader in Quebec, John Gross, emailed me to distill Hizzonner's approach as: "Don't get mad, get even... wimpier."

Well, if the mayor wants to make himself a laughingstock, what's the harm? Only this - that the more rubbish spouted by officials in the wake of these events, the more the averagely well-informed person will resent the dissembling. In that sense, Mayor Miller, M Portelance, Commissioner Paddick et al are colluding in the delegitimizing of the state's institutions. That doesn't seem like a smart move.

One final thought: Miss Phillips is one of Britain's best-known newspaper columnists. She appears constantly on national TV and radio. No publisher has lost money on her. Yet *Londonistan* wound up being published first in New York, and its subsequent appearance in Britain is thanks not to Little, Brown (who published her last big book) but to a small independent imprint called Gibson Square*. I don't know Miss Phillips' agent, but it's hard not to suspect that glamorous literary London decided it would prefer to keep a safe distance from this incendiary subject.

As I always say, that's how nations die - not by war or conquest, but by a thousand trivial concessions, until one day you wake up and you don't need to sign a formal instrument of surrender because you did it piecemeal. How many Muslims in Toronto sympathize with the aims of those arrested last week? Maybe we could use a book on the subject. But which Canadian house would publish it? And would the fainthearts at Indigo-Chapters carry it?

Burning bridges

Gibson Square Books subsequently agreed to publish The Jewel Of Medina, *a novel telling the story of Mohammed's first wife from her betrothal to the Prophet at the age of six. Envisioned by its author, Sherry Jones, as a "bridge-builder" between Islam and the west, the novel was cancelled by its original publisher, Random House in New York, after they received "cautionary advice not only that the publication of this book might be offensive to some in the Muslim community, but also that it could incite acts of violence by a small, radical segment." On September 4th 2008, Martin Rynja at Gibson Square stepped into the breach and announced that he would publish* The Jewel Of Medina *in Britain and the Commonwealth. On September 27th, his home in London was firebombed, and publication was indefinitely postponed.*

III

ISLAM AND THE WEST

The west with its insistence on democracy seems to us eminently gharib, *foreign, because it is a mirror of what frightens us, the wound that 15 centuries have not succeeded in binding: the fact that personal opinion always brings violence. Under the terror of the sword, political despotism has obliged Muslims to defer discussion about responsibility, freedom to think, and the impossibility of blind obedience.*

FATEMA MERNISSI
Islam And Democracy (1992)

In this section we look at the tensions, trivial and profound between Islam and the west, starting with the 2006 Danish cartoons crisis that ensnared my comrade Ezra Levant in the clutches of the "human rights" regime. The decision by a small newspaper in Jutland to print various depictions of Mohammed was whipped up by opportunist imams into a pretext for global rioting – much of it directed not only against Denmark, but against infidels in general. In Lahore, the usual excitable young lads from the religion of pieces destroyed the local McDonald's. Apparently the lively Pakistanis had burned every single Danish target in the city (one early Victor Borge LP left behind by the last British governor) and had been obliged to diversify. So they dragged Ronald McDonald out of the joint, torched him in the street and danced around his flaming remains shouting "Death to America! Death to Britain! Death to Tony Blair!" Which I don't even get. I mean, Ronald and Tony seem kind of similar from a distance but even on the all-infidels-look-alike-to-me-especially-when-they're-alight thesis they're not that *easily confused.*

Ezra Levant's magazine, The Western Standard, *argued that you couldn't cover this story without showing the cartoons. In consequence, it was banned from Canada's bookstore chains. Paul McNally of McNally Robinson defended his action thus:*

> We feel there is nothing to gain on the side of freedom of expression and much to lose on the side of hurting feelings.

Not exactly Voltaire, is it? "I disagree strongly with what you say but I will fight to the death for your right to say it as long as it doesn't hurt anybody's feelings." Maybe it could be Canada's new national motto. What's clear is that the weak response to each assault on liberty only invites more:

116

THE CARTOON CRISIS
Unfit to print

The Western Standard, March 13th 2006

AS PERICLES told the war-battered Athenians, "To a man of spirit, cowardice and disaster coming together are far more bitter than death striking him unperceived at a time when he is full of courage and animated by the general hope."

Yes, I know. Bit of a downer for an opening number, but that's the way I feel. I am by nature a happy warrior, but in this last month I've seen way too much cowardice and disaster coming together.

The Danish cartoons story was a test, and the civilized world failed it. Not all of us are in the mood to have tests sprung upon us. We have other plans, we're washing our hair, whatever. I can understand that as an initial theoretical position - in the way that in the movie the taciturn loner ex-boxer or semi-alcoholic former fastest gun in the west says, "I nearly killed a man back in '58. I ain't gonna fight again." But in the final reel he discovers he has to, whether he wants to or not. That's the point we reached in the cartoons story.

Many parties have behaved wretchedly in these last few weeks - European Commissioners, the British Foreign Secretary, the US State Department, significant chunks of the incoming Canadian cabinet, the dead-again Christians who lead the United Church of Canada - but the western media have managed to produce a uniquely creepy synthesis of craven capitulation and self-serving pomposity. As the great Australian wag Tim Blair observed:

> *Journalists can spend entire careers mouthing off about their commitment to free speech without ever having the chance to properly demonstrate it. I once had a theory that the lack of repression in modern democracies drove journalists to invent*

McCarthyesque threats, so much did they crave an opportunity to stare down those who would silence them.

This story meets all the clichés of journalistic self-aggrandizement: "Sunlight is the best disinfectant", "News is what someone doesn't want you to put in the paper". But it seems it's one thing to "speak truth to power" when the power's George Bush or John Ashcroft, quite another when it's an Islamist mob coming to burn your building down. Needless to say, reflex blowhardism is so ingrained in the media class they couldn't resist passing off their prioritizing of self-preservation as a bold principled stand. Or as Philip Lee, professor of journalism at St Thomas University in New Brunswick, put it:

Freedom of the press means you can publish, or not. Not publishing is also an expression of freedom.

Up to a point, Lord Jello. That's a valid position if you're the editor of, say, *The Ottawa Citizen* and some fellow mails you some cartoons about Mohammed and you say, "Interesting idea, old boy. Unfortunately, not quite our bag." But that's no longer tenable when the cartoons themselves are the story. Then it's not even simple news judgment; it's the headline and you've no choice in the matter. In Nigeria the other day, 15 Christians were killed by Muslims over these cartoons, because they're "offensive". Exercising Professor Lee's "right to not publish" becomes, in effect, a way of supporting that proposition. It's summed up by the CNN technique: whenever the story comes up, they show the cartoons but with the Prophet's image pixilated. Watching, you wonder briefly if it's not your own face that's pixilated. Maybe you dozed off and fell face down in the blancmange and you're not seeing it properly. But no, you grab a towel and wipe your eyes and, when you look again, they're still doing it: the graphics department of a major news network is obscuring the features of a cartoon face. If you weren't paying attention, you'd assume Mohammed must have entered the witness protection program.

But, of course, its meaning is the exact opposite: it's CNN that's entered the witness protection program, or hopes it has. The BBC, disgracefully, did the Islamists' work for them, spreading around the world the canard that one of the cartoons showed Mohammed as a pig. No. That was one of the three fake cartoons added by the Danish imams - presumably because the original 12 were felt to be insufficiently incendiary. If it's an outrage for an infidel to depict the Prophet, isn't it an even greater one for a believer to do so? Who did those Danish Islamists hire to cook up the phoney cartoons and have they killed him yet?

Anyone who's spent any time in the Muslim world cannot help but be struck by its profound ignorance. The famous United Nations statistic from a 2002 report - more books are translated into Spanish in a single year than have been translated into Arabic in the last thousand - suggests at the very minimum an extraordinarily closed society - which in turn explains its stunted political development. For example, the editor of *The Yemen Observer*, Mohammed al-Asadi, wrote a strong editorial denouncing the Danish cartoons, but, like this magazine's editor, decided to show its readers what they actually looked like. As a result, he's now in jail. The point about Islam is that it's beyond discussion. Whether it's good or bad is neither here nor there: It just *is*. There's nothing to talk about. No corner of the earth would benefit more from the ability to debate ideas openly.

Yet what is Mr al-Asadi to conclude from his jail cell about freedom of expression in the western world? Out of "respect" for Islam, the BBC and CNN and *The New York Times* and *Le Monde* have shown less of those cartoons than his government-published Yemeni paper. If you're a Toronto printer who'd rather pass on a job printing up gay propaganda, our oh-so-correct Human Rights Commission will fine you and sternly remind you that your religious beliefs are fine within the confines of your own home but they've got to be left inside the house when you close the front door behind you each morning. But, if you're a Muslim, your particular conventions - many of them relatively recent and by no means universally observed - have now been extended throughout the public square.

In contrast to Professor Lee, the Boston *Phoenix* was admirably straightforward. It declined to publish the cartoons, it said, "out of fear of retaliation from the international brotherhood of radical and bloodthirsty Islamists who seek to impose their will on those who do not believe as they do... Simply stated, we are being terrorized, and as deeply as we believe in the principles of free speech and a free press, we could not in good conscience place the men and women who work at *The Phoenix* and its related companies in physical jeopardy."

I was the subject of an attack in *The Phoenix* a year or two back. As hit pieces go, it was a pretty feeble effort, and I didn't feel it was worth driving all the way down to Boston just to kill a few members of staff and burn the building down. But it makes you think. In our multicultural society, the best way to get "respect" from others is to despise them; the surest way to have your views boundlessly "tolerated" is to be utterly intolerant of anybody else's. Those who think Islam will apply these lessons only to op-ed cartoons or representations of Mohammed are very foolish.

Meanwhile, we prattle on about "moderate Muslims", telling ourselves that the "vast majority" of Muslims aren't terrorists, don't support terrorists, etc.

Okay, then why don't we hear from them?

Because they live in communities where the ideological bullies set the pace, where the price of speaking out is too high, and so they find it easier to say nothing, keep their heads down. And why would we expect them to do any differently when the mighty BBC and CNN do the same? If there is such a thing as a "moderate Muslim", he's surely thinking, "Well, if the CBC and *The Toronto Star* have to knuckle under to the imams, there's no point me tossing in my two bits."

It's odd to hear so many eminent media mandarins patiently explaining that their principal role is deciding what we don't need to know. Simply as a commercial proposition, for the press to trumpet its professional judgment in knowing when to withhold information seems a surefire way for the slide in circulation to turn into an avalanche: they're going to need great recipe columns and film listings if that's the basis on which they approach news reporting. But, beyond that, for the media to play the role of ceremonial maintainer of the multicultural illusions is to damage their credibility on the central issue of our time.

The Islamists picked the right fight. The Danish cartoonists are not Salman Rushdie; Jutland is not literary London. No modish metropolitan semi-celebrities are flocking to the cause of the latest faraway country of which we know little. Yet it was not an accidental target. Denmark was the first country to recognize the demographic and cultural challenge of Islam and to elect a government committed to do something about it. This is the imams' way of warning Norway and Sweden and Belgium and all the rest not to follow in the footsteps of their neighbour. Judging from the formal statements of Continental politicians, they've got the message loud and clear.

It's often observed that, when President Kennedy famously declared he was a Berliner, what he actually said in his imperfect German was: "I am a donut." If ever there was a time to say "I am a Danish", this is it. Shame on all of those whose cowardice will bring disaster.

THE CARTOON CRISIS
Stout-hearted men?

The Western Standard, March 27th 2006

THE PERICLEAN funeral oration I opened with last issue was a bit of a bummer so here's something to stir the blood: *The New Moon*, the smash Broadway operetta of 1928. It's 1792 and in French colonial New Orleans ...hang on, wasn't New Orleans Spanish in 1792? Oh, well. Fortunately for Sigmund Romberg and Oscar Hammerstein, Spanish Colonialism Denial isn't a crime like Holocaust Denial.

At any rate, Robert Misson, a chevalier lying low as a servant, is dreaming of throwing off the shackles of the French King and establishing a free state on the Isle of Pines. But how can he be so sure the other men will stand with him?

Ha, he scoffs:

> *Give me some men*
> *Who are Stout-Hearted Men*
> *Who will fight for the right they adore!*
> *Start me with ten*
> *Who are Stout-Hearted Men*
> *And I'll soon give you ten thousand more!*
> *Shoulder to shoulder, and bolder and bolder*
> *They grow as they go to the fore...*

You may have seen the 1940 film version with Nelson Eddy tramping through the woods as stout-hearted torch-bearing yeomen fall in behind him.

Which brings me to our publisher, Ezra Levant. I'm not suggesting Ezra's as camp as Nelson Eddy, but I am saying he might reasonably have expected to have attracted a similar size of crowd. In publishing the Danish cartoons, he'd started with our editor, Kevin

Libin, and another ten stout-hearted men from the *Western Standard* office, and he had the right to assume he'd be joined by ten thousand more from the Vancouver *Province* and *The Toronto Sun* and *La Presse* and the Charlottetown *Guardian*.

But he wasn't. Nor were the other handful of publishers and editors in France, Germany and elsewhere who reprinted the Danish cartoons. And the ramifications of that will echo through our culture for years. As I said last time round, one can have different opinions on the merits of the original cartoons. After I posted them at my website, Rosie Witty of Christchurch, New Zealand - by the way, isn't it a little culturally insensitive to call a city "Christchurch"? - anyway, Ms Witty wrote to say that she found the cartoons "rude, crude and lewd... The freedom of the press sometimes is wise; sometimes it is not."

That's a valid argument if you're writing to *Jyllands-Posten*, the originating newspaper in Denmark. Had this or that imam done as Ms Witty did, many a dispassionate observer might have agreed. But, instead of writing to the newspapers, the imams embarked on a campaign that led to embassies being burned, Turkish priests being murdered, and over a hundred others dying in associated riots. Once that happened, the issue was not the appalling nature of the cartoons but the appalling nature of the reaction to them. The 12 cartoonists are now in hiding. According to the chairman of the Danish Liberal Party, a group of Muslim men showed up at a local school looking for the daughter of one of the artists.

When that racket starts, no cartoonist or publisher or editor should have to stand alone. The minute there were multimillion-dollar bounties on those cartoonists' heads, *The Times* of London and *Le Monde* and *The Washington Post* and all the rest should have said, "This Thursday we're all publishing all the cartoons. If you want to put bounties on all our heads, you'd better have a great credit line at the Bank of Jihad. If you want to kill us, you'll have to kill us all. You can kill ten who are stout-hearted men but you'll have to kill ten thousand more. We're standing shoulder to shoulder, and bolder and bolder."

But it didn't happen. There was a photograph from one of the early Muslim demonstrations in London that I cut out and kept: a masked protester promising to behead the enemies of Islam, and standing shoulder to shoulder with him two Metropolitan Police officers, dispatched by the state to protect him and enable him to incite the murder of others. When those Muslim men return to that Danish school, I only hope that that little girl is as well protected by the forces of authority.

I realized the other day, talking to a novelist of my acquaintance, that I'd had the conversation before - the one where some writer of repute tells me that he had a great idea for a story involving certain, um, aspects of the, er, geopolitical scene and his publisher (or sometimes even his agent) hemmed and hawed and eventually said well, it sounds like a good idea but in the, ah, current climate maybe we should put that on hold for a year or two, and how about that plot you mentioned a while back about the redneck Baptist serial killer in Alabama? Pitch certain proposals and even the cockiest New York editor at the back of her mind has the vague feeling that her swank Manhattan office could wind up as vulnerable as that Danish grade school. One consequence of the faint-hearted defence of free speech this time round is that more and more publishers and editors will take the path of least resistance next time.

The free world is shuffling into a psychological bondage whose chains are mostly of our own making. "Extreme cases make bad law," we say. But extreme cases can also make the best defence of principle. In 1847, a man called Don Pacifico, a Portuguese Jew living in Greece, had his house burned in an anti-Semitic riot. He appealed to the Greek government for redress (the sons of some ministers had been involved) and got nowhere. But he chanced to have been born on Gibraltar and thus was, technically, a British subject. And so he turned to Her Majesty's Government. And, although to most Englishmen's eyes a century and a half ago no one could have seemed less English than this greasy dago Jew moneylender, Lord Palmerston began a naval blockade of Greece - on the grounds that Don Pacifico was a British subject like any other. And, when the government in Athens backed down, Palmerston addressed the House of Commons thus:

As the Roman in days of old held himself free from indignity when he could say Civis Romanus sum, *so also a British subject, in whatever land he may be, shall feel confident that the watchful eye and the strong arm of England will protect him against injustice and wrong.*

Civis Britannicus sum: that was all Don Pacifico had to say.

Today, in the face of more riots and more burnings, Palmerston's successor Jack Straw, like the foreign ministers of Canada and Europe, is craven and shifty. We in the media could at least recognize our own responsibilities and commercial interests here. The Danish cartoonists are the Don Pacificos of the modern media empire. They're not Thomas Friedman or Naomi Klein, just some nobodies on the fringes of the map. But the mob has threatened them with death, and if they get away with it they will do it again. For that reason - on Islam, eco-terrorism and anything else - the press should act on the principle that a death threat against one newspaper is a death threat against all and will invite automatic republishing of the offending item. We should all be stout-hearted men - before it's too late.

SHAGGERS vs NUTTERS
Mustapha Rethink

The Chicago Sun-Times, February 12th 2006

FROM EUROPE's biggest-selling newspaper, *The Sun*:

> *Furious Muslims have blasted adult shop [ie, sex shop] Ann Summers for selling a blowup male doll called Mustafa Shag.*

Not literally "blasted" in the Danish Embassy sense, or at least not yet. Quite how Britain's Muslim Association found out about Mustafa Shag in order to be offended by him is not clear. It may be that there was some confusion: given that "blowup males" are one of Islam's leading exports, perhaps some believers went along expecting to find Ahmed and Walid modeling the new line of Semtex belts. Instead, they were confronted by just another filthy infidel sex gag. The Muslim Association's complaint, needless to say, is that the sex toy "insults the Prophet Muhammad - who also has the title al-Mustapha."

In a world in which Danish cartoons insult the prophet and Disney Piglet mugs insult the prophet and Burger King chocolate ice-cream swirl designs insult the prophet, maybe it would just be easier to make a list of things that don't insult him. Nonetheless, the Muslim Association wrote to the Ann Summers sex-shop chain, "We are asking you to have our Most Revered Prophet's name 'Mustafa' and the afflicted word 'shag' removed."

If I were a Muslim, I'd be "hurt" and "humiliated" that the revered prophet's name is given not to latex blowup males but to so many real blowup males: The leader of the 9/11 plotters? Mohammed Atta. The British Muslim who self-detonated in a Tel Aviv bar? Asif Mohammed Hanif. The gunman who shot up the El Al counter at LAX? Heshamed Mohamed Hedayet. The former US Army sergeant who masterminded the slaughter at the embassy bombings in Kenya and Tanzania? Ali Mohamed. The murderer of Dutch filmmaker Theo van Gogh? Mohammed Bouyeri. The notorious Sydney gang rapist? Mohammed Skaf. The Washington sniper? John Allen Muhammed. If I were a Muslim, I would be deeply offended that the prophet's name is the preferred appellation of so many killers and suicide bombers on every corner of the earth.

But apparently that's not as big a deal as Mustafa Shag. When Samuel Huntington formulated his famous "clash of civilizations" thesis, I'm sure he hoped it would play out as something nobler than shaggers vs nutters. But in a sense that's the core British value these days. If it's inherent in Muslim culture to take umbrage at everything, it's inherent in English culture to turn everything into a lame sex gag. The "Mustafa" template is one of the most revered in the English music-hall tradition: "I've been reading the latest scholarly monograph - *Sexual Practices Of The Middle East* by Mustapha Camel..."

In their determination to appease the surging Muslim demographic in their own country, the British could conceivably withdraw from Iraq and Afghanistan. But it's hard to imagine they could withdraw from vulgar sex jokes and still be recognizably British. They are, in the Muslim Association's choice of word, "afflicted" with shag fever.

In theory, this should have been the perfect moment for Albert Brooks to release his new film *Looking For Comedy In The Muslim World*. Instead, life is effortlessly outpacing art. Brooks had an excellent premise and, somewhere between studio equivocation and his sense of self-preservation, it all got watered down, beginning with the decision to focus the plot on a trip to India. Which is a, er, mostly Hindu country. But the Arab world refused to let Brooks film there, and, even if they had, he'd have been lucky to get out alive. Needless to say, the movie doesn't mention that. So a film whose title flaunts a bold disdain for political correctness is, in the end, merely another concession to it.

You can't blame Brooks, not in a world of surreal headlines like "Cartoon Death Toll Up To Nine" (*The Sunday Times* of Australia). Instead of looking for comedy in the Muslim world, the Muslim world's come looking for comedy in the west and doesn't like what it's found. If memory serves, it was NBC who back in the Seventies used to have every sitcom joke about homosexuality vetted by a gay dentist in New Jersey. Apprised of this at a conference on censorship, the producer of "The Mary Tyler Moore Show" remarked, "You mean there really is a tooth fairy?" Alas, the Islamist Advisory Commission on Koran-Compatible Humor will be made of sterner stuff, and likely far more devastating to the sitcom biz.

And the good news is that that body's already on its way. The European Union's Justice and Security Commissioner, Franco Frattini, said on Thursday that the EU would set up a "media code" to encourage "prudence" in the way they cover, ah, certain sensitive subjects. As Signor Frattini explained it to *The Daily Telegraph*, "The press will give the Muslim world the message: We are aware of the consequences of exercising the right of free expression… We can and we are ready to self-regulate that right."

"Prudence"? "Self-regulate our free expression"? No, I'm afraid that's just giving the Muslim world the message: You've won, I surrender, please stop kicking me.

But they never do. Because, to use the Arabic proverb with which Robert Ferrigno opens his new novel, *Prayers For The Assassin*, set in an Islamic Republic of America, "A falling camel attracts many knives." In Denmark and France and the Netherlands and Britain, Islam senses the camel is falling and this is no time to stop knifing him.

The issue is more basic than "freedom of speech" or "the responsibilities of the press" or "sensitivity to certain cultures". The issue, as it has been in all these loony tune controversies going back to the Salman Rushdie fatwa, is the point at which a free society musters the will to stand up to thugs. British Muslims march through the streets waving placards reading "BEHEAD THE ENEMIES OF ISLAM". If they mean that, bring it on. As my columnar confrère John O'Sullivan argued, we might as well fight in the first ditch as the last.

But then it's patiently explained to us for the umpteenth time that they're not representative, that there are many many "moderate Muslims".

I believe that. I've met plenty of "moderate Muslims" in Jordan and Iraq and the Gulf states. But, as a reader wrote to me a year or two back, in Europe and North America they aren't so much "moderate Muslims" as quiescent Muslims. The few who do speak out wind up living in hiding or under 24-hour armed guard, like the Dutch Member of Parliament Ayaan Hirsi Ali.

So when the EU and the BBC and *The New York Times* say that we too need to be more "sensitive" to those fellows with "Behead the enemies of Islam" banners, they should look in the mirror: They're turning into "moderate Muslims", and likely to wind up as cowed and silenced and invisible.

CULTURAL SENSITIVITY
My Sharia Amour

After escaping the riots in Nigeria, which claimed more than 200 lives, Miss World contestants were safely installed in their ever-decreasing numbers inside a Heathrow hotel yesterday... Last week, a reporter for This Day, a Nigerian newspaper, wrote an article suggesting that Prophet Mohammed would 'probably' have chosen a wife from one of the contestants, a comment which sparked the unrest...

A number of alternative venues, such as Alexandra Palace, Wembley Arena and the Grosvenor House hotel on Park Lane, are being considered.

Glenda Jackson, the Labour MP for Hampstead, said: 'They should call the whole thing off...' – The Daily Telegraph

The Daily Telegraph, November 30th 2002

"RUN THIS BY me again," I said as we circled Lagos Airport. "We're doing a new 'culturally sensitive' Miss World?"

"That's right," said Julia Morley. "I got the idea from all those stringy London feminists droning on about how we're only promoting a narrow exploitative western image of women. And to be honest, after a week in England listening to their bitching and whining, I'm glad to be back in Nigeria. The locals'll go crazy for this."

"I hope not," I said. But I was pleasantly surprised as we landed smoothly and taxied down the runway. "Look, Julia, a gun salute!"

"Duck, girls!" she yelled, as a SAM missile pierced the window, shot through the First Class curtain and took out the Economy toilet.

"Now don't you worry, Mark," she said once we were safely in the limo. "Your material's hardly been changed at all. Just remember, when you and Tony Orlando do 'Thank Heaven For Little Girls',

130

there's a Sudanese warlord in a third-row aisle seat who's got a new 12-year-old wife you don't want to be caught looking at."

"Got it," I said. The house band, made up entirely of Hausa band members, played the opening strains of Stevie Wonder's classic love song and Julia pushed the revised culturally sensitive lyrics into my hand. It was then that the first nagging doubts began to gnaw at the back of my mind. But what the hell, I was in my tux and they were playing my song.

I bounced out on stage, grabbed the mike and punched the air:

My Sharia Amour
Hot enough for Gulf emirs
My Sharia Amour
But I'm the guy she really fears...

The audience seemed wary and an alarming number appeared to be reaching into their robes. But I ploughed on:

My Sharia Amour
Pretty little thing in her chador
One of only four that I beat raw
How I wish that I had five.

There was a momentary silence, just long enough for me to start backing upstage nervously. And then the crowd went wild! The guys in the balcony cheered deliriously and hurled their machetes across the orchestra pit, shredding my pants. An Afghan wedding party grabbed their semi-automatics and blew out the chandeliers, sending them hurtling to the aisle, where they killed a Japanese camera crew. Tough luck, fellers, but that's what happens when you get between me and my audience.

I took my usual seat with the celebrity judges, in between "Baywatch" hunk David Hasselhoff and Princess Michael of Kent. Lorraine Kelly said: "And now, ladies and gentlemen, let's give our panel a really big hand!" A really big hand landed on the table with a dull thud, courtesy of a Saudi prince in the royal box.

"How'd they like you?" I asked Princess Michael.

"Well, by the end of 'Man, I Feel Like A Woman', I had the crowd with me all the way. But I shook 'em off at Kaduna."

"Who's the bloke next to you?"

"Oh, he's a judge."

I rolled my eyes. "Well, *duh*!"

"No, I mean, he's a real judge. He's some Fulani bigshot who's here to decide who gets stoned."

"And which mother of a Mick Jagger love-child is on the panel this year?"

"That's Marsha Hunt. Had an affair with him in the late Sixties."

The small talk was somewhat stilted. "Have you ever been stoned?" asked the judge. Marsha tittered.

Princess Michael explained that the fellow on Marsha's left was Alhaji Abdutayo Ogunbati, the country's leading female circumcisionist, there to ensure every contestant was in full compliance, and next to him was Hans Blix, there to ensure every involuntary clitorectomy was in accordance with UN clitorectomy inspections-team regulations.

I glanced at my watch. "For crying out loud, when are they going to raise the curtain?"

"They *have* raised the curtain," said David. "Those are the girls."

I peered closer at the shapeless line of cloth, and he was right: there they all were, from Miss Afghanistan to Miss Zionist Entity.

I sighed. "How long till the swimsuit round?"

"This *is* the swimsuit round," said David.

THE ONE-WAY STREET
Facing down the crazies

The Chicago Sun-Times, March 26th 2006

FATE CONSPIRES to remind us what this war is really about: civilizational confidence. And so history repeats itself: first the farce of the Danish cartoons, and now the tragedy - a man on trial for his life in post-Taliban Afghanistan because he has committed the crime of converting to Christianity.

The cartoons of the Prophet Muhammad were deeply offensive to Muslims, and so thousands protested around the world in the usual restrained manner: rioting, torching, killing, etc.

The impending execution of Abdul Rahman for embracing Christianity is, of course, offensive to westerners, and so around the world they reacted equally violently by issuing blood-curdling threats like that made by State Department spokesman Sean McCormack:

"Freedom of worship is an important element of any democracy," said Mr McCormack. "And these are issues as Afghan democracy matures that they are going to have to deal with increasingly."

The immediate problem for Mr Rahman is whether he'll get the chance to "mature" along with Afghan democracy. The President, the Canadian Prime Minister and the Australian Prime Minister have all made statements of concern about his fate, and it seems clear that Afghanistan's dapper leader Hamid Karzai would like to resolve this issue before his fledgling democracy gets a reputation as just another barbarous Islamist sewer state. There's talk of various artful compromises, such as Mr Rahman being declared unfit to stand trial by reason of insanity on the grounds that (I'm no Islamic jurist so I'm paraphrasing here) anyone who converts from Islam to Christianity must ipso facto be out of his tree.

On the other hand, this "moderate" compromise solution is being rejected by leading theologians. Let this guy Rahman cop an insanity plea and there goes the neighborhood. "We will not allow God to be humiliated. This man must die," says Abdul Raoulf of the nation's principal Muslim body, the Afghan Ulama Council. "Cut off his head! We will call on the people to pull him into pieces so there's nothing left." Needless to say, Imam Raoulf is one of Afghanistan's leading "moderate" clerics.

For what it's worth, I'm with the Afghan Ulama Council in objecting to the insanity defense. It's not enough for Rahman to get off on a technicality. Afghanistan is supposed to be "the good war", the one even the French supported, albeit notionally and mostly retrospectively. Karzai is kept alive by a bodyguard of foreigners. The fragile Afghan state is protected by American, British, Canadian, Australian, Italian, German and other troops, hundreds of whom have died. You cannot ask Americans or Britons to expend blood and treasure to build a society in which a man can be executed for his choice of religion. You cannot tell a serving member of the Princess Patricia's Canadian Light Infantry in Kandahar that he, as a Christian, must sacrifice his life to create a Muslim state in which his faith is a capital offense.

As always, we come back to the words of Osama bin Laden: "When people see a strong horse and a weak horse, by nature they will like the strong horse." That's really the only issue: the Islamists know our side has tanks and planes, but they have will and faith, and they reckon in a long struggle that's the better bet. Most prominent western leaders sound way too eager to climb into the weak-horse suit and audition to play the rear end. Consider, for example, the words of the Prince of Wales, speaking a few days ago at al-Azhar University in Cairo. This is "the world's oldest university", though what they learn there makes the average Ivy League nuthouse look like a beacon of sanity. Anyway, this is what His Royal Highness had to say to 800 Islamic "scholars":

FACING DOWN THE CRAZIES

The recent ghastly strife and anger over the Danish cartoons shows the danger that comes of our failure to listen and to respect what is precious and sacred to others. In my view, the true mark of a civilized society is the respect it pays to minorities and to strangers.

That's correct. But the reality is our society pays enormous respect to minorities - President Bush holds a month-long Ramadan-a-ding-dong at the White House every year; the immediate reaction to the slaughter of 9/11 by the President, the Prince, the Prime Ministers of Britain, Canada and everywhere else was to visit a mosque to demonstrate their great respect for Islam. One party to this dispute is respectful to a fault: after all, to describe the violence perpetrated by Muslims over the Danish cartoons as the "recent ghastly strife" barely passes muster as effete Brit toff understatement.

Unfortunately, what's "precious and sacred" to Islam is its institutional contempt for others. In his book *Islam And The West*, Bernard Lewis writes:

The primary duty of the Muslim as set forth not once but many times in the Koran is 'to command good and forbid evil'. It is not enough to do good and refrain from evil as a personal choice. It is incumbent upon Muslims also to command and forbid.

Or as the shrewd Canadian columnist David Warren put it: "We take it for granted that it is wrong to kill someone for his religious beliefs. Whereas Islam holds it is wrong not to kill him." In that sense, those blood-curdling imams are right, and Karzai's attempts to finesse the issue are, sharia-wise, wrong.

I can understand why the President and the Secretary of State would rather deal with this through back-channels, private assurances from their Afghan counterparts, etc. But the public rhetoric is critical, too. At some point we have to face down a culture in which not only the mob in the street but the highest judges and academics talk like crazies.

Abdul Rahman embodies the question at the heart of this struggle: If Islam is a religion one can only convert to not from, then in the long run it is a threat to every free person on the planet. What can we do? Well, for a start governments with troops in Afghanistan could pass joint emergency legislation conferring their citizenship on this poor man and declaring him, as much as Karzai, under their protection.

In my forthcoming book, I recall an incident from a more culturally confident age. In India, the British were faced with the practice of "suttee" - the tradition of burning widows on the funeral pyres of their husbands. General Sir Charles Napier was impeccably multicultural:

You say that it is your custom to burn widows. Very well. We also have a custom: When men burn a woman alive, we tie a rope around their necks and we hang them. Build your funeral pyre; beside it, my carpenters will build a gallows. You may follow your custom. And then we will follow ours.

India today is better off without suttee. If we shrink from the logic of that, then in Afghanistan and many places far closer to home the implications are, as the Prince of Wales would say, "ghastly".

THE MODERATE MOSQUE
A state within

National Review, January 29th 2007

"MOSQUE" IS a term that covers a multitude of architectural sins these days, but the one at Regent's Park in London is the real deal. Big golden dome above the tree tops, 140-foot minaret. I used to live nearby and I must have strolled past it hundreds of times and, if I ever did give it a second glance in those days, it was only to marvel: "Wow! That Hindu temple is totally awesome."

I walked by it the other week for the first time in a long time. How did it get to sit on such a piece of prime London real estate? Well, you can thank His Majesty's Government for that. In 1940, Lord Lloyd of Dolobran, Secretary of State for the Colonies, former Governor of Bombay and High Commissioner for Egypt, sent a memo to the Prime Minister pointing out that "in our empire which actually contains more Moslems than Christians it was anomalous and inappropriate that there should be no central place of worship for Mussulmans". So the government allocated a hundred thousand pounds to buy land for a London mosque. The British Empire's Muslim soldiers had fought and died honorably in the service of the Crown, and the broader community of His Majesty's Muslim subjects around the globe were on the whole supportive of the war against the Axis powers. It seemed appropriate that this bravery and loyalty should be acknowledged in the heart of the metropolis. King George VI opened the first Islamic Cultural Centre on the site in 1944, and with funding from the Saudi royal family the lavish and splendid mosque proper was completed in 1977. Today, it's the best attended mosque in Britain. If there is a "moderate" Islam in the west, this is it.

So what goes on there? Well, if you swing by the bookstore, you can pick up DVDs of hot preachers like Sheikh Feiz, who does these hilarious pig noises every time he mentions the Jews – "Oh, Muslim, behind me is the Jew. [snort-snort] Come and kill him. [snort-snort]." You can also buy tapes from Sheikh Yasin, a celebrity American "revert" (ie, convert) to Islam, in which he explains that you should "beat women lightly", and that a Muslim can never be friends with a non-Muslim, and that Christian missionaries deliberately introduced Aids to Africa by putting it in the vaccines for other diseases. Another "revert", Jermaine Lindsay, got the jihad fever at the mosque and then went and self-detonated in the July 7th Tube bombings.

If the Regent's Park mosque has been "radicalized", then there are no non-radical mosques.

When I lived in the neighborhood, you'd see t-shirted tourists snapping each other with the dome in the background. That's what it was for most of us: an exotic backdrop. Inside, one assumed, they talked about Allah and Mohammed, and where's the harm in that? We looked on it in multicultural terms – that's to say, as a heritage issue: a link for immigrants back to the old country. It never occurred to us that it was an ideological bridgehead. But listen to Dr Ijaz Mian, secretly taped by Britain's Channel 4 at the Ahl-e-Hadith mosque in Derby:

> *You cannot accept the rule of the kaffir. We have to rule ourselves and we have to rule the others... King, Queen, House of Commons: if you accept it, you are a part of it. If you don't accept it, you have to dismantle it. So you being a Muslim, you have to fix a target. There will be no House of Commons. From that White House to this Black House, we know we have to dismantle it. Muslims must grow in strength, then take over... You are in a situation in which you have to live like a state-within-a-state - until you take over.*

Where's the religious content? Where's the contemplation of the divine? Don't look for it at the Sparkbrook mosque in Birmingham recently praised by Tony Blair for its contribution to tolerance and diversity. Last June they were celebrating the killer of a British Muslim soldier in Afghanistan:

The hero of Islam is the one who separated his head from his shoulders.

These aren't sermons and these men aren't preachers. They're ideological enforcers on an explicitly political project with branch offices on Main Streets across the western world. Imagine the Second World War with St Adolf's Parish Church on every English village green, or the Cold War with a Soviet Orthodox Church in every mid-sized town in all 50 states.

Dr Mian trained in Saudi Arabia. The bookstore at the Regent's Park mosque is run by a company headed by a Saudi diplomat, Dr Ahmad al-Dubayan. The Saudis control mosques, and schools, and think-tanks, and prison chaplaincy programs and much else, too. I'd be calling for a blue-ribbon commission to investigate Saudi subversion of the US but pretty much everyone who'd wind up sitting on it would be on the Saudi gravy train one way or another. As Christopher Hitchens put it:

If, when reading an article about the debate over Iraq, you come across the expression 'the realist school' and mentally substitute the phrase 'the American friends of the Saudi royal family', your understanding of the situation will invariably be enhanced.

Very droll. The trouble is there are so many "American friends of the Saudi royal family". Jimmy Carter's Carter Center was founded on King Fahd's mountain of cash and, in the last year, its biggest donors included Saudi Prince Al-Walid bin Talal. It never occurred to me in the fall of 2001 that five years on nothing would have changed, except that we'd be shoveling even more gazillions of petrodollars into Saudi Arabia and they in turn would be shoveling even more back at us in a brilliantly synergized subversion operation, funding not only the radical imams and their incendiary progeny but also the think-tanks and study groups and Nobel Prize winners who ponder the best way to appease them. The Saudis are hollowing out Britain from within, and in America are hollowing out significant non-military components of national power - diplomatic, academic and cultural. Listen to the men in those mosques and then ask: Where's our ideological offensive?

The logic of madness

National Review, April 16th 2007

ON THE DAY Iran's British hostages were released, I chanced to be reading a poem from *Reflections On Islam*, a terrific collection of essays by George Jonas. The verse is by Nizar Qabbani, and it is his ode to the intifada:

> *O mad people of Gaza,*
> *a thousand greetings to the mad*
> *The age of political reason*
> *has long departed*
> *so teach us madness*

Or as the larky motto you used to find on the wall of the typing pool put it: You don't have to be crazy to work here but it helps. For the madness of the intifada and the jihad and Islamist imperialism is calculated, and highly effective. There is, as Jonas sees it, method in their madness.

Do you remember that little difficulty a few months back over the Pope's indelicate quotation of Manuel II? Many Muslims were very upset about his speech (or his speech as reported on the BBC et al), so they protested outside Westminster Cathedral in London demanding "capital punishment" for the Pope, and they issued a fatwa in Pakistan calling on Muslims to kill His Holiness, and they firebombed a Greek Orthodox Church and an Anglican Church in Nablus, and they murdered a nun in Somalia and a couple of Christians in Iraq. As Tasnim Aslam of the Foreign Ministry in Islamabad helpfully clarified, "Anyone who describes Islam as a religion as intolerant encourages violence." So don't say we're violent or we'll kill you. As I wrote in *National Review* at the time, *quod erat demonstrandum*.

But that's a debating society line. Islam isn't interested in winning the debate, it's interested in winning the real fight – the clash of civilizations, the war, society, culture, the whole magilla. That's why it doesn't care about the inherent contradictions of the argument: in the Middle East early in 2002, I lost count of the number of Muslims I met who believed simultaneously (a) that 9/11 was pulled off by the Mossad and (b) that it was a great victory for Islam. Likewise, it's no stretch to feel affronted at the implication that you're violently irrational and to threaten to murder anyone who says so. Western societies value logic because we value talk, and talks, and talking, on and on and on: that's pretty much all we do, to the point where, faced with any challenge from Darfur to the Iranian nuclear program, our objective is to reduce the issue to just something else to talk about interminably. But, if you don't prize debate and you merely want to win, getting hung up on logic is only going to get in your way. Take the most devastating rapier wit you know – Oscar Wilde, Noel Coward – and put him on a late-night subway train up against a psycho with a baseball bat. The withering putdown, the devastating aphorism will avail him naught.

The quality of your argument is only important if you want to win by persuasion. But it's irrelevant if you want to win by intimidation. I'm personally very happy to defend my columns in robust debate, but after five years I'm a bit bored by having to respond to Muslim groups' demands (in America) that I be fired and (in Canada) that I be brought before the totalitarian-lite kangaroo courts of the country's ghastly "human rights commissions". Publishers like hate-mail; they're less keen on running up legal bills defending nuisance suits. So it's easier just to avoid the subject – as an Australian novelist recently discovered when his book on a, ah, certain topical theme was mysteriously canceled.

That's the advantage of madness as a strategy. If one party to the dispute forswears sanity, then the obligation is on the other to be sane for both of them. Thus, if a bunch of Iranian pirates kidnap some British seamen in Iraqi waters, it is the British whom the world calls on to show restraint and to defuse the situation. If an obscure Danish newspaper prints some offensive cartoons and in reaction Muslims murder people around the planet, well, that just shows we all need to be more sensitive about Islamophobia. But, if Muslims blow up dozens of commuters on the London Underground and in reaction a minor talk-show host ventures some tentative remarks about whether Islam really is a religion of peace, well, that also shows we all need to be more sensitive about Islamophobia. Do this long enough and eventually you'll achieve the exquisite sensitivity of the European Union's Monitoring Center on Racism and Xenophobia. In 2003, their report on the rise of anti-Semitism in Europe found that "many anti-Semitic incidents were carried out by Muslim and pro-Palestinian groups", and so (according to *The Daily Telegraph*) a "political decision" was taken not to publish it because of "fears that it would increase hostility towards Muslims".

Got that? The EU's principal "fear" about an actual ongoing epidemic of hate crimes against Jews is that it could hypothetically provoke an epidemic of hate crimes against Muslims.

And so the more the enemies of free society step on our feet the more we tiptoe around. After the release of the Royal Navy hostages, the Right Reverend Tom Burns, Roman Catholic Bishop of the Armed Forces, praised the Iranians for their "forgiveness". "Over the past two weeks," said the Bishop, "there has been a unity of purpose between Britain and Iran, whereby everyone has sought justice and forgiveness."

Really? In what alternative universe is that? Maybe the insanity is contagious. As the columnist Jack Kelly wrote, "The infidels Allah wishes to destroy, he first makes mad." And so these twin psychoses – Islamist rage and our determination never to see it – continue their *valse macabre* on the brink of catastrophe.

REALITY TV

Survivor

National Review, December 3rd 2007

EVER SINCE this here Internet thingy came along, I spend the first hour of each morning trying to figure out which if any of the gazillions of overnight e-mails is genuine. This one struck me as obviously fake: a press release for a new reality TV show in which non-Muslims get to live under sharia.

But, inevitably, it turns out to be bona fide. Filmed in Harrogate, one of the least Muslim towns in Yorkshire, the series will air on Britain's Channel 4 and feature infidels trying to live as a Muslim for three weeks. It's not as easy as it looks. One participant, offered a cold baked potato at the end of his fast, stomped off to the pub for a pint of beer and a pork pie. "That incident was completely unprompted," the producer Narinder Minhas told *The Guardian*, "and the scene with Suliman, one of the mentors, and Luke, the gay hairdresser, in the clothes shop is one of my favorites."

Luke the gay hairdresser? Yes, Mr Minhas has chosen a scientifically representative sample of early 21st century infidels: a gay hairdresser, a "glamour model" partial to flashing her breasts, an atheist taxi driver with a porn habit, etc. Evidently, Harrogate has changed somewhat from the genteel spa town it was when I took tea and crumpets there some years ago. Anyway, the gay coiffeur and the porno cabbie et al have to live without pork, alcohol, immodest ladies' clothing and non-marital sex. Which pretty much eliminates every pillar of the Yorkshire infidel lifestyle.

Minhas, previously the producer of "Priest Idol" and "Indian Finishing School", says he and Channel 4 wanted their new reality series to be "fun". "We were a bit tired," he explained wearily, "of seeing guys with beards who are a bit scary." Indeed. Who among us has not found himself fighting vainly the old ennui at the umpteenth fire-breathing imam exhorting the lads to one more chorus of "Death to the Great Satan"? It was unclear from the publicity what happens if you find the three-week sharia tough-sledding. Do you get voted off the island? Or beheaded off the island? It had the vague feel of sharia-lite, the Islamic equivalent of Richard Gere Buddhism. A day or two later, I awoke to an e-mail about a British teacher in Sudan facing 40 lashes and blasphemy charges for having been careless enough to let her pupils name a classroom teddy bear "Mohammed". Don't know what precise sura references the matter of cuddly-toy nomenclature, but apparently it's a big deal. You can't help feeling Luke the gay hairdresser would have a livelier sharia-for-a-day session in the Khartoum spin-off.

Meanwhile, away from reality TV, reality plods on. In Pakistan, the suicide bomber who killed 170 people at Benazir Bhutto's homecoming rally is believed by police to be a one-year old child involuntarily conscripted by his jihadist father. Miss Bhutto had glimpsed the kid and beckoned dad over for a baby-kissing photo-op, but someone got between them and her motorcade swept on, fortunately for her. In the west, not many of us would wire up our one-year olds, and, if we did, they'd soon be outnumbered. I said in my book that Europe's demographically shriveled liberal progressives had in effect adopted the same strategy as the 19th century Shakers, who were forbidden to reproduce and so could increase their numbers only by conversion. Result: There aren't a lot of Shakers around today. At the time I wrote it, a year and a half back, I meant it as a cheap metaphorical crack at the expense of European fertility rates. After all, it would be absurd to suggest that liberal progressives were formally enjoined to desist from going forth and multiplying.

But I'm reminded of some advice I once got from a showbiz veteran: the easiest way to make a million bucks is to take your favorite gag and play it for real. My little Shaker crack has been eagerly taken up and made literal by the environmental movement: As the *Daily Mail* headline put it, "Meet The Women Who Won't Have Babies – Because They're Not Eco-Friendly". The best way to save the earth for the next generation is not to have a next generation. So Toni and Sarah, at the peak of their reproductive years, both decided to have themselves sterilized to "protect the planet". As Toni explained, "Every person who is born uses more food, more water, more land, more fossil fuels, more trees and produces more rubbish, more pollution, more greenhouse gases, and adds to the problem of overpopulation." We are the pollution, and sterilization is the solution. It's the ultimate reality TV show: a series of Survivor where *everyone* gets voted off the island.

Toni and Sarah assume they're saving the planet for Al Gore's polar bears, and the spotted owl, and the three-toed tree sloth, and the green-cheeked parrot. In fact, they're saving the planet for the cultures whose womenfolk don't get themselves sterilized. Forty per cent of children in London primary schools now speak a language other than English at home. No matter how frantically Toni and Sarah and all their chums tie their tubes, England grows ever more crowded.

The culture that built the modern world is playing "Civilizational Survivor". Alas, sharia isn't a TV show. For one thing, it never gets canceled.

ANTI-ISLAMIC ACTIVITY

That's all, folks!

The New York Sun, January 28th 2008

MY FAVORITE headline of the year so far comes from *The Daily Mail* in Britain:

Government Renames Islamic Terrorism As 'Anti-Islamic Activity' To Woo Muslims.

Her Majesty's Government is not alone in feeling it's not always helpful to link Islam and the, ah, various unpleasantnesses with suicide bombers and whatnot. Even in his cowboy Crusader heyday, President Bush liked to cool down the crowd with a lot of religion-of-peace stuff. But the British have decided that that kind of mealy-mouthed "respect" is no longer sufficient. So, henceforth, any terrorism perpetrated by persons of an Islamic persuasion will be designated "anti-Islamic activity". Britain's Home Secretary, Jacqui Smith, unveiled the new brand name in a speech a few days ago. "There is nothing Islamic about the wish to terrorize, nothing Islamic about plotting murder, pain and grief," she told her audience. "Indeed, if anything, these actions are anti-Islamic."

Well, yes, one sort of sees what she means. Killing thousands of people in Manhattan skyscrapers in the name of Islam does, among a certain narrow-minded type of person, give Islam a bad name, and thus could be said to be "anti-Islamic" – in the same way that the Luftwaffe raining down death and destruction on Londoners during the Blitz was an "anti-German activity". But I don't recall even Neville Chamberlain explaining, as if to a five-year old, that there is nothing German about the wish to terrorize and invade, and that this is entirely at odds with the core German values of sitting around eating huge sausages in beer gardens while wearing lederhosen.

Still, it should add a certain surreal quality to BBC news bulletins: "The Prime Minister today condemned the latest anti-Islamic activity as he picked through the rubble of Downing Street looking for his 2008 Wahhabi Community Outreach Award. In a related incident, the anti-Islamic activists who blew up Buckingham Palace have unfortunately caused the postponement of the Queen's annual Ramadan banquet."

A few days ago, a pre-trial hearing in an Atlanta courtroom made public for the first time a video made by two Georgia Tech students. Syed Haris Ahmed and Ehsanul Islam Sadequee went to Washington and took footage of key buildings, and that "casing video" then wound up in the hands of Younis Tsouli, an al-Qaeda recruiter in London. As the film shot by the Georgia students was played in court, Ehsanul Islam Sadequee's voice could be heard on the soundtrack: "This is where our brothers attacked the Pentagon."

"Allahu Akbar," responds young Ahmed. God is great.

How "anti-Islamic" an activity is that? Certainly, not all Muslims want to fly planes into the Pentagon. But those that do do it in the name of their faith. And anyone minded to engage in an "anti-Islamic activity" will find quite a lot of support from leading Islamic scholars. Take, for example, the "moderate" imam Yusuf al-Qaradawi, who once observed that "we will conquer Europe, we will conquer America! Not through the sword, but through *da'wa*" – ie, the non-incendiary form of Islamic outreach, the call to live according to the will of Allah.

What could be more moderate than that? No wonder Mr al-Qaradawi is an associate of the Islamic Society of Boston, currently building the largest mosque in the north-east, and also a pal of the present Mayor of London. Just goes to show all this "conquest" talk doesn't have to be blood-curdling, does it? Which is true. But, by insisting on re-labeling terrorism committed by Muslims in the name of Islam as "anti-Islamic activity", Her Majesty's Government is engaging not merely in Orwellian Newspeak but self-defeating Orwellian Newspeak. The broader message it sends is that ours is a weak culture so unconfident and insecure that if you bomb us and kill us our first urge is to find a way to flatter and apologize to you.

Here's another news item out of Britain this week: A new version of *The Three Little Pigs* was turned down for some "excellence in education" award on the grounds that "the use of pigs raises cultural issues" and, as a result, the judges "had concerns for the Asian community" – ie, Muslims. Non-Muslim Asians – Hindus and Buddhists – have no "concerns" about anthropomorphized pigs.

This is now a recurring theme in British life. A while back, it was a local government council telling workers not to have knick-knacks on their desks representing Winnie-the-Pooh's porcine sidekick, Piglet. As Martin Niemöller famously said, first they came for Piglet and I did not speak out because I was not a Disney character and, if I was, I'm more of an Eeyore. So then they came for the Three Little Pigs, and Babe, and by the time I realized my country had turned into a 24/7 Looney Tunes it was too late, because there was no Porky Pig to stammer "Th-th-th-that's all, folks!" and bring the nightmare to an end.

Just for the record, it's true that Muslims, like Jews, are not partial to bacon and sausages. But the Koran has nothing to say about cartoon pigs. Likewise, it is silent on the matter of whether one can name a teddy bear after Mohammed. What all these stories have in common is the *excessive* deference to Islam. If the Three Little Pigs are verboten when Muslims do not yet comprise ten per cent of the British population, what else will be on the blacklist by the time they're, say, 20 per cent?

A couple of days later, Elizabeth May, leader of Canada's Green Party (the fourth largest political party), spoke out against her country's continued military contribution to the international force in Afghanistan. "More ISAF forces from a Christian/Crusader heritage," she said, "will continue to fuel an insurgency that has been framed as a jihad." As it happens, Canada did not send troops to the Crusades, mainly because the fun was over several centuries before Canada came in existence. Six years ago, it was mostly the enemy who took that line,

Osama bin Laden raging at the Great Satan for the fall of Andalusia in 1492, which, with the best will in the world, it's hard to blame on Halliburton. But since then, the pathologies of Islamism have proved surprisingly contagious among western elites.

You remember the Three Little Pigs? One builds a house of straw, and another of sticks, and both get blown down by the Big Bad Wolf. Western civilization is a mighty house of bricks, but who needs a Big Bad Wolf when the pig's so eager to demolish it himself?

THE BOMBAY MASSACRES
Who's vulnerable?

The Orange County Register, December 6th 2008

IN THE WAKE of the late unpleasantness in Bombay, the Associated Press filed a story about (what else?) how Muslims "found themselves on the defensive once again about bloodshed linked to their religion."

Oh, I don't know about that. In fact, you'd be hard pressed from most news reports to figure out the bloodshed was "linked" to any religion, least of all one beginning with "I-" and ending in "-slam." In the years since 9/11, the media have more or less entirely abandoned the offending formulations — "Islamic terrorists," "Muslim extremists" — and by the time of the assault on Bombay found it easier just to call the alleged perpetrators "militants" or "gunmen" - or "teenage gunmen," as in the opening line of this report in *The Australian*: "An Adelaide woman in India for her wedding is lucky to be alive after teenage gunmen ran amok…"

Kids today, eh? Always running amok in an aimless fashion.

The veteran British TV anchor Jon Snow, on the other hand, opted for the more cryptic locution "practitioners". "Practitioners" of what, exactly?

Hard to say. And getting harder. In *The Wall Street Journal*, Tom Gross produced a jaw-dropping round-up of Bombay media coverage: The discovery that, for the first time in an Indian terrorist atrocity, Jews had been attacked, tortured, and killed produced from *The New York Times* a serene befuddlement: "It is not known if the Jewish center was strategically chosen, or if it was an accidental hostage scene."

Hmm. Greater Bombay forms one of the world's five biggest cities. It has a population of nearly 20 million. But only one Jewish center, located in a building that gives no external clue as to the bounty waiting therein. An "accidental hostage scene" that one of the "practitioners" just happened to stumble upon? "I must be the luckiest jihadist in town. What are the odds?"

Meanwhile, the New Age guru Deepak Chopra laid all the blame on American foreign policy for "going after the wrong people" and inflaming moderates, and "that inflammation then gets organized and appears as this disaster in Bombay."

Really? The inflammation just "appears"? Like a bad pimple?

The "fairer" we get to the, ah, inflamed militant practitioners, the unfairer we get to everyone else. At the Chabad House, the murdered Jews were described in almost all the western media as "ultra-Orthodox," "ultra-" in this instance being less a term of theological precision than a generalized code for "strange, weird people, nothing against them personally, but they probably shouldn't have been over there in the first place." Are they stranger or weirder than their killers? Two "inflamed moderates" entered the Chabad House, shouted "Allahu Akbar!", tortured the Jews and murdered them, including the young Rabbi's pregnant wife. Their two-year-old child escaped because of a quick-witted (non-Jewish) nanny who hid in a closet and then, risking being mown down by machine-gun fire, ran with him to safety.

The *Times* was being silly in suggesting this was just an "accidental" hostage opportunity - and not just because, when Muslim terrorists capture Jews, it's not a hostage situation, it's a mass murder-in-waiting. The sole surviving "militant" revealed that the Jewish center had been targeted a year in advance. The 28-year-old rabbi was Gavriel Holtzberg. His pregnant wife was Rivka Holtzberg. Their orphaned son is Moshe Holtzberg, and his brave nanny is Sandra Samuels. Remember their names, not because they're any more important than the Indians, Britons, and Americans targeted in the attack on Bombay, but because they are an especially revealing glimpse into the pathologies of the perpetrators.

In a well-planned attack on iconic Bombay landmarks symbolizing great power and wealth, the "militants" nevertheless found time to divert 20 per cent of their manpower to torturing and killing a handful of obscure Jews helping the city's poor in a nondescript building. If they were just "teenage gunmen" or "militants" in the cause of Kashmir, engaged in a more or less conventional territorial dispute with India, why kill the only rabbi in Bombay? Dennis Prager got to the absurdity of it when he invited his readers to imagine Basque separatists attacking Madrid: "Would the terrorists take time out to murder all those in the Madrid Chabad House? The idea is ludicrous."

And yet we take it for granted that Pakistani "militants" in a long-running border dispute with India would take time out of their hectic schedule to kill Jews. In going to ever more baroque lengths to avoid saying "Islamic" or "Muslim" or "terrorist," we have somehow managed to internalize the pathologies of these men.

We are enjoined to be "understanding," and we're doing our best. A Minnesotan suicide bomber (now there's a phrase) originally from Somalia returned to the old country and blew up himself and 29 other people last October. His family prevailed upon your government to have his parts (or as many of them as could be sifted from the debris) returned to the United States at taxpayer expense and buried in Burnsville Cemetery. Well, hey, in the current climate, what's the big deal about a federal bailout of jihad operational expenses? If that's not "too big to fail," what is?

Last week, a Canadian critic reprimanded me for failing to understand that Muslims feel "vulnerable." *Au contraire*, they project tremendous cultural confidence, as well they might: They're the world's fastest-growing population. A prominent British Muslim announced the other day that, when the United Kingdom becomes a Muslim state, non-Muslims will be required to wear insignia identifying them as infidels. If he's feeling "vulnerable," he's doing a terrific job of covering it up.

We are told that the "vast majority" of the 1.6-1.8 billion Muslims (in Deepak Chopra's estimate) are "moderate." Maybe so, but they're also quiet. And, as the AIDs activists used to say, "Silence=Acceptance." It equals acceptance of the things done in the name of their faith. Rabbi Holtzberg was not murdered because of a territorial dispute over Kashmir or because of Bush's foreign policy. He was murdered in the name of Islam - "Allahu Akbar."

I wrote in my book, *America Alone*, that "reforming" Islam is something only Muslims can do. But they show very little sign of being interested in doing it, and the rest of us are inclined to accept that. Spread a rumor that a Koran got flushed down the can at Gitmo, and there'll be rioting throughout the Muslim world. Publish some dull cartoons in a minor Danish newspaper, and there'll be protests around the planet. But torture, rape and slaughter the young pregnant wife of a rabbi in Bombay in the name of Allah, and that's just business as usual. And, if it is somehow "understandable" that for the first time in history it's no longer safe for a Jew to live in India, then we are greasing the skids for a very slippery slope. Muslims, the AP headline informs us, "worry about image." Not enough.

THE DAY AFTER the assault on Bombay, *The Toronto Star* ran a column by Haroon Siddiqui, one of the last prominent defenders of the Canadian government's powers of censorship under Section 13 of the country's Human Rights Code. Apropos my now notorious book excerpt in *Maclean's*, Mr Siddiqui writes:

> *Alan Borovoy of the Canadian Civil Liberties Union, a lifelong proponent of free speech, told me:*
>
> *'Let's just take one statement that Steyn made: "Not all Muslims are terrorists, though enough are hot for jihad to provide an impressive support network." I interpret that as saying that a significant number of Muslims support terrorism... How much worse can you get? Doesn't that expose them to hatred? This looks to me like an awful exercise in rationalization by those who say this isn't hatred.'*

I'd be interested to know what's in that ellipsis, since the quotation doesn't quite jibe with the evolution of Mr Borovoy's thinking on state censorship. But, assuming that he's being quoted correctly, the day after a Muslim terrorist assault on key landmarks of a major Indian city that left dozens dead, saw British and American tourists taken hostage, and the city's anti-terrorism chief and other municipal law enforcement figures gunned down on the street doesn't seem the most tactful moment for Messrs Siddiqui and Borovoy to protest at *Maclean's* even raising the subject of how many Muslims support terrorism and its goals. That's an entirely responsible subject for the media to raise. And, given what's going on in the streets of Bombay, it's irresponsible for the media not to raise it - unless, that is, like Mr Siddiqui, you see yourself not as a journalist but as an enforcer for PC orthodoxy.

THE OLDEST HATRED

Gaza west

The Orange County Register, January 10th 2009
National Review, January 13th, 14th 2009

SPEAKING on the BBC's flagship morning show, Sir Jeremy Greenstock, former British Ambassador to the UN, explains that the Hamas kill-the-Jews routine is nothing to worry about:

They are not intent on the destruction of Israel. That's a rhetorical statement of resistance and not part of their program.

It's like an Obama pledge to close Gitmo or withdraw from Iraq - just part of the meaningless banter of public discourse, but nothing that's going to happen anytime soon.

Good to know. The rhetoric's certainly catchy, though. Here's a "pro-Palestinian" demonstration from Copenhagen:

Vi vil gerne dræbe alle jøderne verden over, alle jøder skal dræbes.

My Danish is a little rusty but I think that translates to: "We want to kill all the Jews everywhere, all Jews should be killed." Still, you don't have to know the lingo to get the opening shot from the demonstrators, helpfully chanted in English:

Down down, democracy!

Indeed. Meanwhile, in Alberta, the neo-Nazi Aryan Guard get the prestigious second place in Calgary's "pro-Palestinian" parade. Presumably, they just dig the rhetoric, too.

In Toronto, anti-Israel demonstrators yell "You are the brothers of pigs!", and a protester complains to his interviewer that "Hitler didn't do a good job."

In Fort Lauderdale, Palestinian supporters sneer at Jews, "You need a big oven, that's what you need!"

In Amsterdam, the crowd shouts, "Hamas, Hamas! Jews to the gas!"

In Paris, the state-owned TV network France-2 broadcasts film of dozens of dead Palestinians killed in an Israeli air raid on New Year's Day. The channel subsequently admits that, in fact, the footage is not from January 1st 2009, but from 2005, and, while the corpses are certainly Palestinian, they were killed when a truck loaded with Hamas explosives detonated prematurely while leaving the Jabaliya refugee camp in another of those unfortunate work-related accidents to which Gaza is unusually prone. Conceding that the Palestinians supposedly killed by Israel were, alas, killed by Hamas, France-2 says the footage was broadcast "accidentally".

In Toulouse, a synagogue is firebombed; in Bordeaux, two kosher butchers are attacked; at the Auber RER train station, a Jewish man is savagely assaulted by 20 youths taunting, "Palestine will kill the Jews"; in Villiers-le-Bel, a Jewish schoolgirl is brutally beaten by a gang jeering, "Jews must die."

In Helsingborg, the congregation at a Swedish synagogue takes shelter as a window is broken and burning cloths thrown in; in Odense, principal Olav Nielsen announces that he will no longer admit Jewish children to the local school after a Dane of Lebanese extraction goes to the shopping mall and shoots two men working at the Dead Sea Products store; in Brussels, a Molotov cocktail is hurled at a synagogue; in Antwerp, lit rags are pushed through the mail flap of a Jewish home; and, across the Channel, "youths" attempt to burn the Brondesbury Park Synagogue.

In London, the police advise British Jews to review their security procedures because of potential revenge attacks. *The Sun* reports "fears" that "Islamic extremists" are drawing up a "hit list" of prominent Jews, including the Foreign Secretary, Amy Winehouse's record producer and the late Princess of Wales' divorce lawyer. Meanwhile, *The Guardian* reports that Islamic non-extremists from the British Muslim Forum, the Islamic Foundation and other impeccably respectable "moderate" groups have warned the government that the

Israelis' "disproportionate force" in Gaza risks inflaming British Muslims, "reviving extremist groups", and provoking "UK terrorist attacks" - not against Amy Winehouse's record producer and other sinister members of the International Jewish Conspiracy but against targets of, ah, more general interest.

Forget, for the moment, Gaza. Forget that the Palestinian people are the most comprehensively wrecked people on the face of the Earth. For the past 60 years they have been entrusted to the care of the United Nations, the Arab League, the PLO, Hamas and the "global community" - and the results are pretty much what you'd expect. You would have to be very hardhearted not to weep at the sight of dead Palestinian children, but you would also have to accord a measure of blame to the Hamas officials who choose to use grade schools as launch pads for Israeli-bound rockets, and to the UN refugee agency that turns a blind eye to it. And, even if you don't despise Fatah and Hamas for marinating their infants in a sick death cult in which martyrdom in the course of Jew-killing is the greatest goal to which a citizen can aspire, any fair-minded visitor to the West Bank or Gaza in the decade and a half in which the "Palestinian Authority" has exercised sovereign powers roughly equivalent to those of the nascent Irish Free State in 1922 would have to concede that the Palestinian "nationalist movement" has a profound shortage of nationalists interested in running a nation, or indeed capable of doing so. There is fault on both sides, of course, and Israel has few good long-term options. But, if this was a conventional ethno-nationalist dispute, it would have been over long ago.

So, as I said, forget Gaza. And, instead, ponder the reaction to Gaza in Scandinavia, France, the United Kingdom, Canada, and golly, even Florida. As the delegitimization of Israel becomes first routine and then universally accepted, we are assured that criticism of the Jewish state is not the same as anti-Semitism. We are further assured that anti-Zionism is not the same as anti-Semitism, which is a wee bit more of a stretch. Only Israel attracts an intellectually respectable movement querying its very existence. For the purposes of comparison, let's take a state that came into existence at the exact same time as the Zionist Entity, and involved far bloodier population displacements. I happen to think the creation of Pakistan was the greatest failure of post-war British imperial policy. But the fact is that Pakistan does exist, and if I were to launch a movement of anti-Pakism it would get pretty short shrift.

But, even allowing for that, what has a schoolgirl in Villiers-le-Bel to do with Israeli government policy? Just weeks ago, terrorists attacked Bombay, seized hostages, tortured them, killed them, and mutilated their bodies. The police intercepts of the phone conversations between the terrorists and their controllers make for lively reading:

PAKISTAN CALLER 1: *Kill all hostages, except the two Muslims. Keep your phone switched on so that we can hear the gunfire.*

BOMBAY TERRORIST 2: *We have three foreigners, including women. From Singapore and China.*

PAKISTAN CALLER 1: *Kill them.*

(Voices of gunmen can be heard directing hostages to stand in a line, and telling two Muslims to stand aside. Sound of gunfire. Sound of cheering voices.)

"Kill all hostages, except the two Muslims." Tough for those Singaporean women. Yet no mosques in Singapore have been attacked. The large Hindu populations in London, Toronto and Fort Lauderdale have not shouted "Muslims must die!" or firebombed Halal butchers or attacked hijab-clad schoolgirls. CAIR and other Muslim lobby groups' eternal bleating about "Islamophobia" is in inverse proportion to any examples of it. Meanwhile, "moderate Muslims" in Britain warn the government: "I'm a peaceful fellow myself, but I can't speak for my excitable friends. Nice little G7 advanced western democracy you got here. Shame if anything were to happen to it."

But why worry about European Muslims? The European political and media class essentially shares the same view of the situation – to the point where state TV stations are broadcasting fake Israeli "war crimes".

As I always say, the "oldest hatred" didn't get that way without an ability to adapt: Once upon a time on the Continent, Jews were hated as rootless cosmopolitan figures who owed no national allegiance. So they became a conventional nation state, and now they're hated for that. And, if Hamas get their way and destroy the Jewish state, the few who survive will be hated for something else. So it goes.

But Jew-hating has consequences for the Jew-hater, too. And even among my own readers, contempt for the Jew seems to be blinding them to what recent events portend: the Israelification of European life. Mandatory Palestine was, in the old joke, the twice promised land - hence, a western democracy and a disaffected Muslim population exist in opposing solitudes but claim the same piece of real estate. As it happens, that's also how more and more Muslims see Europe – and beyond. When young Muslim men on the streets of Montreal chant "Hezbollah! Nasrallah!" and *"Les juifs sont nos chiens"*, it's easy to think all this stuff is just about the Jew troublemakers, and who cares about them, right? But the thuggery on display in western cities is meant to intimidate not the despised Jew dogs but the citizenry at large, and it seems to be doing the job. Consider this bizarre response from the French government to a Molotov cocktail attack on a synagogue in St-Denis:

> *Interior Minister Michele Alliot-Marie said France has faced a 'very clear increase' in anti-Semitic and anti-Muslim attacks since Israel started an offensive against the militant group Hamas in Gaza on December 27th.*

Would it be too much for a French reporter to ask Mme Alliot-Marie to provide an example of an "anti-Muslim attack" since December 27th? None seems to have been reported in the French press, unlike the daily attacks on synagogues, kosher butchers, schools, and individual Jews in Paris, Toulouse, Bordeaux, etc. So the Interior

160

Minister would appear to be promoting a wholly false equivalence. Why would she do this?

Well, for a clearer picture, look at the Internet video of another "pro-Palestinian" protest in Central London and the Metropolitan Police retreating up St James's Street to Piccadilly in the face of a mob jeering, "Run, run, you cowards!" and "Fatwa!" The west's deluded multiculti progressives should understand: In the end, this isn't about Gaza, this isn't about the Middle East. It's about you. And in the coming Europe, you're the Jews.

ISLAM AND FREE EXPRESSION
Death is too easy

The New York Sun, June 24th 2007

A YEAR OR SO after the Ayatollah Khomeini took out an Islamist mob contract on Salman Rushdie, the novelist appeared, after elaborate security arrangements, on a television arts show in London. His host was Melvyn Bragg, a long-time British telly grandee, and what was striking was how quickly the interview settled down into the usual lit.crit. chit-chat. Lord Bragg took Rushdie back to his earlier pre-fatwa work. "After your first book," drawled Bragg, "which was not particularly well-received…"

That's supposed to be the worst a novelist has to endure. His book will be "not particularly well-received" – ie, some twerp reviewers will be snotty about it in *The New Yorker* and *The Guardian*. In the cosy world of English letters, it came as a surprise to find that being "not particularly well-received" meant foreign governments putting a bounty on your head and killing your publishers and translators. Even then, the literary set had difficulty taking it literally. After news footage of British Muslims burning Rushdie's book in the streets of English cities, BBC arts bores sat around on talk-show sofas deploring the "symbolism" of this attack on "ideas".

There was nothing symbolic about it. They burned the book because they couldn't burn Rushdie himself. If his wife and kid had swung by, they'd have gladly burned them, just as the mob was happy to burn to death 37 Turks who'd made the mistake of being in the same hotel in Sivas as one of the novelist's translators. When British Muslims called for Rushdie to be killed, they meant it. From a mosque in Yorkshire, Mohammed Siddiqui wrote to *The Independent* to endorse the fatwa by citing Sura 5 verses 33-34 from the Koran:

162

The punishment of those who wage war against God and His Apostle, and strive with might and main for mischief through the land, is execution, or crucifixion, or the cutting off of hands and feet from opposite sides, or exile from the land.

That last apparently wasn't an option.

Britain got so many things wrong during the Rushdie affair, just as America got so many things wrong during the Iranian embassy siege ten years earlier. But it's now 2007 – almost two decades after Iran claimed sovereignty over British subjects, almost three decades after they claimed sovereignty over US territory. So what have we learned? I was with various British parliamentarians the other day, and we were talking about the scenes from Islamabad, where the usual death-to-the-Great-Satan chappies had burned an effigy of the Queen to protest the knighthood she'd just conferred on Rushdie. I told my London friends that I had to hand it to Tony Blair's advisors: What easier way for the toothless old British lion, after the humiliations inflicted upon the Royal Navy sailors by their Iranian kidnappers, to show you're still a player than by knighting Salman Rushdie for his "services to literature"? Given that his principal service to literature has been to introduce the word "fatwa" to the English language, one assumed that some characteristically cynical British civil servant had waved the knighthood through as a relatively cheap way of flipping the finger to the mullahs.

But no. It seems Her Majesty's Government in London was taken entirely by surprise by the scenes of burning Union Jacks on the evening news.

Can that really be true? In a typically incompetent response, Margaret Beckett, the Foreign Secretary, issued one of those obviously-we're-sorry-if-there's-been-a-misunderstanding statements in which she managed to imply that Rushdie had been honored as a representative of the Muslim community. He's not. He's an ex-Muslim. He's a representative of the Muslim community's willingness to kill you for attempting to leave the Muslim community. But, locked into obsolescent multiculti identity-groupthink, Mrs Beckett instinctively saw Rushdie as a member of a quaintly exotic minority rather than as a free-born individual.

This is where we came in two decades ago. We should have learned something by now. In the Muslim world, artistic criticism can be fatal. In 1992, the poet Sadiq Abd al-Karim Milalla also found that his work was "not particularly well-received": he was beheaded by the Saudis for suggesting Mohammed cooked up the Koran by himself. In 1998, the Algerian singer Lounès Matoub described himself as "*ni Arabe ni musulman*" (neither Arab nor Muslim) and shortly thereafter found himself neither alive nor well. These are not famous men. They don't stand around on Oscar night congratulating themselves on their "courage" for speaking out against Bush-Rove fascism. But, if we can't do much about freedom of expression in Iran and Saudi Arabia, we could at least do our bit to stop Saudi-Iranian standards embedding themselves in the western world.

So many of our problems with Iran today arise from not doing anything about our problems with Iran yesterday. Men like Ayatollah Khomeini despised pan-Arab nationalists like Nasser who tried to impose a local variant of Marxism on the Muslim world. Khomeini figured: Why import the false ideologies of a failing civilization? Doesn't it make more sense to export Islamism to the dying west?

And, for a guy dismissed by most of us as crazy, he made a lot of sense. The Rushdie fatwa established the ground rules: The side that means it gets away with it. Mobs marched through Britain calling for the murder of a British subject – and, as a matter of policy on the grounds of multicultural sensitivity, the British police shrugged and looked the other way. Genuine "moderate Muslims" were cowed into silence, and pseudo-moderate Muslims triangulated with artful evasiveness. Sir Iqbal Sacranie, who went on to become leader of the most prominent British Muslim lobby group, was asked his opinion of the fatwa against Rushdie and mused: "Death is perhaps too easy."

In 1989 Salman Rushdie went into hiding under the protection of the British police. A decade later, despite renewals of the fatwa and generous additions to the bounty, he decided he did not wish to live his life like that and emerged from seclusion to live a more or less normal life. He learned the biggest lesson of all – how easy it is to be forced into the shadows. That's what's happening in the free world incrementally every day, with every itsy-bitsy nothing concession to groups who take offence at everything and demand the right to kill you for every offence. Across two decades, what happened to Rushdie has metastasized, in part because of the weak response in those first months. "Death is perhaps too easy"? Maybe. But slow societal suicide is easier still.

ISLAMOTOPIA
Caliphate

Maclean's, June 9th 2008

T HE DOMINION of Canada. It was nice while it lasted:

> *Nineteen Regular Army divisions, one dozen divisions of the Army National Guard, plus the Second and Fourth Marine Divisions, rolled across the border just before dawn on 11 May, 2020.*
>
> *Despite the gallant resistance put up by the main elements of the Canadian Forces, notably the Royal 22nd and Twelfth Armored, which died in defense of Quebec City, the Royal Canadian Regiment and Royal Canadian Dragoons, shattered in the forlorn defense of Ottawa, and the Princess Patricia's Canadian Light Infantry and Lord Strathcona's Horse, butchered in detail in a hopeless defense of the long western border, Canada — rather the thin strip of well-populated area that roughly paralleled the border with the United States — fell quickly.*

Oh, dear. Only 12 years of "Canadian values" to go. If you want to put in for your hip replacement now, they may just get to you before the tanks roll. It's going to be mighty expensive once the Princess Margaret Hospital is renamed for whichever Halliburton subsidiary winds up running it. The author of the above passage, Tom Kratman, adds:

> *It is both interesting and sad to note that it was only those most despised by the government of Canada, and its ruling party, who actually proved willing to defend that government. Those who had most despised their own forces, and who had themselves signally failed to fight, soon found themselves the center of attention of a country-wide sweep.*

166

Hmm. Do you think he means Grits and Dippers and Péquistes and whatnot? Hey, at least they don't wind up at Gitmo:

Almost as quickly they found themselves in various well-guarded logging and mining camps in the cold, cold lands of Nunavut and the Northwest Territories...

Oh, well, could be worse. Don't ask me how. The lurid and loving description of the fall of the peaceable kingdom comes from Mr Kratman's new novel. No, it's not about Canada. Although the author specializes in military science fiction, a US invasion of the friendly neighbour to the north doesn't require a lot of imagination – unless, that is, the Canucks win, and the beaten demoralized Yanks wind up retreating across the 49th parallel vowing never again to be so foolish as to take on the genetically augmented warriors of big government: "All those stories about more MRI machines in Philadelphia than in the whole of Canada," sighed President Chelsea Clinton Obama. "Why didn't we figure out, if they're not spending the budget on MRI machines, they must be doing something else with it. To think we swallowed that hooey about the 'Toronto General' and the 'Royal Victoria' being just hospitals..." She was about to fire the CIA director but at that point Field Marshal Khadr of the Ontario Human Rights Commission Mounted Division entered the Oval Office on a SARS-breathing winged moose...

Alas, no. Mr Kratman's novel is called *Caliphate*, and is set more or less a century hence in a Muslim Europe at war with an imperial America. The fall of Canada is little more than a bit of backstory to explain how things got that way. On the press release, the publisher includes a recommendation from the technothriller writer John Ringo describing *Caliphate* as "Mark Steyn's *America Alone* with a body count."

Gulp. That's not the kind of quote that's terribly helpful right now. Insofar as I understand the complaints against *Maclean's* before the various "human rights" commissions, it's that my hate speech could lead to body counts all over Canada, and now here comes Tom

Kratman to pretty much prove the point. The thesis of my book is that the western world is becoming more Muslim, and that this will change the nature of our societies – might be for the better, might be for the worse; we'll find out in the fullness of time. But an emerging sub-genre of Islamotopian fiction is beginning to delineate some of the options. Robert Ferrigno has just published *Sins Of The Assassins*, the second novel in his trilogy set circa 2040 in the Islamic Republic of America. He recently took time out from his hectic schedule of book promotion south of the border to profess bewilderment at finding himself part of a "human rights" case up north. As evidence of my "flagrant Islamophobia", the Canadian Islamic Congress claims I "asserted" the following:

1. American will be an Islamic Republic by the year 2040 – there will be a Muslim / Islamist takeover

2. As a result of the Muslim takeover, there will be a break for prayers during the Super Bowl, the stadium will have a stereotypical Muslim name, and the fans will be forced to watch the game in a Muslim prayer posture

4. As a result of the Muslim takeover there will an oppressive religious police enforcing Islamic/Muslim norms on the population, important US icons [such as the USS Ronald Reagan] will be renamed after Osama bin Laden, no females will be allowed to be cheerleaders, and popular American radio and television talk show hosts will have been replaced by Muslim imams...

In fact, I didn't "assert" that any of the above will happen. Robert Ferrigno did – in the plot of the splendid first novel of his trilogy, *Prayers For The Assassin*. As Mr Ferrigno put it, "It's as if that hall monitor saw the two of us walking to class and decided that it was Steyn with the squeaky shoes. Sorry pal, *c'est moi*." The author was as perplexed as any citizen of any free nation should be at the idea that the plot points of a work of fiction – an act of imagination - apparently constitute a hate crime in Canada. But he took particular umbrage at

168

being described by the Canadian Islamic Congress plaintiffs as a "recognized Islamophobe". "For the record," he says, "I am neither Islamophobic nor recognized."

He's right. The hero of his trilogy – and, as the Islamist enforcers at the CIC apparently aren't on top of this whole fiction-type deal, I should explain that the "hero" is the chap that you the reader is meant to identify with – is a Muslim: Rakkim Epps, a veteran of the Fedayeen, "a small, elite force of genetically enhanced holy warriors". He's a cynical fellow – Joel Schwartz in *The Weekly Standard* recently described him as a kind of Muslim Bogart, which is the right general territory; he's Philip Marlowe crossed with certain cabinet ministers I've met from Islamic countries – decent fellows under no illusions about the societies they serve. Ferrigno's second novel puts Rakkim undercover in the part of the old United States that didn't go Muslim – the south-eastern "Bible Belt", a wild raucous land of rough liquor and cartoon religiosity in which the biggest tourist attraction is the daily reenactment of the Waco siege. Mr Ferrigno's Belt sometimes feels like a televangelist theme-park writ large. So, if Christian groups were as litigious as their Muslim equivalents and willing to bandy around accusations of Christophobia, they'd have as much to work with as the Canadian Islamic Congress does. And, to one degree or another, both inheritors of the old United States – the Islamic Republic and the Belt – are societies in decline, living off the accumulated capital of a lost past.

If you're minded to spot Islamophobia in everything, Tom Kratman's *Caliphate* may offer easier pickings. His Islamic Europe is in serious decay – a land of rutted tracks and crumbling ruins. His protagonist is a post-CIA undercover operative in Germany who hooks up with a Catholic cutie sold into slavery and then into an elite brothel. Ferrigno is stronger on character and motivation, but Kratman's dystopia is a brisk page-turner full of startling twists and bad sex. I don't just mean the pneumatic bouts of hooker sex; even the good sex comes off as bad. Whether or not Mr Kratman is an expert in this field, I cannot say. But he's a professional military man who retired as Lieutenant-Colonel and was Director, Rule of War at the US Army War College, so he's certainly up to speed on the military and geopolitical conceits of the book. What I found most intriguing was not so much the 22nd century thriller but the short 21st century interludes between chapters, featuring the great-grandparents of Petra, the child prostitute at the heart of the novel. Robert Ferrigno inaugurates his dystopia with a big bang – simultaneous nuclear detonations that precipitate America's embrace of Islam. Tom Kratman also has bombs, but his 21st century episodes attempt, in an impressionistic way, to capture a subtler societal transition. These scenes are set in the Germany of the here and now, beginning with an Iraq war demonstration and the aftermath of the London Tube bombings. And then slowly and subtly the recent past turns into Kratman's imagined future, as the remorseless Islamization of Europe accelerates.

NUREMBERG, FEDERAL REPUBLIC OF GERMANY,
1 DECEMBER, 2011

Tax in Germany was becoming a problem, even in German terms, and they'd grown used to being nearly as heavily taxed as the French. The country was graying fast. Worse, because there were places where young people could earn more and keep more, places like America, Canada, Australia... young Germans were leaving. This left more tax to be paid by fewer workers, which drove even more to think about leaving...

17 OCTOBER, 2021

In an effort to placate the Muslims and stem the violence, Germany had established Sharia courts under Islamic scholars for Muslim communities...

10 JULY, 2022

It came as quite a shock to her, so much of a shock that she didn't even cry out, when five boys surrounded her, exclaimed, 'This is our sister," dropped a blanket over her head and pulled her into a cellar.

> *Germans and German law had long since stopped defending Muslim women…*

5 MARCH, 2024

'We still take some immigrants from Old Europe,' the [American] consular explained. 'But we don't really need them… You're in the process of losing your own homeland. You brought it on yourselves and it's become irreversible now. So ask yourself: Why should we accept into our country people with a history of destroying the country they live in?'

We'll be seeing a lot more novels like this – although perhaps not in Canada, if the Canadian Islamic Congress and their dopey enablers in the "human rights" commissions succeed in their campaign to get fictional plots rendered actionable. But I was interested to see that apparently the authors of Quebec's Bouchard-Taylor report, according to a story in *Le Journal de Montréal*, accept the notion of an Islamic conquest of Europe as not without foundation. It's a lopsided *valse macabre* between two left-footed dancers. "Why are you so certain everything's going down the tubes?" Gabi, a young German of conventional anti-American multiculti post-nationalist views, asks her Muslim boyfriend as he decides to flee the Continent for life in Boston.

"Because my people could fuck up a wet dream," Mahmoud answers. "And I'm beginning to think that yours can, too."

IV

FREE SPEECH AND THE MULTICULTURAL STATE

Freedom of expression doesn't mean the right to offend.
DUTCH FOREIGN MINISTER MAXIME VERHAGEN
speaking at the Alliance of Civilizations, an international forum to reduce
tensions between the Muslim world and the west
Madrid, January 2008

You remember that business from 2007 when Senator Larry Craig had his unfortunate run-in with the undercover cop in the Minneapolis Airport men's room? When the Canadian "human rights" apparatchiks began investigating my writing north of the border, I was amazed to pick up a newspaper south of the border and read that Senator Craig's lawyer had filed a brief arguing that the inviting hand gestures he supposedly made under the bathroom stall divider were constitutionally protected speech under the First Amendment. What a great country! In Canada, according to the Canadian Islamic Congress, "freedom of speech" doesn't extend to my books and columns. But in America Senator Craig's men's room semaphore is covered by the First Amendment. From now on, instead of writing about radical Islam, I'm only going to hit on imams in bathrooms. It'll be a lot safer.

In countries without a First Amendment, the state has become very comfortable at regulating speech, initially in the interests of approved groups such as gays, and at the expense of non-approved groups such as Christians. So the threat to western liberties isn't Islam, so much as the politically correct enforcers paving the way for tyranny.

At which point, enter Islam. In the last decade, Muslim groups in the west have decided reasonably enough that what's sauce for the gays and the Jews should also be sauce for the imams. One can't blame them for grabbing a slice of the censorship action, but the scale of their project is very different. And for the most part the west greets it with passivity and/or cowardice ever more unconvincingly dignified as "multicultural sensitivity":

MULTICULT

The slipperiest ism

The Western Standard, September 25th 2006

FIVE YEARS after the (a) all too predictable blowback to US foreign policy born of decades of poverty and desperation or (b) controlled explosion by Bush-Cheney-Halliburton-Zionist agents (delete according to taste), I get a lot of mail on the lines of: C'mon, man, cut to the chase - are we gonna win or lose?

Well, let me come at that in an evasive non-chase-cutting manner and circle around to it very gradually. I gave a speech in Sydney last month and among the audience was a lady called Pauline Hanson. A decade ago, Miss Hanson exploded onto the political scene Down Under on an explicitly nativist platform, forming the One Nation Party and arguing that Australia was "in danger of being swamped by Asians". She was mocked mercilessly as a former fish'n'chip shop owner, a 14-year-old school-leaver, an old slapper of dubious romantic attachments, etc. On the last point, I must say, having seen her in a little black number on the TV show "Dancing With the Stars", I thought she was a fine-looking woman, an impression confirmed when she stood up to ask her question.

Nonetheless, her question was a little overwrought. After some remarks about "grave concern for Australia", flag-burning, immigrants who "do not want to assimilate", and "a push for multiculturalism", she ended with: "This is not just happening in Australia. We see it happening worldwide, as you said, in the western societies. I want to ask you who's doing it, why is it happening?"

Now I don't happen to agree with all the "swamped by Asians" stuff (by which she means Chinese and Japanese and whatnot rather than "Asians" in the coyly euphemistic sense in which the British media now use the term). An ability to prioritize is essential in politics and, simply as a practical matter, there's no point in our present struggle in making enemies of large numbers of potential allies. So I took refuge in a big philosophical answer, and said I thought it all went back to the battlefields of the Somme. The ruling classes of the great powers believed they had lost their moral authority in the First World War and, although they rallied sufficiently to defeat Nazism and fascism and eventually communism, they never truly recovered their cultural confidence.

There's always been a market for self-loathing in free societies: after all, the most famous anti-western idea of all was itself an invention of the west, cooked up by Karl Marx while sitting in the Reading Room of the British Library. The obvious defect in Communism is that it's decrepit and joyless and therefore of limited appeal. Fascism, likewise, had many takers in those parts of the cultural west that were politically deficient - ie, continental Europe - but it had minimal support in the heart of the political west - ie, the English-speaking world. So the counter-tribalists came up with something subtler and suppler than Communism and Fascism - the slipperiest ism of all. The great strength of "multiculturalism" is not that it's an argument against the west but that it short-circuits the possibility of argument. If there's no difference between English Common Law and native healing circles and Sharia, then what's to discuss? Even to want to debate the merits is to find oneself on the wrong side - for, if the core belief of multiculturalism is that there's nothing to talk about and everything's equally nice and fluffy, then to favour honest argument puts you, by definition, on the extremist side.

That's the genius of multiculturalism: It renders discussion undiscussable. I'm sure most of my colleagues at *The Western Standard* have found themselves in this situation on call-in shows or at public meetings. You point out, for example, that there are very few "free" Muslim societies. And your questioner retorts: "Well, that's just your opinion." And so you pull up a few facts about GDP per capita, freedom of religion, life expectancy, women's rights, etc. And she says: "Well, you're just imposing your values on them." And you realize that the great advantage of cultural relativism is that it make argument impossible. There is no longer sufficient agreed reality. It's like playing tennis with an opponent who thinks your ace is a social construct.

To be sure, there are still those who are beyond the pale. Indeed, in a culture of boundless tolerance, there are all kinds of things we won't tolerate. Hating Jews, for example, is strictly *verboten*. Well, it's *verboten* if you're an elderly white male of German extraction, like Reni Sentana-Ries (formerly Reinhard Gustav Mueller) of Edmonton. Herr Sentana-Ries was sentenced to 16 months in jail by the Court of Queen's Bench for anti-Semitic screeds on his widely unread website in which he referred to Jews as "subhuman" "debauched" "demons".

On the other hand, if you're not an elderly white male of German extraction, if you're a large crowd of persons of, ahem, non-German extraction and you march through downtown Calgary with placards reading "DEATH TO THE JEWS" (a timeless rallying cry but hitherto relatively unsung on the Canadian prairies), nobody prosecutes you. The President of Iran, like the hapless Herr Sentana-Ries, is also a Holocaust denier and one with rather more advanced plans for assuring it all goes more efficiently next time. But he gets photo ops with the UN Secretary-General and EU officials.

In other words, Jew-hating isn't the problem, only certain types of Jew-haters. Even white men can get away with Jew-hating these days - not the old-school neo-Nazi white-supremacist jackboots-a-go-go Jew-hating, but certainly the new school of Jews-are-today's-Nazis disproportionate ambulance-targeting neo-apartheid Jew-hating.

The Fuhrer isn't coming out of retirement and, even if he does, there aren't enough Jews left in Europe to man a decent genocide. And it seems oddly apposite that the more we fetishize an extinct enemy the more Jews in Britain and Australia and even Montreal are targeted by the new Jew-haters. The question is: What other than Hitler is our society prepared to make a moral judgment over? Bernard Lewis, the west's pre-eminent scholar of Islam, worked for British Intelligence through the grimmest hours of the Second World War. "In 1940, we knew who we were, we knew who the enemy was, we knew the dangers and the issues," he told *The Wall Street Journal* a few months ago. "It is different today. We don't know who we are, we don't know the issues, and we still do not understand the nature of the enemy."

That first is the most important: it's not just that "we don't know who we are" but that cultural relativism strips the question of its basic legitimacy. In Britain, they used to say that the Battle of Waterloo was won on the playing fields of Eton, the sort of line it's easy to mock as a lot of Victorian hooey. But it contains an important truth. This present conflict will be won (if at all) in the kindergarten classes of America's grade schools, and Canada's, and Britain's and Europe's. Because the resolve necessary to win a war can't be put on and taken off like a suit of armour. It has to be bred in the bone, and sustained by the broader institutions of society. And the typical western education, even when it's not telling you that your country's principal contribution to the world is racism and oppression, teaches history in a vacuum - random facts, a few approved figures, but no overarching heroic narrative. And, if the past isn't worth defending, why should the future be?

Which brings me back to where we came in: are we gonna win or lose? I'd say right now the best bet for much of the world is a slow ongoing incremental defeat, the kind most folks don't notice until it's too late. That's to say, in 20 years' time many relatively pleasant parts of the planet are going to be a lot less pleasant. That doesn't mean "Islamofascism" or "radical Islam" or even just plain "Islam" is going to win. But they, like the bigshot analysts in Moscow, Beijing and elsewhere, have concluded that, even in an apparently "unipolar" world, a civilization's overwhelming military dominance, economic dominance and technological dominance count for naught if it's ideologically insecure. The issue is self-defence. If you're a genuine cultural relativist - if you really believe our society is no better or worse than any other — you're about to get the opportunity not just to talk the talk but to walk the walk. Good luck.

THE ILLIBERAL WEST
Time to ban the Bible

The Irish Times, August 9th 2003

I F YOU LIVE pretty much anywhere in the western world these days, you'll notice a certain kind of news item cropping up with quiet regularity. *The Irish Times* had one last week. As Liam Reid reported, the Irish Council for Civil Liberties has warned Catholic bishops that distributing the Vatican's latest statement on homosexuality could lead to prosecution under the 1989 Incitement to Hatred Act, and a six-month jail term.

"The document itself may not violate the Act, but if you were to use the document to say that gays are evil, it is likely to give rise to hatred, which is against the Act," says Aisling Reidy, director of the ICCL. "The wording is very strong and certainly goes against the spirit of the legislation." No Irish bishop has actually called gays evil yet. But best to be on the safe side and shut down all debate.

From Dublin, let us zip 6,000 miles to Quesnel, a small paper-mill town in British Columbia. Chris Kempling is a high-school teacher and a Christian conservative and he likes writing letters to his local newspaper. In one of them, he said that "homosexuality is not something to be applauded". The regulatory body for his profession, the British Columbia College of Teachers, suspended him for a month without pay for "conduct unbecoming a member of the college".

No student, parent or fellow teacher at Correlieu Secondary School has ever complained about Mr Kempling: he was punished by the BCCT for expressing an opinion in the paper. The British Columbia Civil Liberties Association supported the suspension, not because of anything he's done but because of what he might do in the future. He might discriminate against gay and lesbian students in the future. He hasn't done so yet, but, if we don't pre-emptively punish him now, he might well commit a hate crime somewhere down the road.

He didn't say gays are evil. But he did say homosexuality wasn't something to be "applauded". And, if we start letting people decide who they are and aren't going to applaud, there's no telling where it will end. As in Dublin, best to be on the safe side and shut down all debate.

In Sweden, meanwhile, they've passed a constitutional amendment making criticism of homosexuality a crime, punishable by up to four years in jail. Expressing a moral objection to homosexuality is illegal, even on religious grounds, even in church. Those preachers may not be talking about how gays are evil this Sunday. But they might do next week, or next month. As in Ireland and British Columbia, best to be on the safe side and shut down all debate.

Anyone sense a trend here? Even in America, where the First Amendment (on freedom of expression) still just about trumps "hate crimes" law, you can see where things are headed. Thus, in Hollywood, they're famously opposed to censorship, and blacklisting, and leaning on studio executives to end someone's career because of his or her views, and making people answer questions such as: "Are you now or have you ever been a member of the Communist Party?"

But, when it comes to: "Are you now or have you ever been a member of a traditional Judaeo-Christian religion?", that's another question entirely. A couple of years back, the writers of "Frasier" and various other Hollywood colossi successfully chased America's second most popular radio host, Dr Laura, off the TV airwaves by putting pressure on Paramount over her views on the gay agenda.

That's fair enough. If influential people want to lean on advertisers to get rid of someone they disapprove of, it's not pretty but it's an understandable use of muscle - although a bit rich coming from Hollywood. If you're an aged survivor of McCarthyism who's unrepentant about being an apologist for a totalitarian system that murdered untold millions, celebrity lefties will be relaxed and, indeed, supportive. But, if you happen to think that gay marriage is not such a great idea, then getting the major TV studios, networks and affiliates to blacklist you is in the public interest.

But what was interesting was how many ostensibly higher-minded people thought that Dr Laura's defence of traditional Judaeo-Christian morality justified gutting the First Amendment. As the San Francisco Board of Supervisors put it: "At what point do her words become the equivalent of yelling 'Fire!' in a crowded theatre?" - or, in this instance, yelling "Robert Mugabe!" in a crowded bathhouse.

Dr Laura has yet to yell anything in a gay bathhouse. But she might, some day. As in Ireland, British Columbia and Sweden, best to be on the safe side and shut down all debate.

Thirty years ago, in the early days of gay liberation, most of us assumed we were being asked to live and let live. But, throughout the western world, "tolerance" has become remarkably intolerant, and "diversity" demands ruthless conformity. In New Zealand, an appeals court upheld a nationwide ban on importing a Christian video, *Gay Rights/Special Rights: Inside The Homosexual Agenda*. In Saskatchewan, *The Saskatoon Star-Phoenix* was fined by the Human Rights Commission for publishing an advertisement citing not the relevant Biblical passages on homosexuality but merely the chapter and verse numbers. Fining publishers of the Bible surely can't be far off. The coerciveness of the most "liberal" cultures in the western world is not a pretty sight.

Whatever happened to "live and let live"? If I can live with the occasional rustle from the undergrowth as I'm strolling through a condom-strewn park or a come-hither look from George Michael in the men's room, why can't gays live with the occasional expression of disapproval?

Most Christian opponents of gay marriage oppose gay marriage; they don't oppose the right of gays to advocate it. But increasingly gays oppose the right of Christians even to argue their corner. Gay activists have figured that, instead of trying to persuade people to change their opinions, it's easier just to get them banned.

As Rodney King, celebrated black victim of the LAPD, once plaintively wondered: "Why can't we all just get along?" But, if that's not possible, why can't we all just *not* get along? What's so bad about disagreement that it needs to be turned into a crime?

CANADA

"Human rights" ...and wrongs

T HE INTOLERANCE *of the forces of "tolerance" delineated in the previous chapter is justified as a kind of mopping-up operation - just getting rid of a few religious bigots blocking the path to utopia. Yet illiberalism in the cause of "liberalism" can be addictive, and never more so than in the deranged Dominion.*

No sooner had my little difficulties with Canada's "human rights" commissions begun than some of my pickier northern readers demanded to know where have I been on the egregiousness of the kangaroo courts all these years. Well, I've been opposed to them my entire adult life. When The National Post *was launched by Conrad Black in 1998, my very first column in the newspaper's very first week started with the anti-Suharto demonstrators getting pepper-sprayed in British Columbia but wound up with...*

> Canada's much-vaunted niceness is smug and suffocating, but it's our national characteristic. It's what all those *National Lampoon* non-jokes boil down to: "How do you get 40 Canadians into a phone booth?" "You say, 'Pardon me, but would you please all go into the phone booth?'" Etc. The truth is it requires a vast panoply of restrictive legislation to shoehorn us in: Canada's "niceness" has always been somewhat coercive. It's not just anti-totalitarian demonstrators being denied the right to protest, but also fellows like that Mayor of Fredericton, forced by New Brunswick's Human Rights Commission to proclaim officially the city's Gay Pride Week.

Canada's famous "tolerance" has become progressively intolerant. It's no longer enough to be tolerant, to be blithely indifferent, warily accepting, detachedly libertarian about gays – as the Mayor and his voters were. For tolerance is, by definition, somewhat grudging. Instead, gays must be accorded official mandatory fulsome approval, no matter that enforcing Gay Pride means inflicting Straight Humiliation on a hapless mayor and displaying a cool contempt for his electorate. As the Queen put it a couple of Canada Days back, "Let us celebrate the unique Canadian ability to turn diversity to the common good." But the uniquely Canadian thing about "diversity" is the ruthless uniformity with which it's applied.

I'll bet those BC students protesting against Suharto would approve of the New Brunswick Human Rights Commission's ruling that Hizzoner was guilty of discrimination. But the trouble with letting the state restrict free expression in the interests of nice cuddly causes like gay liberation is that you make it a lot easier for them to restrict free expression in the interests of non-nice causes like Suharto. In Canada, we've let the state go too far in policing dissent. Our official niceness has led, inexorably, to official intolerance...

So I wrote in The National Post *of October 29th 1998. And that's the way I've always felt:*

The aim of a large swathe of the left is not to win the debate but to get it cancelled before it starts. You can do that in any number of ways - busting up campus appearances by conservatives, "hate crimes" laws, Canada's ghastly human rights commissions, the more "enlightened" court judgments, the EU's recent decision to criminalize "xenophobia", or merely, as *The New York Times* does, by declaring your side of every issue to be the "moderate" and "non-ideological" position.

That's from The National Post *of August 6th 2002. A couple of years earlier:*

When the left tried dispensing with democracy in the Soviet Union and the Warsaw Pact, it led eventually to counter-revolution and the regimes' collapse. In the US courts, in Canada's human rights commissions and in Europe's bureaucracy, the left may finally have found a form of democratic subversion that works.

That's from The Gazette *in Montreal, March 4th 2000. Contemporary Canada is profoundly hostile to individual liberty, and the "human rights" commissions are the most explicit enforcers of that hostility. As I wrote in* The Calgary Herald *of May 2nd 1998:*

The real choice in Canada is whom to be oppressed by. On the one hand, there's the Parizeau tendency. On the other, there's what I'll call, in deference to the most famous gay in Alberta, the Delwin Vriend tendency.

Let's take Jacques Parizeau first. The old boy travels around Quebec, notes that the overwhelming majority of its population is francophone and feels that this should be reflected in its constitutional arrangements and public face. He can't understand why an anglophone, calling some Quebec City apparatchik to query why his medical card hasn't arrived yet, should feel entitled to service *en anglais*. For propounding these views, Parizeau is reviled throughout English Canada as a dangerous wacko.

The other tendency is represented by Mr Vriend, the human rights commissions and the courts of Canada. It believes that municipalities should be compelled to lend official support to gay pride days, that religious colleges should be compelled to hire people whose behaviour they consider an abomination before God, and that a spouse is no more or less than (in the felicitous words of the Ontario Court of Appeal) someone you "designate" as such - husband, wife, gay partner or, presumably, the next-door neighbour or your favourite goldfish.

For its willingness to break up Canada on a 50-per-cent-plus-one vote, the Parizeau tendency is denounced as profoundly anti-democratic; for their willingness to break up ancient institutions such as the laws of marriage and contract on the basis of no social consensus whatsoever, the Vriend crowd are hailed as reasonable persons of a progressive tolerant bent. That's why we'll have gay marriage long before an independent Quebec: In Canada, it's easier to come out than get out.

At which point, to avoid the attention of the human rights commission myself, I'd better issue the usual disclaimers: some of my best friends are gay; I'm entirely relaxed when it comes to penetrative sex with other men. Hang on, that didn't come out quite right. Anyway, the point is being gay - in the modern, professional, litigious sense - is not primarily about penetrative sex with other men. Rather, it's about the construction of a round-the-clock identity accorded special protection under the law. The courts and commissions do not extend this consideration to all groups. Quite the opposite. If, following Mr Vriend's example, a devout Catholic were to get a job in a gay bathhouse and wander around the cubicles saying Hail Marys, he'd receive short shrift from Canadian justice. We all know that, in media commentary on the Supreme Court decision, "religious", like "rural", is code-speak for "bigot".

In fact, these religious bigots are surprisingly tolerant. For example, I have before me a copy of the Easter edition of *The Mirror*, a Montreal weekly of vaguely leftish views and entertainment listings. On page three is an advertisement for

Resurrection, "the queer dance event of Easter weekend", featuring an oiled, muscular hunk, nude except for several phallic symbols over his washboard stomach and a neon cross over his crotch, his glistening thighs flanked by two urinals. This queer dance event was a benefit party for Montreal Queer Pride/Divers Cité 98, whose corporate sponsors proudly display their logos underneath the twinkling stud: Canadian Airlines, American Airlines, Glaxo Wellcome... In the diversified Dominion, we must be properly sensitive toward persons of colour, persons of orientation and persons of gender, but we can be sneeringly contemptuous of persons of faith, appropriating their most sacred imagery for the crassest of purposes even on the holiest day in the Christian calendar.

That was written a mere decade before my own tribulations, but we've come a long way since then. Of course, not all "persons of faith" get treated so disdainfully: Try putting Mohammed or the Muslim crescent next to a urinal in a Queer Pride poster, and a "human rights" complaint will be the least of your worries. Nevertheless, as interpreted by Canada's "human rights" regime, "tolerance" is little more than fashion: gays are in, Christians are out – and ever more so. This is from The Western Standard *of April 18th 2005:*

So it's no surprise to find that, even though we've only had legalized "same-sex marriage" for ten minutes, and even though Paul Martin & Co have given a lot of fine-sounding assurances on how the new arrangements will respect the deeply held beliefs of ancient religions, gays are already in court suing for the right to marry on church property. In 2003, the Knights of Columbus in Port Coquitlam accepted a booking for a wedding reception in their hall behind Our Lady of the Assumption Church. It's a fairly typical Knights of Columbus hall - crucifixes, photographs of the Pope, paintings of the Virgin Mary, etc. When the Knights discovered that Deborah Chymyshyn and Tracey Smith were, in fact, a lesbian couple, they cancelled the booking as politely as they could under the circumstances, returning the deposit and, on the advice of the Archdiocese, chipping in a further $600 to cover new wedding invitations and an alternative location. The Misses Chymyshyn and Smith immediately went out and signed on with Barbara Findlay - or, to use her preferred style, barbara findlay. If you want to know why she rejects capital letters, you should attend one of her 'unlearning oppression' workshops. The point is, if you're looking for a lower-case crusader who'll get your lower case to a higher court, she's the gal - the Queen 's Counsel who's also BC's most celebrated queens' counsel, the lesbian activist who famously declared in 1997 that "the legal struggle for queer rights will one day be a showdown between freedom of religion versus sexual orientation".

Right now, which would you plunk your chips on? A legal decision here, a legal decision there - a religious institution can't fire a militantly gay employee, a religious school has to allow gay couples to the prom, the sterner admonitions from Leviticus can no longer be quoted in church advertising - and the ratchet effect is well underway...

If I could afford the liability coverage, I'd be happy to put up the dough for a lesbian couple to sue over the right to marry in an Islamic community centre - just to get a sense of how the Grits intend to resolve the internal contradictions of the multicultural society. But militant gays, like Quebec separatists and "abused" natives, know how to pick their targets.

I have a lot of respect for barbara findlay, QC (or qc). She's admirably straightforward about what she wants and how she intends to get it. By contrast, the quiet lifers are deluding either themselves or us by persisting in the belief that one last retreat will do it and we can then draw a line.

There is no bottom line - no line and no bottom, just an ongoing bumpy descent into a brave new world.

The proponents of that brave new world see it as a rainbow utopia of gay rights and women's rights and ethnic rights enforced only at the expense of recalcitrant theocratic bigots. But in the Nineties a far more motivated and less easily demonized crowd of theocrats began making their presence felt in Canada and the west. And what I called multiculturalism's internal contradictions became far harder to ignore...

THE BBC
Kilroy was here

The Daily Telegraph, January 13th 2004

LET ME SEE if I understand the BBC Rules of Engagement correctly: if you're Robert Kilroy-Silk and you make some robust statements about the Arab penchant for suicide bombing, amputations, repression of women and a generally celebratory attitude to September 11th - none of which is factually in dispute - the BBC will yank you off the air and the Commission for Racial Equality will file a complaint to the police which could result in your serving seven years in gaol. Message: this behaviour is unacceptable in multicultural Britain.

But, if you're Tom Paulin and you incite murder, in a part of the world where folks need little incitement to murder, as part of a non-factual emotive rant about how "Brooklyn-born" Jewish settlers on the West Bank "should be shot dead" because "they are Nazis" and "I feel nothing but hatred for them", the BBC will keep you on the air, kibitzing (as the Zionists would say) with the *crème de la crème* of London's cultural arbiters each week. Message: this behaviour is completely acceptable.

So, while the BBC is "investigating" Kilroy, its only statement on Mr Paulin was an oblique but curiously worded allusion to the non-controversy on the Corporation website: "His polemical, knockabout style has ruffled feathers in the US, where the Jewish question is notoriously sensitive." "The Jewish question"? "Notoriously sensitive"? Is this really how they talk at the BBC?

Mr Paulin's style is only metaphorically knockabout. But, a few days after his remarks were published in the Egyptian newspaper *Al-Ahram*, some doughty Palestinian "activists" rose to his challenge and knocked about some settlers more literally, murdering among others five-year-old Danielle Shefi. In a touch of symbolism the critic in Mr

190

Paulin might have found a wee bit obvious, they left her Mickey Mouse sheets soaked in blood.

Evidently Kilroy's "polemical, knockabout style" is far more problematic. For what it's worth, I accept the BBC's right to axe his show. I haven't seen it in a decade and I thought they should have axed it then. I myself got fired by the BBC a while back and, although I had a couple of rough years sleeping in a rotting boxcar at the back of the freight yards, I eventually crawled my way back to semi-insolvency. There's no doubt in my mind that, when the CRE, the BBC, the Metropolitan Police and the Muslim Council of Britain are through making an example of him, he'll still be able to find gainful employment, if not in TV then certainly in casual construction work or seasonal fruit-picking.

But it's not really about Kilroy or Paulin or Jews, or the Saudis beheading men for (alleged) homosexuality, or the inability of the "moderate" Jordanian parliament to ban honour killing, or the fact that (as Jonathan Kay of Canada's *National Post* memorably put it) if Robert Mugabe walked into an Arab League summit he'd be the most democratically legitimate leader in the room. It's not about any of that: it's about the future of the "multicultural" society.

One reason why the Arab world is in the state it's in is because one cannot raise certain subjects without it impacting severely on one's wellbeing. And if you can't discuss issues, they don't exist. According to Ibrahim Nawar of Arab Press Freedom Watch, in the last two years seven Saudi editors have been fired for criticising government policies. To fire a British talk-show host for criticising Saudi policies is surely over-reaching even for the notoriously super-sensitive Muslim lobby.

But apparently not. "What Robert could do," suggested the CRE's Trevor Phillips helpfully, "is issue a proper apology, not for the fact that people were offended, but for saying this stuff in the first place. Secondly he could learn something about Muslims and Arabs - they gave us maths and medicine - and thirdly he could use some of his vast earnings to support a Muslim charity. Then I would say he has been properly contrite."

Extravagant public contrition. Re-education camp. "Voluntary" surrender of assets. It's not unknown for officials at government agencies to lean on troublemaking citizens in this way, but not usually in functioning democracies.

When Catholic groups complain about things like Terrence McNally's Broadway play *Corpus Christi* (in which a gay Jesus enjoys anal sex with Judas), the arts crowd says a healthy society has to have "artists" with the "courage" to "explore" "transgressive" "ideas", etc. But, when Cincinnati Muslims complained about the local theatre's new play about a Palestinian suicide bomber, the production was immediately cancelled: the courageous transgressive arts guys folded like a cheap Bedouin tent. The play was almost laughably pro-Palestinian, but that wasn't the point: the Muslim community leaders didn't care whether the play was pro- or anti-Islam: for them, Islam was beyond discussion. End of subject. And so it was.

Fifteen years ago, when the fatwa against Salman Rushdie was declared and both his defenders and detractors managed to miss what the business was really about, *The Times'* Clifford Longley nailed it very well. Surveying the threats from British Muslim groups, he wrote that certain Muslim beliefs "are not compatible with a plural society: Islam does not know how to exist as a minority culture. For it is not just a set of private individual principles and beliefs. Islam is a social creed above all, a radically different way of organising society as a whole."

Since then, societal organisation-wise, things seem to be going Islam's way swimmingly - literally in the case of the French municipal pool which bowed to Muslim requests to institute single-sex bathing, but also in more important ways. Thus, I see the French Interior Minister flew to Egypt to seek the blessing for his new religious legislation of the big-time imam at the al-Azhar Theological Institute. Rather odd, don't you think? After all, Egypt isn't in the French interior. But, if Egypt doesn't fall within the Interior Minister's jurisdiction, France apparently falls within the imam's.

And so, when free speech, artistic expression, feminism and other totems of western pluralism clash directly with the Islamic lobby, Islam more often than not wins - and all the noisy types who run around crying "Censorship!" if a Texas radio station refuses to play the Bush-bashing Dixie Chicks suddenly fall silent. I don't know about you, but this "multicultural Britain" business is beginning to feel like an interim phase.

Nazi party boy

Prince Harry Ordered To Visit Auschwitz After Wearing Nazi Uniform To Party – NBC News, January 14th 2005

The Daily Telegraph, January 18th 2005

IT'S A GOOD rule of thumb that, no matter how big an idiot someone is, he can never compete with the political class' response to his idiocy. Thus, whatever feelings of unease I might have had about Prince Hitler were swept away the moment the rent-a-quote humbugs started lining up to denounce him. I say to Harry: You go, girlfriend, you Reichstone Cowboy you. It's uniforms night at my pad every Thursday and you're more than welcome, Your Royal Heilness.

First off was Doug Henderson, former Armed Forces Minister, who suggested that the Nazi dress sense should disqualify the young lad from Sandhurst: "I think it would be very inappropriate," huffed Doug, "that someone who had done such a stupid thing as Prince Harry has should join the Army."

The French Sports Minister suggested the "scandal" would undermine Britain's bid to host the Olympics. Londoners should be so lucky. But, if I understand the concern of the sporting world correctly, being a totalitarian state that's killed millions is no obstacle to hosting the Olympics, but going to a costume party wearing the uniform of a defunct totalitarian state that's no longer around to kill millions is completely unacceptable.

German politicians, meanwhile, launched their own rhetorical blitzkrieg, arguing that the prince's choice of fancy dress demonstrated the need for a continent-wide ban on Nazi insignia.

"In a Europe grounded in peace and freedom there should be no place for Nazi symbols," declared Markus Soeder, General Secretary of the Christian Socialist Union party. "They should be banned throughout Europe, as they are with good reason in Germany."

Personally, I found the sight of the Prince of Wales climbing into the full Highgrove hejab for dinner with that bin Laden brother a week after the 9/11 slaughter far more disquieting: it seemed a rather more conscious act of identification than his son's party get-up.

A good indication of societal decadence is when it prefers to obsess over fictional offences rather than real ones. I suppose it's possible that, should fate bring Harry to the throne, he'd turn into a Victor Emmanuel or King Carol of Romania and lend a constitutional figleaf to some Fascist regime. Yet worrying about a minor Royal schoolboy's alleged Nazi bent seems something of an indulgence at a time when the neo-Nazis get as many votes in Saxony's elections as Gerhard Schroeder's Social Democratic Party; when from Marseilles to Paris, Jews are being attacked and their homes, schools, kosher butchers, synagogues and cemeteries burnt and desecrated in a low-level intifada that's been going on so long the political establishment now accepts it as a normal feature of French life; when the wife of the head of the European Central Bank is not above doing sly Holocaust jokes in public; and when the Berlin police advise Jews not to go out in public wearing any identifying marks of their faith. It's not just *Nazi* insignia you don't see in Germany these days; Nazi wise, the uniforms are the least of it.

But if Adolf Hitler were to return from wherever he is right now, what would he be most steamed about? That in some countries there are laws banning Nazi symbols and making Holocaust denial a crime? No, that wouldn't bother him: that would testify to the force and endurance of his ideas - that 60 years on they're still so potent the state has to suppress them.

What would bug him the most is that on Broadway and in the West End Mel Brooks is peddling Nazi shtick in *The Producers* and audiences are howling with laughter. I don't know what kick Prince Harry gets out of his Nazi gear, but once long ago I was obliged for an historical scene to wear an SS uniform and I've never felt so screamingly camp as when mincing around doing that little flip-of-the-wrist mini-Heil thing.

One reason why the English-speaking democracies were just about the only advanced nations not to fall for Nazism or Fascism is that they simply found it too ridiculous. Bertie Wooster's famous riposte to the Mosleyesque Sir Roderick Spode could speak for the entire Anglosphere:

> *The trouble with you, Spode, is that just because you have succeeded in inducing a handful of half-wits to disfigure the London scene by going about in black shorts, you think you're someone. You hear them shouting, 'Heil, Spode!' and you imagine it is the Voice of the People.*
>
> *That is where you make your bloomer. What the Voice of the People is saying is: 'Look at that frightful ass Spode swanking about in footer bags! Did you ever in your puff see such a perfect perisher?'*

That's why British party stores stock Nazi outfits - because they're a joke, and the Brits made them one. So when prissy Krauts want to ban Prince Harry's party gear they should go suck an old bratwurst.

Alas, tyranny doesn't always come with a self-evidently hilarious dress code. And the soft, supple, creeping totalitarian inclinations of our present-day rulers are sometimes harder to resist. If I had to pick the single most revolting remark from this bogus Reichsfuror, it would be this:

> *I think it might be appropriate for him to tell us himself just how contrite he now is.*

That's Michael Howard, the leader of the supposed Conservative Party. What's conservative about demanding people submit to public self-abasement? Wasn't it the Commies who used to insist you recant on TV and then disappear into re-education camp? A conservative party ought to be a refuge from the sanctimonious nannytollahs of the age. But, from his shabby Kerryesque opportunism on the war down, Mr Howard has no discernible coherent political philosophy - except for his all-pervasive authoritarianism, into which his repellent call for a display of princely contrition fits all too neatly.

Since Britain seems to hold three-minute silences for something or other every month now, maybe for the next one we could all get together and Prince Harry (in uniform) and his father (in mufti) can lay a wreath to mark the tragic loss of our sense of proportion.

THE UNITED KINGDOM
Ending the debate

The Daily Telegraph, July 13th 2004

A COUPLE OF years back, I mentioned the fatwa against Salman Rushdie and received a flurry of lively e-mails. It was, you'll recall, Valentine's Day 1989 when the Ayatollah Khomeini issued his extraterritorial summary judgment on a British subject, and shortly thereafter large numbers of British Muslims went marching through English cities openly calling for Rushdie to be killed.

A reader in Bradford told me he'd asked a West Yorkshire officer on the street that day why the various "Muslim community leaders" weren't being arrested for incitement to murder. The officer said they'd been told to "play it cool". The calls for blood got more raucous. My correspondent asked his question again. The policeman told him to "fuck off, or I'll arrest *you*."

Isn't that pretty much how it's likely to go once David Blunkett's new protection for Islam is in place? If you're the "moderate" imam Yusuf al-Qaradawi, you'll be invited to speak at the "Our Children Our Future" conference sponsored and funded by the Metropolitan Police and the Department for Work and Pensions. But, if you express concern about ol' Mullah Moderate, an Islamic lobby group will file an official complaint about you.

Indeed, after Sir John Stevens, Met commissioner and event co-sponsor, said he didn't want his officers on the same stage as the imam, the Muslim Association of Britain filed an official complaint about his comments. By the time you read this, Sir John might have already called for himself to be investigated by a Royal Commission and found guilty of systemic Islamophobia.

As for "Our Children Our Future", when it comes to children, the imam certainly has the future all mapped out: as he has said, "Israelis might have nuclear bombs but we have the children bomb and

198

these human bombs must continue until liberation." Thank heaven for
little girls, they blow up in the most delightful way.

If an Anglican bishop were to commend a career as a suicide
bomber to his Sunday School charges, you'd certainly hope to be free
to question his judgment on the matter. Not that Anglican bishops
ever say such things, of course. They're lost in anguished debate on
whether they should license merely celibate gay deans in long-term
relationships or go for full-blown robustly active gay bishops, and all
the thanks they get for their painful efforts to keep up with the times is
wholesale public mockery of Christianity up and down the land – ie,
my old friend Alistair Beaton's satirical Iraq war song, "We're Sending
You A Cluster Bomb From Jesus".

Meanwhile, Islam is the fastest-growing religion in the western
world, but the Home Secretary wants us to pretend that it's a wee
delicate bloom which has to be sheltered from anything unpleasant.
The other week, the governor of one of those Nigerian states that now
lives under sharia called for the burning of all Christian churches
within his jurisdiction. Every Friday, on state TV and radio
throughout the Arab world and in mosques somewhat closer to home,
the A-list imams call for the killing of Jews and infidels. Well, good for
them. But, if they can dish it out so enthusiastically, couldn't they
learn to take it just an eensy-teensy-weensy bit?

One of the reasons Arab nations are in the state they're in is
because of the inability to discuss Islam honestly. I was in Amman for
the Jordanian election last year and one of the things you notice is that,
although the city does a reasonable impression of a modern dynamic
capital, and its press is, by the standards of the region, free-ish, its
stunted political culture is subordinate to its religious culture. That's
why, for example, Article 340 of the Jordanian Penal Code - which
effectively licenses "honour killings" - always gets renewed when it
comes up in parliament.

That's another reason the British Government should not be in
the business of helping coercive lobby groups further stifle debate.
Islam raises political questions that Judaism or Buddhism doesn't - the

suggestion, for example, that Muslim women should be exempt from the requirement to be photographed on national identity cards. In the absence of Blunkett's law, we might still get the odd crusty type from the shires huffing on BBC phone-ins that if Muslim women think it's insulting to be made to remove their hijab for ID cards, they should bloody well have thought about that before moving to Britain. But, if the Home Secretary's proposals sail through, we'll discuss such questions, if at all, between tightly imposed government constraints explicitly favouring one party to the dispute. I know which one of those options any self-respecting liberal democracy ought to prefer.

In *The River War* (1899), Winston Churchill's account of the Sudanese campaign, there's a memorable passage which I reproduce here while I'm still able to:

> *How dreadful are the curses which Mohammedanism lays on its votaries! Besides the fanatical frenzy, which is as dangerous in a man as hydrophobia in a dog, there is this fearful fatalistic apathy. Improvident habits, slovenly systems of agriculture, sluggish methods of commerce, and insecurity of property exist wherever the followers of the Prophet rule or live. A degraded sensualism deprives this life of its grace and refinement; the next of its dignity and sanctity. The fact that in Mohammedan law every woman must belong to some man as his absolute property - either as a child, a wife, or a concubine - must delay the final extinction of slavery until the faith of Islam has ceased to be a great power among men.*
>
> *Individual Moslems may show splendid qualities. Thousands become the brave and loyal soldiers of the Queen: all know how to die. But the influence of the religion paralyses the social development of those who follow it. No stronger retrograde force exists in the world. Far from being moribund, Mohammedanism is a militant and proselytising faith. It has already spread throughout Central Africa, raising fearless warriors at every step; and were it not that Christianity is sheltered in the strong arms of science - the science against which*

it had vainly struggled - the civilisation of modern Europe might fall, as fell the civilisation of ancient Rome.

Is that grossly offensive to Muslims? Almost certainly. Is it also a rather shrewd and pertinent analysis by one of Britain's most eminent leaders? I think so. If David Blunkett bans the sentiments in that first sentence, the sentiments of the last will prove even more pertinent.

INCIDENTS & INVESTIGATIONS

Crime?
It's a matter of opinion

The Daily Telegraph, December 12th 2005

ALL OVER THE United Kingdom, right now, real crimes are being committed: mobiles are being nicked, front doors are being kicked in, bollards are being lobbed through bus shelters - just to name some of the lighter activities that add so much to the gaiety of the nation. None of these is a "priority crime", as you'll know if you've ever endured the bureaucratic time-waster of reporting a burglary.

So what is a "priority crime"? Well, the other day, the author Lynette Burrows went on a BBC Five Live show to talk about the government's new "civil partnerships" and expressed her opinion - politely, no intemperate words - that the adoption of children by homosexuals was "a risk". The following day, Fulham police contacted her to discuss the "homophobic incident".

A Scotland Yard spokesperson told the *Telegraph*'s Sally Pook that it's "standard policy" for "community safety units" to investigate "homophobic, racist and domestic incidents" because these are all "priority crimes" - even though, in the case of Mrs Burrows, there is (to be boringly legalistic about these things) no crime, as even the zealots of the Yard concede. "It is all about reassuring the community," said the very p.c. Plod to the *Telegraph*. "All parties have been spoken to by the police. No allegation of crime has been made. A report has been taken but is now closed."

So no crime was committed. Yet Mrs Burrows was "investigated" and a report about the "incident" and her involvement in it is now on a government computer somewhere. Oh, to be sure, the vicious homophobe wasn't dragged off to re-education camp - or more likely, given budgetary constraints, an overcrowded women's prison to be tossed in a cell with a predatory bull-dyke who could teach her the error of her homophobic ways.

But, on balance, that has the merit of at least being more obviously outrageous than the weaselly "community reassurance" approach of the Met. As it is, Lynette Burrows has been investigated by police merely for expressing an opinion. Which is the sort of thing we used to associate with police states. Indeed, it's the defining act of a police state: the arbitrary criminalisation of dissent from state orthodoxy.

Mrs Burrows writes on "children's rights and the family", so I don't know whether she's a member of PEN or the other authors' groups. But it seems unlikely the Hampstead big guns who lined up to defend Salman Rushdie a decade and a half ago will be eager to stage any rallies this time round. But, if the principle is freedom of expression, what's the difference between his apostasy (as the Ayatollah saw it) and Mrs Burrows' apostasy (as Scotland Yard sees it)?

I don't suppose the Tories will be eager to take to the ramparts for Mrs B, either. At the last conservative confab I dropped in on, the bigtime A-list party heavyweight was droning on about how "the public sees us as too white, male, middle-class and heterosexual". If it's any consolation, the American lady sitting next to me nudged me in the ribs and said, "He doesn't seem that heterosexual to me." Not for the first time the Tories take too much for granted. But, at any rate, defending Lynette Burrows' right to free speech seems unlikely to play well with the party's marketing gurus.

As for the government, in *The Observer* on Sunday, Tony Blair wrote a piece almost every bland sentence of which had me spraying my cornflakes all over my civil partner, right from the sub-headline: "The most important freedom is harm from others."

Well, up to a point. If you live in one of those parts of, say, Aston in Birmingham where the writ of the British state no longer runs in any meaningful way, that sounds grand. But the police don't seem to have much stomach for enforcing your right to be free from harm in such neighbourhoods. The Prime Minister was writing principally about the great Asbo – that's not the powerful God-like being from *The Lion, The Witch And The Wardrobe*, although, from Mr Blair's touching faith in Asbo as an instrument of righteousness and justice, it might as well be. Technically, Asbo is an Anti-Social Behaviour Order, one of those "so-called summary powers", as the Prime Minister puts it. The trouble is the British police are a lazy lot and, if it's a choice between acting against intimidating thugs who've made the shopping centre a no-go area or investigating the non-crime of a BBC radio interview, they'll take the latter. I leave it to Scotland Yard to decide whether the Asbo's reach already extends to "homophobia" and "Islamophobia", but whether it does or not, sticking Mrs Burrows' "homophobic incident" in a police file is certainly an Anti-Social Behaviour Notice, de facto if not de jure.

"Freedom from harm" is all very well, "freedom from being offended" is extremely dangerous - a way of extending the already harmful phenomenon of "libel chill" and making it freely available to every noisy lobby group. If Sir Iqbal Sacranie and co get their way on "religious hatred", every BBC Five Live discussion on Islam will be followed by a call from an aggrieved listener and a visit from the Fulham police. And, for every Lynette Burrows, insisting she'll continue to exercise her right to free speech, there'll be a hundred more who keep their heads down and opt for a quiet life.

Hollywood stars are forever complaining about the "crushing of dissent" in Bush's America, by which they mean Tim Robbins having a photo-op at the Baseball Hall of Fame cancelled because he's become an anti-war bore. But, thanks to the First Amendment, he can say anything he likes without the forces of the state coming round to grill him. It's in Britain and Europe where dissent is being crushed. Following the murder of Theo van Gogh in the Netherlands, film directors and museum curators and all the other "brave" "transgressive" artists usually so eager to "challenge" society are voting for self-censorship: "I don't want a knife in my chest," explained Albert Ter

CRIME? IT'S A MATTER OF OPINION

Heerdt, announcing his decision to "postpone" a sequel to his hit multicultural comedy *Shouf Shouf Habibi!*

But who needs to knife him when across Europe the authorities are so eager to criminalise him? No society with an eye to long-term survival should make opinion a subversive activity. Here's a thought: we should be able to discuss homosexuality, Islam and pretty much everything else in the same carefree way *Guardian* columnists damn Bush's America as "neo-fascist".

LIBEL TOURISM
Alms and the man

The New York Sun, August 6th 2005

HOW WILL WE lose the war against "radical Islam"?

Well, it won't be in a tank battle. Or in the Sunni Triangle or the caves of Tora Bora. It won't be because terrorists fly three jets into the Oval Office, Buckingham Palace and the Basilica of St Peter's on the same Tuesday morning.

The war will be lost incrementally because we are unable to reverse the ongoing radicalization of Muslim populations in South Asia, Indonesia, the Balkans, Western Europe and, yes, North America. And who's behind that radicalization? Who funds the mosques and Islamic centers that in the last 30 years have set up shop on just about every Main Street around the planet?

For the answer, let us turn to a fascinating book called *Alms For Jihad: Charity And Terrorism In The Islamic World* by J Millard Burr, a former USAID relief coordinator, and the scholar Robert O Collins. Can't find it in your local Barnes & Noble? Never mind, let's go to Amazon. Everything's available there. And sure enough, you'll come through to the *Alms For Jihad* page and find a smattering of approving reviews from respectably torpid publications: "The most comprehensive look at the web of Islamic charities that have financed conflicts all around the world," according to Canada's *Globe And Mail*, which is like *The New York Times* but without the jokes.

Unfortunately, if you then try to buy *Alms For Jihad*, you discover that the book is "Currently unavailable. We don't know when or if this item will be back in stock." Hang on, it was only published last year. At Amazon, items are either shipped within 24 hours or, if a little more specialized, within four-to-six weeks, but not many books from 2006 are entirely unavailable with no re-stock in sight.

Well, let us cross the ocean thousands of miles from the Amazon warehouse to the High Court in London. Last week, the Cambridge University Press agreed to recall all unsold copies of *Alms For Jihad* and pulp them. In addition, it has asked hundreds of libraries around the world to remove the volume from their shelves. This highly unusual action was accompanied by a letter from the publishers to Sheikh Khalid bin Mahfouz, in care of his English lawyers, explaining their reasons:

> *Throughout the Book there are serious and defamatory allegations about yourself and your family, alleging support for terrorism through your businesses, family and charities, and directly.*
>
> *As a result of what we now know, we accept and acknowledge that all of those allegations about you and your family, businesses and charities are entirely and manifestly false.*

Who is Sheikh Khalid bin Mahfouz? Well, he's a very wealthy and influential Saudi. Big deal, you say. Is there any other kind? True, but even by the standards of very wealthy and influential Saudis, this guy is plugged in: He was the personal banker to the Saudi royal family and head of the National Commercial Bank of Saudi Arabia, until he sold it to the Saudi government. He has a swanky pad in London and an Irish passport and multiple US business connections, including to Thomas Kean, the chairman of the 9/11 Commission. I'm not saying the 9/11 Commission is a Saudi shell operation, merely making the banal observation that, whenever you come across a bigshot Saudi, it's considerably less than six degrees of separation between him and the most respectable pillars of the American establishment.

As to whether allegations about support for terrorism by the Sheikh and his "family, businesses and charities" are "entirely and manifestly false", the Cambridge University Press is going way further than the US or most foreign governments would. Of his bank's funding of terrorism, Sheikh Mahfouz's lawyer has said: "Like upper management at any other major banking institution, Khalid Bin

207

Mahfouz was not, of course, aware of every wire transfer moving through the bank. Had he known of any transfers that were going to fund al-Qaida or terrorism, he would not have permitted them." Sounds reasonable enough. Except that in this instance the Mahfouz bank was wiring money to the principal Mahfouz charity, the Muwafaq (or "Blessed Relief") Foundation, which in turn transferred them to Osama bin Laden.

In October 2001, the Department of the Treasury named Muwafaq as "an al-Qaeda front that receives funding from wealthy Saudi businessmen" and its chairman as a "specially designated global terrorist". As the Treasury concluded, "Saudi businessmen have been transferring millions of dollars to bin Laden through Blessed Relief." Indeed, this "charity" seems to have no other purpose than to fund jihad. It seeds Islamism wherever it operates. In Chechnya, it helped transform a reasonably conventional nationalist struggle into an outpost of the jihad. In the Balkans, it played a key role in replacing a traditionally moderate Islam with a form of Mitteleuropean Wahhabism. Pick a Muwafaq branch office almost anywhere on the planet and you get an interesting glimpse of the typical Saudi charity worker. The former head of its mission in Zagreb, Croatia, for example, is a guy called Ayadi Chafiq bin Muhammad. Well, he's called that most of the time. But he has at least four aliases and residences in at least three nations (Germany, Austria and Belgium). He was named as a bin Laden financier by the US government, and disappeared from the United Kingdom shortly after 9/11.

So why would the Cambridge University Press, one of the most respected publishers on the planet, absolve Khalid bin Mahfouz, his family, his businesses and his charities to a degree that neither (to pluck at random) the US, French, Albanian, Swiss and Pakistani governments would be prepared to do?

Because English libel law overwhelmingly favors the plaintiff. And, like many other bigshot Saudis, Sheikh Mahfouz has become very adept at using foreign courts to silence American authors - in effect, using distant jurisdictions to nullify the First Amendment. He may be a wronged man, but his use of what the British call "libel chill" is designed not to vindicate his good name but to shut down the discussion. Which is why Cambridge University Press made no serious attempt to mount a defense. He's one of the richest men on the planet, and they're an academic publisher with very small profit margins. But, even if you've got a bestseller, your pockets are unlikely to be deep enough: *House Of Saud, House Of Bush* did boffo biz with the anti-Bush crowd in America, but there's no British edition - because Sheikh Mahfouz had indicated he was prepared to spend what it takes to challenge it in court and Random House decided it wasn't worth it.

We've gotten used to one-way multiculturalism: the world accepts that you can't open an Episcopal or Congregational church in Jeddah or Riyadh, but every week the Saudis can open radical mosques and madrassahs and pro-Saudi think-tanks in London and Toronto and Dearborn, Michigan and Falls Church, Virginia. And their global reach extends a little further day by day, inch by inch, in the lengthening shadows, as the lights go out one by one around the world. Suppose you've got a manuscript about the Saudis. Where are you going to shop it? Think Cambridge University Press will be publishing anything anytime soon?

THE PROGRESSIVE DELUSION
Passivity

National Review, February 19th 2007

I HAVE THE most professional publishers I've ever had. Regnery, that is. They're in the business of shifting product in large quantity, and to that end they've had me staggering from one radio or TV interview to another for months on end, plugging my book on the dangerously enfeebled state of western civilization. Mostly to the usual suspects, I have to admit: Fox, right-wing talk-radio, and so on. But a few weeks ago I suggested to my publicist that, much as I enjoyed taking calls that began, "Your book is the best book I've read in my entire adult life", I wouldn't mind doing a few shows from the other side, down the NPR/PBS end of things.

My publicist pursed her lips. "We could book you on those shows," she said. "But I'm not sure it's a good idea."

"Don't worry, I can handle it," I insisted. "It'll keep me sharp, on my toes, thinking on my feet, responding vigorously to hostile questioning."

"I didn't mean that," she replied. "I meant going on those shows doesn't sell a lot of books." As she sees it, your nutso right-wing author does ten minutes on WZZZ Hate-Talk AM at three in the morning and the local Borders sells out the next day. Whereas he's interviewed for an hour by Terri Gross on NPR, and it sends precisely two listeners out to their bookstore, and only to buy that Andrew Sullivan doorstopper on everything that's gone wrong with conservatism.

"It's not about sales," I protested. "What profiteth a man if he maketh a gazillion bucks but loseth hith entire thivilithathion?" As she wiped the Niagara of saliva off her face, I explained that we can't keep preaching to the choir, we've got to try and persuade folks of the merits of the case, etc. Well, she promised to do her best, and so I've found myself taking the first tentative steps into the hostile territory of various public radio shows.

And a bit dispiriting it is, too. I don't mind the conspiracy guys and the all-about-oil obsessives. I'm cool with the fellows who say, well, America sold Saddam all his weapons anyway: it's always fun to point out that, according to analysis by the International Peace Research Institute of Stockholm, for the years between 1973 and 2002 the American and British arm sales combined added up to under 2 per cent of Iraq's armaments – or less than Saddam got from the Brazilians.

That's all good knockabout. But what befuddles me are the callers who aren't foaming and partisan but speak in almost eerily calm voices like patient kindergarten teachers and say things like "I find it very offensive that your guest can use language that's so hierarchical" - ie, repressive Muslim dictatorships are worse than pluralist western democracies - and "We are confronting violence with violence, when what we need is non-violent conflict resolution that's binding on all sides" – ie …well, ie whatever.

Half the time these assertions are such watery soft-focus blurs of passivity, there's nothing solid enough to latch on to and respond to. But, when, as they often do, they cite Martin Luther King or Mahatma Gandhi, I point out that we're not always as fortunate to find ourselves up against such relatively benign enemies as British imperial administrators or even American racist rednecks. King and Gandhi's strategies would not have been effective against fellows who gun down classrooms of Russian schoolchildren, or self-detonate at Muslim weddings in Amman, or behead you live on camera and then release it as a snuff video, or assassinate politicians and as they're dying fall to the ground and drink their blood off the marble. Come to that, King and Gandhi's strategies would not have been effective against the prominent British Muslim who in a recent debate at Trinity College, Dublin announced that the Prophet's message to infidels was "I am here to slaughter you all." Good luck with the binding non-violent conflict resolution there.

And at that point there's usually a pause and the caller says something like "Well, that's all the more reason why we need to be even more committed to non-violence." Or as a lady called Kay put it: "We have a lot of work to do then so that someday a long way down the road they won't want to slaughter us."

There may, indeed, come a day when they won't want to slaughter us, but it may be because by that day there's none of us left to slaughter. She had just told me that "we're all in this together. I don't care if you're Jewish, Christian, Muslim, Buddhist." Good for you. Unfortunately, they *do* care. In Gaza, in Sudan, in Kashmir, in southern Thailand, and even in Europe and North America, they care very much. But the great advantage of cultural relativism is that it absolves you of the need to know anything. For, if everything's of equal value, why bother learning about any of the differences?

On the whole I prefer those Americans who tune out the foreign-policy bores for wall-to-wall Anna Nicole Smith coverage. At least they've got an interest – ask them about the latest scoop on the identity of the father of her child and they'll bring you up to speed. By contrast, a large number of elite Americans are just as parochial and indifferent to the currents of the age; the only difference is that they choose to trumpet it as a moral virtue. And you can't avoid the suspicion that, far from having "a lot of work to do", a lot of us are heavily invested in a belief in "pacifism" precisely because it involves doing no work at all – apart from bending down once every couple of years and slapping the "CO-EXIST" bumper sticker on your new car.

Or as I said somewhat tetchily to one caller, "Life isn't a bumper sticker."

Which, come to think of it, would make rather a good bumper sticker.

THOUGHTSTOPPERS UBIQUITOUS
The showboating rabbi

National Review Online, March 9th 2008

"MY THEOLOGY," writes Rabbi Dow Marmur in *The Toronto Star*, "prompts me to opt for a concept of liberty that includes the free choice not to exercise it." Weighing in on the Danish cartoons, Canada's "human rights" thought police and related matters, the rabbi comes down on the side of self-censorship in the interests of multicultural sensitivity. But, en passant, he observes:

> *This was my stance more than a decade ago when* Show Boat *was staged in Toronto and some members of the black community objected on the grounds that it was racist. Many of my friends thought otherwise. For all I know, they may have been right, because it's difficult to describe* Show Boat *as a racist musical. Nevertheless, I felt that if some blacks thought that it was, their feelings were more important to me than my own artistic judgment. I think tolerance is also about that.*

Show Boat is a "racist musical" only in the sense that the blacks get the best roles and the best songs – "Ol' Man River", "Bill", "Can't Help Lovin' That Man Of Mine". Its authors were classic New York liberals - Oscar Hammerstein went on to write "You've Got To Be Carefully Taught" (to hate persons of another color) in the score for *South Pacific*, a song which so offended theater owners in the south they insisted it be cut from the film version. The Hal Prince revival referenced above subsequently opened on Broadway, and I remember Paul Simon, a latterday New York liberal, telling me how much he loved the show.

If you throw over *Show Boat*, one of the great works of the American theatre, because somebody's "feelings" (however

213

manufactured) are more important, what else are you prepared to lose? In such a world, there will be nothing left. To discard a work like *Show Boat* is to deny history, which is to deny reality, and that's rarely a smart move. In the name of "tolerance", you'll wind up in a society that tolerates nothing - nothing genuinely enquiring or provocative, or even mildly controversial. Even liberal rabbis should know better.

Watching a grown man congratulating himself for placing "their feelings" over objective truth, Kathy Shaidle put it more bluntly:

> *It is sad to see someone like Dow Marmur still stuck in that illusory mindset, all these years later, trying, in public, to talk himself into believing something he knows full well is absolute rubbish.*

In a letter unconnected to the rabbi's thoughts, a British reader Peter Monro nevertheless reminded me of something that seems relevant, Orwell's far-sighted concept of *1984* – "Crimestop":

> *Crimestop means the faculty of stopping short, as though by instinct, at the threshold of any dangerous thought. It includes the power of not grasping analogies, of failing to perceive logical errors, of misunderstanding the simplest arguments if they are inimical to Ingsoc*, and of being bored and repelled by any train of thought which is capable of leading in a heretical direction. Crimestop, in short, means protective stupidity.*

There's a lot of that about.

**"Ingsoc", you'll recall, is a contraction deriving from "English Socialism". Poor old Orwell got so much right but even he couldn't foresee that the very word "English" would be deemed beyond the pale in a scrupulously sensitive post-national Britain. Still, it's not hard to imagine a smiley-face government regulatory agency of "Canadian values" called "Canval".*

Whoops, don't want to give anybody any ideas.

THE STEYN-HUGGER
Saying the unsayable

Maclean's, April 21st 2008

IN *THE VILLAGE VOICE* the other week, the playwright David Mamet recently outed himself as a liberal apostate and revealed that he's begun reading conservative types like Milton Friedman and Paul Johnson. If he's wondering what he's in for a year or two down the line, here's how *Newsweek*'s Jonathan Tepperman began his review this week of another literary leftie who wandered off the reservation:

> *Toward the end of* The Second Plane, *Martin Amis's new book on the roots and impact of 9/11, the British novelist describes a fellow writer as 'an oddity: his thoughts and themes are ... serious - but he writes like a maniac. A talented maniac, but a maniac.' Amis is describing Mark Steyn, a controversial anti-Islam polemicist, but he could just as well be describing another angry, Muslim-bashing firebrand: himself. Talented, yes. Serious, yes. But also, judging from the new book, a maniac.*

Poor chap. What did Martin Amis ever do to deserve being compared to me? As Mr Tepperman concludes, the new Amis is "painful for the legion of Amis fans who still love him for novels like *The Rachel Papers* and his masterpiece, *London Fields*." But the masterpieces were in the fast fading good old days before he transformed himself into a fellow who, as a recent profile in Britain's *Independent* put it, "chooses to promote the writings of a Canadian former disc-jockey called Mark Steyn". I'm not sure which half of that biographical précis is intended to be more condescending. At least the "disc-jockey" bit is "former", whereas the Canadianness is, alas, immutable: You can take the disc-jockey out of Canada but you can't

215

take the Canada out of the disc-jockey. In fact, it was *The Independent* which "chose" to promote the writings of the ghastly colonial platter-spinner. Having obtained an exclusive interview – the first with Mr Amis since he found himself declared beyond the literary pale – the *Indy*'s man "chose" to spend most of his brief time with the eminent novelist bemoaning the non-eminent disc-jockey. It's a very curious interviewing technique: "But enough about what I think of Steyn. What do *you* think of Steyn?"

The profile concluded that Amis had descended into a kind of schizophrenia, torn between "the left-wing… nuclear-disarming multiracialist" and the "Steyn-hugger". An even more renowned literary personage sent me a note after *The Independent*'s piece appeared saying that, if you'd held a competition a decade ago to invent the phrase least likely ever to be appended to Martin Amis, "Steyn-hugger" would be pretty hard to beat. It's faintly surreal to find oneself cited as the principal reason for someone else's fall from media grace, and it's not terribly fair to dear old Amis. His approval of me is very limited: Steyn, he says, "is a great sayer of the unsayable".

In Canada, depending on how *Maclean's* forthcoming "human rights" show trial shakes out, it's legally unsayable. But Britain has not (yet) reached the benighted condition of a land policed by "human rights" commissions, and so for the moment Martin Amis refers only to what's merely socially "unsayable". He seems to have concluded that across the last 30 or 40 years the citizens of enlightened western democracies have allowed their public discourse to wither to the point where they almost literally lack a language in which to examine the critical challenges to our society.

Amis wrote the central essay in *The Second Plane* – "The Age Of Horrorism" – a couple of years back. It dwells on the "extreme incuriosity of Islamic culture" and remarks that "the impulse towards rational inquiry is by now very weak among the rank and file of the Muslim male." Which is all but unarguable. But, ever since, he's found himself writing pieces to which editors append headlines like "Amis:

Why I Am Not A Racist" and "No, Look, Honestly, I'm Not A Racist".

He has a point. Islam is everything but a race. It's a religion – which is to say (if you're an atheist like Amis and his friend Christopher Hitchens) an ideology. It's also a political platform and an imperialist project, as those terms are traditionally understood. It has believers of every colour on every continent. So, if Islam is a race, then everything's a race – from the Elks Lodge to the Hannah Montana Fan Club to the British Airways frequent flyer program. Moreover to denounce as "racist" any attempt to discuss Islam is to accept that being Muslim, like being black, is a given, fixed, unchangeable. That's what many of its adherents believe: According to one poll, 36 per cent of young Muslims think that anyone attempting to leave Islam should be killed. That's not young Muslims in Yemen or Waziristan, by the way, but 36 per cent of young Muslims in the United Kingdom. However, there's no good reason for British non-Muslims to endorse the view that one can only be Muslim unto death. "Racist", of course, no longer has anything very much to do with skin colour. It merely means you have raised a topic that discombobulates the scrupulously non-judgmental progressive sensibility. I wonder if one reason we seem so bizarrely fixated on "climate change" and the flora and fauna is because it's one of the few subjects we can talk about without having any dissenting view greeted by cries of "Racist!" For the moment.

So much is "unsayable", isn't it? I mentioned a week or two back that 57 per cent of Pakistani Britons are married to their first cousins. Forty years ago, the notion of a Yorkshire grade-school class in which a majority of the pupils are the children of first cousins would have been unthinkable. Now it's "unsayable". Many non-Pakistani Britons are a little queasy about the marital preferences of their neighbours but no longer know quite on what basis to object to it. "The ethos of relativism," writes Amis, "finds the demographic question so saturated in revulsions that it is rendered undiscussable." Dissenting from recent immigration proposals, the NDP's Olivia Chow said she worried about possible government bias: "My fear is they will choose immigrants who they think are 'good for Canada'." And we can't have that, can we? A progressive nation must demonstrate its multicultural bona fides by taking a position of scrupulous disinterest in such matters: If 12, 17, 43, 91 per cent of our immigrants turn out to be cousin-marriers, who are we to be judgmental? And so we string along, with cousin marriage, and polygamy, and more.

Unlike most writers, who chose to sit this one out, Martin Amis has struggled since September 11th 2001 to find a lingo in which to mull these questions. The pen is mightier than the sword, but not if the ink you're using is so diluted by "the ethos of relativism". Before his descent into Steyn-hugging, Mr Amis was a famously "cool" media personality, and you get the sense that he would prefer to accommodate the tensions of our time in a voice of amused detachment – a non-"maniacal" voice, as that *Newsweek* guy would say. But it doesn't seem to do the job. He writes a short story about Mohammed Atta suffering from constipation and can't quite pull it off. He decides to decry the media shorthand for the day of infamy: "9/11". "My principal objection to the numbers is that they are numbers," he writes. "The solecism, that is to say, is not grammatical but moral-aesthetic — an offense against decorum; and decorum means 'seemliness,' which comes from *soemr*, 'fitting,' and *soema*, 'to honour.' 9/11, 7/7: who or what decided that particular acts of slaughter, particular whirlwinds of plasma and body parts, in which a random sample of the innocent is killed, maimed, or otherwise crippled in body and mind, deserve a numerical shorthand? Whom does this 'honour'? What makes this 'fitting'?"

Mr Amis' objection to me is that Steyn "writes like a nutter". But in the above passage it's the urge to write like a non-nutter that leaves the prose mincing like a pretentious sommelier asked to bring a bottle of Baby Duck. He's struggling to find an aspect of the situation against which he can strike a writerly pose, and it smells fake because we know that's not what engages him about the situation. Not really.

He wants to write something more primal, more visceral, more *felt*. But, when he does, the media call him racist.

When he reviewed my book, he felt the jokes were inappropriate. And he had a point, at least to the extent that just about the first gag, way up front in the book's second paragraph, was at his expense. I quoted a passage of his from the Eighties, outlining his plans for coping with the impending Thatcher-Reagan nuclear Armageddon:

> *'Suppose I survive,' he fretted. 'Suppose my eyes aren't pouring down my face, suppose I am untouched by the hurricane of secondary missiles that all mortar, metal and glass has abruptly become: suppose all this. I shall be obliged (and it's the last thing I feel like doing) to retrace that long mile home, through the firestorm, the remains of the thousands-miles-an-hour winds, the warped atoms, the grovelling dead. Then - God willing, if I still have the strength, and, of course, if they are still alive - I must find my wife and children and I must kill them.'*

And then I added: "But the Big One never fell. And instead of killing his wife Martin Amis had to make do with divorcing her."

Mean and petty? Yes, indeed. And I feel a bit bad about it. But a couple of pages on and I was soon cheerfully hooting and jeering at the head-hackers and clitorectomy enforcers in much the same fashion. Mr Amis felt jihadist snuff videos and the like were no laughing matter, but each of us gets through "the age of horrorism" as he can. If I didn't laugh, I'd weep – and feel I'd already half-surrendered, for, as the late Ayatollah Khomeini pronounced, "There are no jokes in Islam." I hope Martin Amis recovers a bit of his old drollery: He's on the right side in this struggle and should bring the best weapon to the fight. It's time for a great novel on the theme, a *London Fields* for a transformed London.

V

TRUDEAUPIA VS INDIVIDUAL LIBERTY

Prime Minister Stephen Harper's office confirmed Thursday he will be on hand Friday for the groundbreaking ceremony for the Canadian Museum for Human Rights in Winnipeg.

THE WINNIPEG FREE PRESS

December 18th 2008

They took all the rights
And put 'em in a rights museum
And they charged the people a loonie-and-a-half just to see 'em
Don't it always seem to go
That you don't know what you've got till it's gone?
They paved paradise
And put up a Human Rights Commission…

If you'd said to me in mid-2007 that in twelve months' time I'd be a poster boy for (according to taste) either "hate" or the campaign to restore Canada's lost liberties, I'd have roared my head off. But a year later, shortly before the British Columbia "Human Rights" Tribunal put my "flagrant Islamophobia" on trial, Michel Vonn of the BC Civil Liberties Association gave an interview to a journalism ethics bore from the Centre for Journalism Ethics at the University of British Columbia. In the course of her remarks, Ms Vonn observed: "The feeling is that it doesn't matter which way Steyn is going to go, it's probably going to get appealed."

It took me a moment to realize that "Steyn" was no longer a "he" but an "it". I used to be a writer, now I'm a case. That's not a promotion. In this section, here's some snapshots from the battle to recover freedom of speech in a country that so carelessly lost it:

THE STATE vs YOUR OPINIONS
That's for sure

Maclean's, January 28th 2008

OUR LESSON for today comes from Shirlene McGovern:

You're entitled to your opinions, that's for sure.

Clichés are the reflex mechanisms of speech - "Yeah, sure, it's a free country. Everyone's entitled to his opinion, right?" And we get so careless with them that we don't even notice when they become obsolescent.

But Shirlene McGovern should. Because it's her job to determine whether you - yes, you, Gordy Schmoe of 37b Hoser Crescent - are entitled to your opinions. Miss McGovern is a "human rights agent" with Alberta's "Human Rights" Commission, and she was officially interrogating Ezra Levant as to why, in his capacity as publisher of *The Western Standard*, he had reproduced in his magazine the so-called "Danish cartoons". As you'll recall from a year or so back, these were representations of the Prophet Muhammad published in the widely unread newspaper *Jyllands-Posten*, but which nevertheless prompted the usual surprisingly coordinated campaign of vandalism, violence, mayhem and murder by the more excitable Muslims in various parts of the world. I doubt, had I been the editor of *Jyllands-Posten*, I would have published the original cartoons, because most of them weren't terribly good. But once the drawings became an international news story it seems absurd to publish reports on the controversy without also showing what all the fuss is about. CNN did show the cartoons, but with the Prophet's face all blurry and pixilated — the first time, I believe, that this familiar technique of investigative TV journalism has been applied not to a human being but to a, er, drawing.

Back in Jutland, the cartoonists had originally accepted the Muhammad assignment in order to test the boundaries of freedom of speech in Denmark. And they failed only insofar as the episode tested freedom's boundaries not in Denmark, where nobody has been prosecuted; nor in the US, where CNN's craven straddle artfully finessed the issue; nor in France, where the sole editor to publish the cartoons was subsequently fired by his boss, as is a private employer's right; nor even at the European Union, whose commissioner for justice and security proposed a "media code" that would encourage, ah, "prudence" in the way the press covers, ahem, certain touchy subjects, but who was at least at pains to emphasize that these restraints would be "self-regulated" by the press themselves.

No, the western jurisdiction in which the Danish cartoons have most comprehensively demonstrated the constraints on free expression is our own decayed Dominion: only in Canada have the commissars of the state launched an official investigation for the alleged "crime" of publishing the cartoons. Last week, sitting across the table from Shirlene McGovern, Ezra Levant launched into an impassioned denunciation of his interrogation. He took the quaint view that his "freedom of expression" was not the generous if qualified gift of Trudeaupian bureaucrats but his inalienable right and one bolstered in this country by 800 years of English Common Law as well as more modish innovations such as the 1946 UN Universal Declaration on Human Rights. Canada likes that last one so much it sticks it on the back of the $50 bill, even though we are in sustained and systemic breach of its provisions on free expression. Yes, yes, I know: so are Sudan and North Korea, but come on, is that really the league you want to play in?

In the course of his interrogation, Mr Levant also pointed out that the time and money Canada's "human rights" pseudo-courts cost publishers has a broader "chilling effect" - on all the stories that will never see the light of day because at the back of some editor's mind is the calculation of the expense of fending off Shirlene McGovern. And, at the end of this exchange, Agent McGovern, licensed to chill, looked blandly across the table and shrugged:

You're entitled to your opinions, that's for sure.

No, sorry. That cliché is no longer operative in Canada. Today you're only entitled to your opinions if Agent McGovern says you are – "for sure". Ezra Levant was of the opinion that he should publish the Danish cartoons. That opinion is now on trial. Ken Whyte, the executive honcho at *Maclean's*, was of the opinion he should publish an excerpt from my book. That opinion comes up for trial at the British Columbia "Human Rights" Tribunal in June, and at the Canadian "Human Rights" Tribunal shortly thereafter, and most likely at the Ontario "Human Rights" Tribunal a little way down the road.

Because I've always been opposed to "human rights" commissions in theory (I like proper courts with things like "due process"), I failed to appreciate until *Maclean's* present predicament how much worse they are in practice. These commissions were supposedly intended to investigate discrimination in housing and the like, but then came the very poorly drafted Section 13, which makes it a crime to communicate anything electronically "likely to expose a person or persons to hatred or contempt". "Likely", eh? What does that mean? Well, according to the key determination, subsequently endorsed by the Supreme Court, in Canadian legalese "likely" now means "highly unlikely". That's to say, notwithstanding the absence of any evidence by the plaintiffs of anyone at all ever having been exposed to actual hatred or contempt, nor even any coherent argument as to why there is a hypothetical possibility of someone unspecified being exposed to theoretical hatred or contempt in the decades ahead, a commission can still deem such hatred or contempt "likely".

In the three decades of the Canadian "Human Rights" Tribunal's existence, not a single "defendant" has been "acquitted" of a Section 13 crime – except for something called the "Canadian Nazi Party", a complaint against whom was dismissed on the grounds that there was no evidence any such "Canadian Nazi Party" actually existed.

But, if you do happen to exist, the odds are a lot tougher. Would you bet on *Maclean's* bucking this spectacular 100 per cent conviction rate? "Sentence first, verdict afterwards," declares the Queen in *Alice In Wonderland*. Canada's not quite there yet, but at the "Human Rights" Commission, it's "Verdict first, trial afterwards". So I'm guilty and Ken Whyte's guilty and *Maclean's* is guilty because that's the only verdict there is.

Who has availed themselves of the "human rights" protected by Section 13? In its entire history, over half of all cases have been brought by a sole "complainant", one Richard Warman. Indeed, Mr Warman has been a plaintiff on every single Section 13 case before the federal "human rights" star chamber since 2002 - and he's won every one. That would suggest that no man in any free society anywhere on the planet has been so comprehensively deprived of his human rights. Well, no. Mr Warman doesn't have to demonstrate that he personally has been deprived of his human rights, only that it's "likely" (ie, "highly un-") that someone somewhere will be deprived of some right sometime.

Who is Richard Warman? What's his story? Well, he's a former employee of the Canadian "Human Rights" Commission: an investigator. Same as Shirlene McGovern.

Isn't there something a little odd about a supposedly indispensable Canadian "human rights" system used all but exclusively by one lone Canadian who served as a long-time employee of that system? Why should Richard Warman be the only citizen to have his own personal inquisition? You can hardly blame the Canadian Islamic Congress and the Islamic Supreme Council of Canada and no doubt the Supreme All-Powerful Islamic Executive Council of Swift Current, Saskatchewan, for belatedly figuring they'd like a piece of the human rights action.

In a free society, justice must not only be done, but must be seen to be done. And when you see what's being done at the CHRC it's hard not to conclude that the genius of the English legal system - the balance between prosecutor, judge, and jury - has been all but destroyed. The American website Pundita has a sharp analysis of Section 13, comparing it to Philip K Dick's sci-fi novel *The Minority Report*, set in a world in which citizens can be sentenced for "pre-crime" - for criminal acts which have not occurred but are "likely" to. Who needs futuristic novels when we're living it here and now in one of the oldest constitutional democracies on the planet?

What kind of countries have tribunals with 100 per cent conviction rates that replace the presumption of innocence with the presumption of guilt and in which truth is not only no defence but compelling evidence of that guilt? Consider this statement, part of the criteria by which the star chamber determines when a Section 13 crime has occurred. What does it look for as evidence?

Messages that make use of allegedly true stories, news reports, pictures and references to apparently reputable sources in an attempt to lend an air of objectivity and truthfulness to the extremely negative characterization of the targeted group have been found to be likely to expose members of the targeted group to hatred and contempt.

Read that again slowly. Citing news reports, reputable sources, facts, statistics, documentation, quotations, references, scholarly studies, etc, has been "found" to be clear evidence of your "likely" pre-crime.

Canadians are uncomfortable even confronting what's going on in their name. On last week's letters page, Lauren Demaree of Windsor seemed closest to "mainstream" "moderate" Canadian opinion:

Placing limits on free speech is a slippery slope, but that is not the only issue in play here. There is often a fine line that is crossed between opinion and hate propaganda and our laws need to reflect this more effectively. Where do we draw the line? When a group of people is harassed or when someone is beaten? How about killed? When your writer Andrew Coyne sits on a high horse spouting the ideals of free speech, he doesn't stop and think about the consequences of his words.

Who has been "killed" or "beaten" or "harassed" by Coyne-Steyn "hate propaganda"? The killings and bombings, as Ezra Levant pointed out, occur in countries without freedom of expression - because when you criminalize words the only expression left is action. How sad to see Canada pursuing, as the federal "Human Rights" Commission puts it, "A Watch On Hate". Not "hate crimes" or even "hate speech", but just "hate" - thoughts, feelings, emotions. Mohamed Elmasry of the Canadian Islamic Congress is a world-class hater who thinks all Israeli civilians over 18 are legitimate targets for murder. Bully for him. Yet, in Elmasry's pursuit of *Maclean's*, Lauren Demaree sees the hater as the pin-up crusader who'll abolish hate. No free society can do that. But it can certainly abolish, incrementally, freedom of expression and the presumption of innocence in relentless pursuit of such a banal happy-face chimera. The arbitrary absurdity of *Alice In Wonderland*'s Queen yoked to the Cheshire Cat smile. This is your fight, too, Lauren, even if you don't yet know it.

SUBTERRANEAN CONVERSATION
Alarums

Maclean's, February 18th 2008

SINCE *MACLEAN'S* got into a spot of bother with Canada's "human rights" pseudo-courts, I've been pleasantly surprised by the number of our media confrères who don't think it should be a "crime" for magazines to publish excerpts from books by yours truly. Nevertheless, it has to be said that not all my defenders are as full-throated as one might wish. "Mark Steyn's book about Muslim demographics may contain some cynical statistics and Islamic stereotypes," wrote Peter Jackson in *The Telegram* of St John's, Newfoundland, "but his observations are not totally without merit."

"Not totally without merit", eh? That's not exactly what Broadway producers call a money quote. I prefer Kathy Shaidle's approach: "If your response to the *Maclean's*/Steyn case isn't tainted with outrage, sarcasm and a profound sense of urgency, there is something wrong with you," she wrote. "I'm getting as worried by these prissy attitudes emerging around this case as I am about the case itself." She's right. I don't mind the mass mailings of dreary identical insert-name-of-outraged-reader-here form letters run off by the Supreme Islamic Council of Moose Jaw or some other cockamamie pressure group, but a certain recurring shtick in the mainstream commentary is even more wearisome. In defending free speech in general, journalists usually feel obliged to deplore my exercise of it in particular:

> Maclean's *published an alarmist screed by Mr Steyn...*
> (THE ECONOMIST)

> *While the book may be alarmist...* (CFRB)

> *Steyn's argument is indeed alarmist...* (THE GUARDIAN)

And, oh dear, even:

LIGHTS OUT

The fear of 'a Muslim tide' was alarmist...
(Tarek Fatah and Farzana Hassan in MACLEAN'S)

Okay, enough already. I get the picture: Alarmist, alarmist, alarmist. My book's thesis – that most of the western world is on course to become at least semi-Islamic in its political and cultural disposition within a very short time – is "alarmist".

The question then arises: Fair enough, guys, what would it take to alarm you? The other day, in a characteristically clotted speech followed by a rather more careless BBC interview, the Archbishop of Canterbury said that it was dangerous to have one law for everyone and that the introduction of sharia – Islamic law – to the United Kingdom was "inevitable". No alarm bells going off yet? Can't say I blame you. After all, de facto creeping sharia is well established in the western world. Last week, the British and Ontario governments confirmed within days of each other that thousands of polygamous men in their jurisdictions receive welfare payments for each of their wives. Still no alarm bells? I see British Muslim nurses in public hospitals riddled with C difficile are refusing to comply with hygiene procedures on the grounds that scrubbing requires them to bare their arms, which is unIslamic. Would it be alarmist to bring that up – say, the day before your operation?

Sharia in Britain? Taxpayer-subsidised polygamy in Toronto? Yawn. Nothing to see here. True, if you'd suggested such things on September 10th 2001, most Britons and Canadians would have said you were nuts. But a few years on and it doesn't seem such a big deal, and nor will the next concession, and the one after that. It's hard to deliver a wake-up call for a civilization so determined to smother the alarm clock in the soft fluffy pillow of multiculturalism and sleep in for another ten years. The folks who call my book "alarmist" accept that the western world is growing more Muslim (Canada's Muslim population has doubled in the last ten years), but they deny that this population trend has any significant societal consequences.

Sharia mortgages? Sure.

Polygamy? Whatever.

Honour killings? Well, okay, but only a few.

The assumption that you can hop on the Sharia Express and just ride a couple of stops is one almighty leap of faith. More to the point, who are you relying on to "hold the line"? Influential figures like the Archbishop of Canterbury? The bureaucrats at Ontario Social Services? The western world is not run by fellows noted for their line-holding: Look at what they're conceding now and then try to figure out what they'll be conceding in five years' time.

The other night at dinner, I found myself sitting next to a Middle Eastern Muslim lady of a certain age. And the conversation went as it often does when you're with Muslim women who were at college in the Sixties, Seventies or Eighties. In this case, my dining companion had just been at a conference on "women's issues", of which there are many in the Muslim world, and she was struck by the phrase used by the "moderate Muslim" chair of the meeting: "authentic women" – by which she meant women wearing hijabs. And my friend pointed out that when she and her unveiled pals had been in their twenties *they* were the "authentic women": The covering routine was for old village biddies, the Islamic equivalent of gnarled Russian babushkas. It would never have occurred to her that the assumptions of her generation would prove to be off by 180 degrees – that in middle age she would see young Muslim women wearing a garb largely alien to their tradition not just in the Middle East but in Brussels and London and Montreal. If you had said to her in 1968 that westernized Muslim women working in British hospitals in the early 21st century would reject modern hygiene because it required them to bare their arms, she would have scoffed with the certainty of one who assumes that history moves in only one direction.

In another of those non-alarmist nothing-to-see-here stories, a British government minister tentatively raised the matter of severe birth defects among the children of Pakistani Muslims. Some 57 per cent of Pakistani Britons are married to their first cousins, and this places their progeny at increased risk of certain health problems. This is the only way a culturally relativist west can even raise some of these topics: Nothing against cousin marriage, old boy, but it puts a bit of a strain on the old health care budget. Likewise, it's not the polygamy, it's the four welfare cheques you're collecting for it.

But this is being penny-wise and pound-blasé. What does it mean when 57 per cent of Pakistani Britons are married to first cousins and 70 per cent are married to relatives? At the very least, it tells you that this community is strongly resistant to traditional immigrant assimilation patterns. Of course, in any society, certain groups are self-segregating - the Amish, the Mennonites and whatnot. But when that group is not merely a curiosity on the fringe of the map but the principal source of population growth in all your major cities, the challenge posed by that self-segregation is of a different order. There are now towns in northern England where cousin marriage is the norm: Pakistanis aren't assimilating with "the host community"; the host community has assimilated with Pakistan. Again, if you had told a Yorkshireman in 1970 that by the early 21st century it would be entirely normal for half the kindergarten class to be the children of first cousins, he would have found it preposterous.

But it happened. By "alarmist", *The Economist* and co really mean "raising the subject". Last year, the British novelist Martin Amis raised the subject of my book with Tony Blair and asked him if, when he got together with his fellow prime ministers, the Continental demographic picture was part of the "European conversation". Mr Blair replied, with disarming honesty, "It's a subterranean conversation."

"We know what that means," wrote Amis. "The ethos of relativism finds the demographic question so saturated in revulsions that it is rendered undiscussable." The "multiculturist ideologue", he added, "cannot engage with the fact that a) the indigenous populations of Spain and Italy are due to halve every 35 years, and b) this entails certain consequences."

Whether or not it's "alarmist" to ponder what those consequences might be, under Canada's "human rights" kangaroo courts it might soon be illegal. All Section 13 cases brought to the federal "Human Rights" Commission end in defeat for the defendant, so, if *Maclean's* fails to buck the 100 per cent conviction rate, it would be enjoined from publishing anything that might relate to the "hate speech" in question – in other words, we would be legally prevented from writing about Islam and the west, demographic trends in Canada, and many other topics.

What would we be permitted by the state to write about? How about Nazis? It's been years since I've run into one, but apparently they're everywhere. A British blogger, pooh-poohing my book, said there are more Nazis than Muslims in England. Really? In Canada, meanwhile, defenders of Section 13 of the Human Rights Code – the one that makes "criminals" of *Maclean's* – warn that if the private member's motion of Keith Martin, MP proposing its repeal were to succeed, Nazis would be free to peddle their dangerous Nazi ideas to simpleminded Canadians who might lack the fortitude to resist. As evidence of the Nazi tide waiting to engulf the Dominion once Section 13 is repealed, Liberal spin-doctor Warren Kinsella posted on his website a photograph he'd taken in a men's room stall showing the words "WHITE POWER" and a swastika scrawled on the wall at knee height. Why Mr Kinsella is photographing public toilets on his knees I don't know, but every guy needs a hobby. At any rate, Warren sees this loser's graffiti as critical evidence of the imminent Nazi threat to the peaceable kingdom.

As I often say, I'm a phobiaphobe. I don't subscribe to the concepts of "homophobia" and "Islamophobia". They're a lame rhetorical sleight to end the argument by denying it's an argument at all: "Why, you poor thing, you don't have a philosophical disagreement with me over gay marriage or sharia, you have a mental illness! But don't worry, we can give you counselling and medication and your 'phobia' will eventually go away."

Yet "Naziphobia" is the real thing – an irrational fear of non-existent Nazis. And so Canada's leading "human rights" hero is Richard Warman, a man whose Naziphobia is so advanced he hauled the "Canadian Nazi Party" before the "Human Rights" Tribunal even though, as the Tribunal was reluctantly forced to rule, no such party exists.

Our heroes pursue phantoms as the world transforms. Is sharia, polygamy, routine first-cousin marriage in the interests of Canada or Britain or Europe? Oh, dear, even to raise the subject is to tiptoe into all kinds of uncomfortable terrain for the multicultural mindset. It's easier just to look the other way, or go Nazi-hunting in the men's room. Nobody wants to be unpleasant, or judgmental, do they?

What was it they said in the Cold War? Better dead than Red. We're not like that anymore. Better screwed than rude.

"ALLOWING" SPEECH

First they came for the giant space lizard conspiracy theorists...

Maclean's, March 10th 2008

WHAT DOES *Maclean's* have in common with a labiaplasty and blood-drinking space lizards from the star system Alpha Draconis?

Well, they're all part of the wacky world of Canadian "human rights".

First things first: What is a labiaplasty? Well, it's a cosmetic procedure performed on the female genitalia for those who are dissatisfied with them. I think I speak for many sad male losers living on ever more distant memories when I say that I find it hard to imagine ever being dissatisfied with female genita...

What's that? Oh, it's the *women* who are dissatisfied are them? Ah, right. Well, there's the rub. The Ontario "Human Rights" Commission is currently weighing whether or not to become the (at last count) third "human rights" commission in Canada to prosecute *Maclean's* for the crime of running an excerpt from my book. *The Globe And Mail's* Margaret Wente was interested to know what Canada's vast "human rights" machinery does when it isn't sticking it to privately owned magazines, so she swung by the Ontario "Human Rights" Tribunal to check out the action. And it seems the reason they haven't yet dragged *Maclean's* into court is because they're tied up hearing the case of two women who claim they were denied their human right to a labiaplasty by a Toronto plastic surgeon who

235

specializes in that particular area. The women proved to be post-operative transsexuals who were unhappy with some of the aesthetic results of their transformation, and Dr Stubbs declined to perform the procedure on the grounds that he usually operates on biological females and is generally up to speed on what goes where and, when it comes to transsexuals, he had no idea what he was, so to speak, getting into. Had he done it and it had all gone horribly wrong, the plaintiffs would have sued his pants off. So, as a private practitioner, he chose to decline the business, and as a result now finds himself in "Human Rights" Commission hell.

As Ms Wente pointed out, you can see what got the "human rights" commissars' juices going. Here was an opportunity to lay down a lot of landmark "jurisprudence" on the issue of "transsexuals' access to medical care", and if, in the end, it destroys Dr Stubbs and his business, hey, that's a price worth paying: The human right to a labiaplasty is too important to a free society. So the Ontario "Human Rights" Tribunal is solemnly deliberating on whether the party of the first part is obliged to take apart the party of the second part's parts.

Dr Stubbs is a bigshot plastic surgeon, so, like *Maclean's*, he can probably withstand a few years of "human rights" heat. The system is risk-free for the plaintiff: the Crown picks up the tab for the "complainant", while the "respondent" – ie, defendant – has to pay his own legal bills no matter what the eventual verdict is. Ted Kindos of Burlington, Ontario has already spent $20,000 of his own dough defending himself against a "human rights" complaint and estimates he'll add another six figures to that before it's all done. Mr Kindos owns a modest restaurant, Gator Ted's Tap and Grill. So what outrageous "human right" did he breach? Well, he asked a guy smoking "medical marijuana" in the doorway of his restaurant if he wouldn't mind not doing it. Mr Kindos felt that his customers – including young children – shouldn't have to pass through a haze of pot smoke being to enter his establishment. But apparently in Canada there's a human right to light up a spliff in some other fellow's doorway. The other man's grass is always greener, and in this case the plaintiff's grass will cost Mr Kindos an awful lot of green. He faces financial ruin, while there's no cost to the complainant.

Canadians are not notably "hateful" people. To be sure, deep in the human heart lurk dark prejudices that may occasionally be furtively expressed to likeminded persons over a drink or two. But discrimination in housing and employment on the grounds of gender and race – the original justification for creating the "human rights" pseudo-courts – is all but extinct, so a self-perpetuating nomenklatura has moved on to invent new rights – like the human right to a labiaplasty or a joint on someone else's property. You'll recall the Osgoode Hall law students who objected to my book excerpt in *Maclean's* demanded a five-page cover story in response, unedited, with the students determining the artwork and the cover art, along with a financial contribution to their "cause". As any self-respecting publisher would, Kenneth Whyte told them he would rather go bankrupt – much as Mr Kindos seems likely to. The Osgoode students have since explained that they went to the "human rights" enforcers because they were only trying to "start a debate", and mean old *Maclean's* was preventing their voices from being heard. They have repeated this mournful plea in lengthy editorials they've written for, at last count, *The Globe And Mail, The National Post, The Toronto Star, The Toronto Sun, The Ottawa Citizen, The Calgary Herald,* the Montreal *Gazette,* the Halifax *Chronicle-Herald, The London Free Press,* and no doubt a few other publications. That's the reality of Canada's "Islamophobic" media: They've been given acres of op-ed real estate to yell that their voices are being silenced and all they want to do is start a debate – even though, in none of their many columns, do they actually start it.

Incidentally, although they characterize themselves as the "complainants" in these suits, they're not. In the two "human rights" complaints against *Maclean's* that are going forward, the complainants in British Columbia are Dr Mohamed Elmasry, president of the Canadian Islamic Congress, and Naiyer Habib, and, in the federal case, Dr Elmasry alone. Mohamed Elmasry is the man who announced on Canadian TV that he approved of the murder of any and all Israeli civilians over the age of 18. One can understand why such an unlikely poster boy for the cause of "anti-hate" campaigns would prefer to hide behind his fresh-faced Osgoode sock puppets. But the fact that every major newspaper in Canada has opened its page to turgid recitations of imagined victimhood by three students who have no standing in these cases tells you everything about how "excluded" and "marginalized" they are. That's the "racist" Canadian media of 2008: All you have to do is claim to represent some community with a grievance and, even though there's no evidence you represent anything other than your own peculiar obsessions and you have nothing substantive to say, nine out of ten editors will turn their pages over to you - no matter what your interminable victimological prose does to their circulation.

Dr Keith Martin, a Liberal Member of Parliament, the Canadian Association of Journalists, PEN Canada (ie, John Ralston Saul and the rest of the CanCon literati) support the repeal of Section 13 of the Human Rights Code, under which *Maclean's* and Ezra Levant, former publisher of *The Western Standard*, have been hauled before the "thought police". Others talk of *Maclean's* appealing its case (after we lose, as all federal Section 13 defendants do) to the Supreme Court. Last time round, their lordships upheld Section 13 by a four-three majority, announcing confidently that there was "little danger that subjective opinion as to offensiveness will supplant the proper meaning". Of course, that's exactly what has happened, as could have been foreseen by anyone but a Supreme Court judge. This is a philosophically flawed and corruptly administered system that is an affront to Canada's legal inheritance.

That may be why, as even Liberal MPs and PEN Canada understand what's happening, the only defenders of the system are its beneficiaries, like Pearl Eliadis, the former director of the Ontario Human Rights Commission, who accused me in the Montreal *Gazette* of "disturbing tactics" for having the impertinence to resist being ruled a hatemonger by a kangaroo court. She claims that I am trying to "disentitle" acknowledged human-rights experts, by which she means herself and other members of a small and unrepresentative clique that has done huge damage to *real* human rights like the presumption of innocence. "Human rights" plaintiffs are professional activists: Since filing her complaint, the lead transsexual in the labiaplasty case has been given a government job investigating the health status of transsexuals. Richard Warman, the plaintiff in over half of all federal Section 13 cases, is not even a transsexual or a member of any other approved victim group. You can write a piece about Jews, gays, Muslims, transsexuals that offends not a single Jew, gay, Muslim or transsexual. But if Mr Warman, a former employee of the CHRC, decides to get offended on their behalf he'll drag you before the kangaroo court. He has been a plaintiff on every single federal Section 13 case in the last six years. No other provision of Canada law has such a deformed profile that it is, in effect, the personal plaything of one very strange man.

Oh, and the bit at the top about the space lizards? That's a chap called David Icke, former Coventry City goalie and BBC sports anchor turned ...well, "turned" pretty much covers it. One day, David was anchoring the World Cup. The next, he'd called a press conference to announce he was the Son of God. Shortly thereafter he concocted a grand conspiracy theory to explain everything that happens anywhere in the world. David believes in a secret world government run by child-abusing Satanist Illuminati controlled by the Queen and the Bush family who are, he says, reptilian humanoids descended from the blood-drinking space lizards of the star system Alpha Draconis. As I recall, a friend of the late Princess of Wales has confirmed to him Her Royal Highness' belief that the Royal Family are shape-shifting space reptiles. I apologize to David if I've lost a bit in translation. It has been many years since he and I shared a BBC talkshow sofa together, and our paths have diverged somewhat. At any rate, Richard Warman took against him and decided to shut him down, telling *The Independent On Sunday* in London:

> *He has taken all the conspiracy theories that have ever existed and melded them together to create an even greater conspiracy theory of his own. His writings may be the work of a madman, or*

*of a genuine racist. Either way, they are very dangerous. There is
an unpleasant anti-Semitic undercurrent in his work that must
be brought to people's attention. If he's unstable, then so are his
followers, who hang on to his every word. What benefit can there
be in allowing him to speak?*

If you want to know what's gone wrong with the Canadian state's
conception of human rights, it's perfectly distilled in that one line from
the Canadian "Human Rights" Commission's longtime investigator
and current serial plaintiff: "What benefit can there be in allowing him
to speak?"

Look, if David Icke was a racist, he wouldn't find it prudent to
give seven-hour speeches in Brixton. Icke isn't a racist, he's a kook who
believes the world is run by shape-shifting space lizards. Why should it
be illegal to advance that theory? Has the Queen or any other shape-
shifter filed a "Human Rights" Commission complaint alleging that
Icke has exposed her to "hatred or contempt"? No. I should imagine
Her Majesty is laughing the socks off her sinister reptilian feet over it.
Which is the healthy reaction. But instead Richard Warman decided to
get affronted on her behalf. And this is the standard that the Canadian
government's former senior speech investigator sets:

What benefit can there be in allowing him to speak?

Who died and made Richard Warman Speech God? Er, well, the
Canadian government did the latter. And it's freedom of expression, in
any meaningful sense, that's died. A longtime "human rights" officer
thinks that it's the state's role to "allow" citizens to speak if they can
demonstrate some "benefit" in doing so. With human rights like that,
who needs lack of human rights? The question is not whether I'm
"disentitling" Canada's human rights nomenklatura, but who entitled
them in the first place, to the point where Mr Warman and Ms Eliadis
think the state commissars should be determining who should be
"allowed" to speak. Sorry, but that's not my definition of human
rights. And I'd rather take my chances with a shape-shifting space

lizard than an endlessly morphing, ever expanding star chamber that shames Canada.

In his way, Richard Warman is nuttier than David Icke. Icke has flown the coop. He's out there in Alpha Draconis having a ball. But Warman is still more or less in the real world, and the assumptions underpinning that rhetorical question to *The Independent* have advanced dramatically, from neo-Nazi losers in basements to conspiracy-theorist gurus and now to Canada's leading news weekly. In such a world, how many more of us will discover the state can find no "benefit" in "allowing" us to speak?

TRUDEAUPIA ABROAD
The Witchpointer-General

National Review Online, April 5th 2008

ONE OF THE striking features of my current troubles with Canada's "Human Rights" Commissions is the way, in the name of ersatz "human rights", these pseudo-courts trample on one of the bedrock human rights: the presumption of innocence. Instead, you're presumed guilty unless you can prove that you're not. That's why Section 13 has a 100 per cent conviction rate. So I'm sorry to see the Aussies going down the same grim path. According to the Melbourne *Age*:

> *Race Discrimination Commissioner Tom Calma wants the burden of proof in cases of racial discrimination to fall on the alleged offender, instead of the person making the complaint.*
>
> *Mr Calma said Australia's laws made it difficult to prove there had been discrimination.*

Well, you never know: That might be because there hasn't been. But best not to take any chances. Australia's Human Rights and Equal Opportunity Commission looked at how the system works in Britain, America and, inevitably, Canada, and found that "the onus of proof shifts to the person who has been accused of discrimination once the complainant has established an initial case", whereas down under "the burden of proof rests on the person making the complaint".

Oh, dear. As *The Age* reported, "Mr Calma said if people were forced to defend themselves, it might make them think twice before offending."

The Herald Sun's Andrew Bolt has an excellent response:

> *OK, Calma - I'll start your ball rolling to hell. I accuse you of being a damn racist. Which, under your new regime, means a*

242

racist you are until you can prove you are not. In the meantime you should stand down, because a racist can't hold your job, surely?

Indeed. I'm shocked to find that that damned filthy racist Calma hasn't resigned yet.

THE FIRST VERDICT
Drive-by justice

Steynposts, April 9th, 12th 2008

WHEN THE CANADIAN Islamic Congress decided to get belatedly affronted by an excerpt from my book, they took their complaint to no less than three of these cockamamie "human rights" commissions. So we were facing potentiall three trials, before the Canadian "Human Rights" Tribunal, the British Columbia "Human Rights" Tribunal and the Ontario "Human Rights" Tribunal. As we know, in any civilized justice system, double jeopardy is a no-no, but triple jeopardy is apparently fine and dandy. Today, the Ontario "Human Rights" Commission announced that they'd decided not to hear the case. That's the good news. The bad news is they decided to issue a verdict anyway. So they added the following:

> *While freedom of expression must be recognized as a cornerstone of a functioning democracy, the Commission strongly condemns the Islamophobic portrayal of Muslims, Arabs, South Asians and indeed any racialized community in the media, such as the Maclean's article and others like them, as being inconsistent with the values enshrined in our human rights codes. Media has a responsibility to engage in fair and unbiased journalism.*

So in effect the Ontario "Human Rights" Commission, the world leaders in labiaplasty jurisprudence, have decided that, even though they don't have the guts to hear the case, they might as well find us guilty. Ingenious! After all, if the federal "Human Rights" Commission hadn't been so foolish enough to drag Marc Lemire to trial, their bizarre habits of playing dress-up Nazis on the Internet and posting their own hate messages using telecommunications fraud and identity theft would never have come to light. If they'd simply skipped the trial and declared Mr Lemire guilty anyway, they wouldn't be in the mess they're in.

Over the years I've written in newspapers and magazines in dozens of countries and have attracted my share of libel suits and other legal difficulties. But today's a first for me. The Ontario "Human Rights" Commission, having concluded they couldn't withstand the heat of a trial, decided to cut to the chase and give us a drive-by conviction anyway. Who says Canada's "human rights" racket is incapable of reform? As kangaroo courts go, the Ontario branch is showing a bit more bounce than the Ottawa lads.

If I'm charged with holding up a liquor store, I enjoy the right to the presumption of innocence and to defend myself in court. But when it comes to so-called "Islamophobia" – a word which was only invented a few years ago and which enjoys no legal definition – all the centuries old safeguards of English Common Law go out the window. I'd be interested to know whether the Justice Minister of Ontario thinks this is appropriate behaviour. At one level, Chief Commissioner Barbara Hall appears to have deprived *Maclean's* and me of the constitutional right to face our accusers. But, at another, it seems clear the OHRC enforcers didn't fancy their chances in open court. So, after a botched operation, they've performed a cosmetic labiaplasty and hustled us out.

Oh, and in the full statement they say:

The Commission intends to further consider these issues in the coming months as it embarks on its new mandate.

"A new mandate", eh? That sounds reassuring, doesn't it? In what Paul Wells calls her "barely lucid, rambling meditation", Ontario's head commissar gives the game away: Unfortunately she doesn't have the jurisdiction to jail Steyn for "Islamophobia", but she would if she could - so she's going to seek the power to do so when the Ontario "Human Rights" Commission is "reformed". I hope the Government of Ontario is dumb enough to give her the extra powers she seeks, and perhaps then she'll be man enough to haul me and Ken

Whyte into her pseudo-courtroom and actually convict us of the crime rather than merely issuing the verdict in a press release.

TODAY'S EDITION of *The Globe & Mail* is well worth picking up. This is Canada's establishment paper, and it doesn't like what it's hearing from Barbara Hall, Chief Commissar of the Ontario "Human Rights" Commission, the world leaders in labiaplasty jurisprudence.

First, star columnist Rex Murphy:

The press release wasn't limited, however, to lamenting the absence of competence and declaring the HRC wouldn't be proceeding in the matter.

It went on, seizing the educative moment, to light into Maclean's *for its 'Islamophobia' over 'a number of articles', illustrating a 'type of media coverage [that] has been identified as contributing to Islamophobia and promoting societal intolerance towards Muslim, Arab and South Asian Canadians.' More, it regretted that in Ontario, with the statute as written, it is not 'possible to challenge any institution that contributes to the dissemination of destructive, xenophobic opinions.' Meaning* Maclean's *and whatever of that ilk trails in the familiar and long-tenured magazine's presumed xenophobic and racist wake.*

I'm not a lawyer, so I merely ask the question: Is it normal when declining a case (or, in this case, a complaint) for a commission, court or tribunal to then deliver a guilty verdict? For that's what the press statement, directly, or by forceful implication, did.

And hasn't it always been in free society a human right (old-fashioned, I know) not to be judged without a hearing? But here there was no hearing. Neither Maclean's *nor Mr Steyn made a case or presented arguments. And yet the commission's release damned them in harsh and condemnatory language that was a verdict in everything but name.*

Furthermore, it did so before — mark that, before — two other tribunals, which, we presume, listen to and read this HRC's words, have themselves even begun proceedings on the same complaint. Do judges in real courts act this way? Do they telegraph verdicts to other jurisdictions? Do they make up what they are delighted to call their minds in vacuo? Do they decline cases, then pass judgment anyway, and issue stern and rebuking releases?

And Mr Murphy's column bears the headline:

Vive Le Canada Libre!

Oh, well, columnists are (or were) licensed to peddle eccentric and contrarian views. What of the sensible sorts who pen the Globe editorials? What have these solid citizens got to say? Here's their headline:

Alarmingly Pro-Active

And here's how they begin:

'Looking forward' was an explicit theme of Wednesday's press release from the Ontario Human Rights Commission (OHRC), which, without a hearing, attributed Islamophobic racism to Maclean's *magazine and the writer Mark Steyn.*

The commission is looking ahead to a pro-active new role... The broad, if not vague, criterion of the public interest will be the basis for the commissioners' own initiating of inquiries into such practices, whatever they may be.

In turn, the commission's appointees can enter any premises (except a dwelling), without a search warrant, and demand any relevant 'document or thing', and remove such things, not quite for indefinite periods, but for 'a reasonable time'. Hindering all this is forbidden...

The closing, 'looking-forward' paragraph of Wednesday's press release evokes the OHRC's 'broader role in addressing the tension and conflict that such writings [as the Maclean's *article in question] cause in the community'.*

Or to put it in a nutshell, as the editorial concludes:

Be afraid.

This was the Globe's second editorial on the subject. Yesterday the editors wrote:

> *When is a decision not a decision? The Ontario Human Rights Commission (OHRC) performed just such a deft manoeuvre on Wednesday, announcing there would be no hearing on whether* Maclean's *magazine and Mark Steyn had violated human rights. Nonetheless, the commission concluded in a press release that they were both guilty of racism...*
>
> *One of the most basic maxims of justice is* Audi alteram partem: *Listen to the other side. By pronouncing Maclean's and Mr Steyn to be racist, the commission has violated that fundamental principle.*

Well, so much for the writers and editors. But what do the readers, that great mass of moderate centrist reasonable Canadian opinion, think about all this? Under the headline "Commissioners, Not Commissars", James Marvin of Toronto writes:

> *A case could be made that, instead of berating Mark Steyn and* Maclean's, *the Ontario Human Rights Commission should have been defending them (Unproven Racism – editorial, April 11). We don't want a situation where commissioners act like commissars and hate laws become gag laws.*

So that's what a casual *Globe & Mail* reader will see on a quick scan of the paper this weekend: "*Vive le Canada libre!*"; "Alarmingly Pro-Active"; and "Commissioners, Not Commissars". I wonder if even Commissar Hall is so secure in her cocoon of cowardly bureaucratic thuggery that she doesn't realize she and the grotesque system so embodies so perfectly have fewer friends by the week.

WEIMAR CANADA

More hate, please

Maclean's, May 5th 2008

LAST WEEK'S letters page included a missive from Jennifer Lynch, QC, Chief Commissioner of the Canadian "Human Rights" Commission, defending her employees from the accusation of "improper investigative techniques" by yours truly. Steyn, she writes, "provides no substantiation for these claims", and then concludes:

> *Why is this all important? Because words are important. Steyn would have us believe that words, however hateful, should be given free rein. History has shown us that hateful words sometimes lead to hurtful actions that undermine freedom and have led to unspeakable crimes. That is why Canada and most other democracies have enacted legislation to place reasonable limits on the expression of hatred.*

Hmm. "History has shown us that hateful words sometimes lead to hurtful actions that undermine freedom and have led to unspeakable crimes." Commissar Lynch provides, as she would say, "no substantiation for these claims". But then she's a "hate speech" prosecutor and, as we know, Canada's "human rights" procedures aren't subject to tiresome requirements like evidence. So she's made an argument from authority: The great Queen's Counsel has risen from her throne in the Star Chamber and pronounced, and let that suffice. Those of us who occupy less exalted positions in the realm might wish to ponder the evidence for her assertions.

It's true that "hurtful actions that undermine freedom" and lead to "unspeakable crimes" usually have some figleaf of intellectual justification. For example, the ideology first articulated by Karl Marx has led to the deaths of millions of people around the planet on an

249

unprecedented scale. Yet oddly enough, no matter how many folks are murdered in the name of Marxism-Leninism, you're still free to propound its principles at every college in Canada.

Ah, but that's the Good Totalitarianism. What about the Bad Totalitarianism? You know, the one everybody disapproves of: Nazism. Isn't it obvious that in the case of Adolf Hitler "hateful words" led to "unspeakable crimes"? This argument is offered routinely: If only there'd been "reasonable limits on the expression of hatred" seventy years ago, the Holocaust might have been prevented.

There's just one teensy-weensy problem with it: Pre-Nazi Germany had such "reasonable limits". Indeed, the Weimar Republic was a veritable proto-Trudeaupia. As Alan Borovoy, Canada's leading civil libertarian, put it:

> *Remarkably, pre-Hitler Germany had laws very much like the Canadian anti-hate law. Moreover, those laws were enforced with some vigour. During the fifteen years before Hitler came to power, there were more than two hundred prosecutions based on anti-semitic speech. And, in the opinion of the leading Jewish organization of that era, no more than 10 per cent of the cases were mishandled by the authorities. As subsequent history so painfully testifies, this type of legislation proved ineffectual on the one occasion when there was a real argument for it.*

Inevitably, the Nazi Party exploited the restrictions on "free speech" in order to boost its appeal. In 1925, the State of Bavaria issued an order banning Adolf Hitler from making any public speeches. The Nazis responded by distributing a drawing of their leader with his mouth gagged and the caption, "Of 2,000 million people in the world, one alone is forbidden to speak in Germany."

The idea that "hate speech" led to the Holocaust is seductive because it's easy: If only we ban hateful speech, then there will be no hateful acts. But, as Professor Anuj C Desai of the University of Wisconsin Law School points out, "Biased speech has been around since history began. As a logical matter, then, it is no more helpful to say that anti-Semitic speech caused the Holocaust than to say organized government caused it, or, for that matter, to say that oxygen caused it. All were necessary ingredients, but all have been present in every historical epoch in every country in the world."

Just so. Indeed, the principal ingredient unique to the pre-Hitler era was the introduction of Jennifer Lynch-type hate-speech laws that supposedly protect vulnerable minorities from "unspeakable acts". You might as well argue that Weimar's "reasonable limits" on free speech led to the Holocaust: after all, while anti-Semitism is "the oldest hatred", it didn't turn genocidal until the "reasonable limits" proponents of the day introduced group-defamation laws to Germany. 'Tween-wars Europe was awash in prototype hate-crimes legislation. For example, the Versailles Conference required the new post-war states to sign on to the 1919 Minorities Protection Treaty, with its solemn guarantees of non-discrimination. I'm sure Canada's many Jews of Mitteleuropean origin will be happy to testify to what a splendid job that far-sighted legislation did.

The problem the Jews found themselves up against in Germany and elsewhere was not the lack of hate-speech laws but the lack of protection of the common or garden laws – against vandalism and property appropriation and suchlike. One notes, by the way, that property rights are absent from Canada's modish Charter of Rights. The reductio ad Hitlerum is the laziest form of argument, so it's no surprise to find the defenders of the "human rights" regime taking refuge in it. But it stands history on its head. Most of us have a vague understanding that Hitler used the burning of the Reichstag in February 1933 as a pretext to "seize" dictatorial powers. But, in fact, he didn't "seize" anything because he didn't need to. He merely invoked Article 48 of the Weimar Republic's constitution, allowing the state, in the interests of the greater good, to set – what's the phrase? – "reasonable limits" on freedom of the press, freedom of expression, freedom of association, freedom from unlawful search and seizure and surveillance of postal and electronic communications. The Nazis didn't invent a dictatorship out of whole cloth. They merely took advantage of the illiberal provisions of a supposedly liberal constitution.

Oh, and by the way, almost all those powers the Nazis "seized" the morning after the Reichstag fire the "human rights" commissions already have. In the name of cracking down on "hate", Canada's "human rights" apparatchiks can enter your premises without a warrant and remove any relevant "document or thing" (as the relevant Ontario legislation puts it) for as long as they want it. And without anybody burning the House of Commons or even the Senate.

As for "freedom of the press", in her now celebrated decision to dismiss the Canadian Islamic Congress complaint against Maclean's, Barbara Hall of the Ontario "Human Rights" Commission acknowledged that she did not have jurisdiction over magazines. So she ruled that, while she didn't have the power to toss us in the clink, she'd certainly like to and we certainly deserve it. Commissar Hall suggested that if my words had appeared on a sign rather than in a magazine article, she would be free to haul my hatemongerin' ass into the dock. Makes sense to me. So I've now put the offending excerpt from my book on a placard and I'll be in Toronto in the first week of May to drop it off at her office. I look forward to the prosecution. Given that we've already been found guilty, I don't think I've got much to fear from the trial.

Happily, beginning on July 1st, under Ontario's "human rights" reforms, Commissar Hall will have far greater powers to initiate prosecutions against all and sundry. Under the new proposals, "'hate incident' means any act or omission, whether criminal or not, that expresses bias, prejudice, bigotry or contempt toward a vulnerable or disadvantaged community or its members." "Act or *omission*"? Of course. The act of not acting in an insufficiently non-hateful way can itself be hateful. Whether or not the incident is a non-incident is incidental. I quote from *Concepts Of Race And Racism And Implications For OHRC Policy* as published on the OHRC website:

> *The denial of racism used by so many whites in positions of authority ranging from the supervisor in a work place to the chief*

of Police and ministers of government must be understood for what it is: an example of White hegemonic power over those considered 'other'.

Got that? Your denial of racism merely confirms your racism – because simply by being a "White hegemon" (like Barbara Hall or Jennifer Lynch) you wield racist power. The author, Frances Henry, cites the thinking of "modern neo-Marxist theorists" as if these are serious views that persons of influence in Canada's "human rights" establishment ought to be taking into account, rather than just the latest variant of an ideology that's led to the death of millions in Russia, China and everywhere else it's been put into practice. Yet, underneath the blather about "omissions" and "denials" of racism is the bleak acknowledgment that, alas, Canadians just aren't hateful enough to justify the cosy sinecure of taxpayer-funded hate police. "I would say that for a province as large and as diverse as Ontario, to have 2,500 formal complaints a year, that that's a very low level," Commissar Hall said. C'mon, you Ontario deadbeats, can't you hate a little more? Or complain a little more? To modify Brecht, we need to elect a new people, if only to file more "human rights" complaints.

Oh, and again, isn't that kind of a Nazi thing to do? Exaggerate the threat in order to justify government powers to deal with it?

Well, look, the defenders of the "human rights" racket started this whole free-speech-leads-to-the-Holocaust line. I'm not saying that Canada's thought-crime enforcers are planning to murder millions of people, only that (as Jennifer Lynch might put it) history has shown us that extraordinary government powers in the name of "reasonable limits" often lead to hurtful actions that undermine freedom and have led to unspeakable crimes. Whether or not I'm the new Fuhrer and *Maclean's* is *Mein Kampf*, Commissars Lynch and Hall are either intentionally inverting the historical record or, to be charitable, simply ignorant. But, if it's the latter, why should they have extraordinary powers to regulate public discourse?

I don't have as low an opinion of Canadians as Barbara Hall and Jennifer Lynch do. I don't believe your liberty is the conditional discretionary gift of hack bureaucrats advised by Marxist theorists. You defeat bad ideas – whether Nazism, Marxism, jihadism, Steynism or Trudeaupian pseudo-"human rights" mumbo-jumbo – in the bracing air and light of day, in vigorous open debate, not in the fetid corridors of power policed by ahistorical nitwits.

It's not a left/right thing. It's not a gay/straight thing. It's not a Jew/Muslim thing. It's not a hateful Steyn/nice fluffy caring compassionate Canadian thing.

It's a free/unfree thing.

STARTING THE DEBATE

Islamophobe meets Sock Puppets

I N MAY 2008 *the paperback edition of* America Alone *was launched in Canada, and my publicist booked me for a week of interviews in Toronto. As a routine courtesy to SteynOnline readers, we always link to the shows' websites and, in the course of so doing the day before an appearance on TVOntario, discovered that the broadcast in question had, unbeknown to us, scheduled an interview with the Sock Puppets for immediately after my own appearance. The lads at "The Agenda" had alerted the Socks to my visit, but had neglected to inform me of theirs.*

For five months the Socks – Khurrum Awan, Naseem Mithoowani and Muneeza Sheikh – had been pretending to be the plaintiffs in these "human rights" suits, fronting for Dr Mohamed Elmasry, the real complainant, but, alas, a figure too controversial to have any credibility as the poster boy for a hate-free Canada. So instead he sent out the Socks to pose as plaintiffs - rather as if I had responded to media requests for interviews with Canada's Number One hatemonger by sending in some spindly but telegenic Dickensian urchin boy as my body double. The media were, naturally, happy to string along with the fraud, and gave space to the Socks week after week to drone that all they wanted to do with me and Maclean's was "start a debate".

So, upon belatedly discovering that Elmo's Socks were going to be on the show, I thought this would be a perfect opportunity to have that debate they were so anxious to start. Here's how things unfolded:

Steynposts, May 5th 2008

A S YOU CAN see from the "forthcoming attractions" précis at their website, the current plan for tomorrow night's broadcast of

"The Agenda" is to interview me and then have the Sock Puppet Three come on to do their usual schlocko summer-stock routine of pretending to be "the complainants". It's like "Little Human Rights Commission On The Prairie": terrible acting, lavishly subsidized, and running forever.

Anyway, it seemed a bit of a bore to me, so we've put in a request to let me go *mano a mano* with the Sock Puppets. Don't care how many there are: One, two, or all three… I'd much rather go *mano a mano* with the real complainant, Mohamed Elmasry, but his *mano* is stuck up the Sock Puppets so I guess it's unavailable.

We'll let you know whether Steve Paikin's gonna go for it.

Steynposts, May 6th 2008

AFTER BLEATING for five months about how all they want to do is "start a debate", the Sock Puppet Three finally got the chance to have one - on TVO's "Agenda" with Steve Paikin, tonight at 8pm. Unfortunately, the Sock nellies are refusing, which is an interesting insight into the sincerity of their we-only-want-to-start-a-debate mantra. Here's the latest email from TVO's producer to my publicist:

After our agreement last evening for Mark to join the debate after the 1x1, we have informed the three panellists about our change of plans. We have just received a negative response from them.

Their main reason is that this is not what they have initially agreed to and that they would not have the time to prepare for such a debate. The other reason they offered is that their complaint is with Maclean's *magazine and not Mark Steyn personally.*

Given this picture, I think we need to go back to our original plan of keeping the combatants apart.

Wodek

To which Kathleen replied:

Hi Wodek-

> *If these students refuse to debate despite the fact that they have been publically trashing Mark for four months now (including at their press conference two weeks ago when Ms Sheikh called him 'Islamophobic',) then it is only fair that these interviews be done in the same order as a Canadian court of law. The students can make their accusations first and Mark, the accused, gets to defend himself only after those accusations.*
>
> *If they say they are not accusing Mark of anything then why have you juxtaposed them on the same show?*

Paikin's crowd never told us about the Sock Puppets and weren't planning to, but evidently they told the Socks about me, which is in itself interesting. If I were of a suspicious bent, I might be asking, as Mark Bourrie does, "Is Steyn being set up?" Instead, when I heard about it, I immediately said, great, let's have a debate. No point me being in the same studio as the Sock Puppets and being kept in a hermetically sealed compartment.

Yet even with a three-to-one advantage the Socks pussied out.

This is Islam as represented by the likes of the Canadian Islamic Congress. They don't want any kind of honest open debate, because they can't handle it. That's why they prefer to use government agencies to shut down debate on the specious grounds of invented crimes like "Islamophobia". And apparently TV producers, having been complicit in the fraud that the Sock Puppets are "the complainants", are willing to protect the sensitive little souls from the consequences of their charade.

Ah, well. We're still negotiating. I think the latest pitch is for me to show up just to trash the set. God Almighty, given the amount of money Canadian taxpayers are giving to the Canadian Islamic Congress to pursue this prosecution, you'd think they could find one Sock Puppet who'd be up to 15 minutes of honest debate. Maybe next time they should be like "Little Mosque On The Prairie" and get the Muslim roles played by non-Muslims.

See you on TV in a couple of hours…

'We just wanted a chance for open debate, the right to respond.'

'We just wanted a chance for debate, but not directly or have to respond to others.'

'We just wanted a chance to tell our side of the story without any chance of debate.'

'We just want everyone to think just like us.'

'Everyone needs to think like us ...or else.'

Is it a natural progression?

A COMMENTER AT JAY CURRIE'S WEBSITE

If you didn't watch it tonight you missed out on the most exciting current events programming I've ever watched. Mark Steyn confronted the three Muslim students who initiated a human rights complaint against Maclean's *magazine, chiefly because of one of his articles published therein. Even though they had gone on record saying that all they want is to start a debate, they refused to debate him on the show. Instead Steyn was to be interviewed and then they were to be interviewed separately. In the midst of his interview he repeatedly offered to have the debate, right then and there, on live TV.*

ED SKELTON, KITCHENER, ONTARIO

Thinking like a moderator, Paikin commented that there weren't enough chairs which led to Steyn's uproarious retort that 'this isn't a chair issue...'

As Steyn himself was the first to admit, it wasn't exactly 'Must-See TV' but it was enough to clearly illustrate the characters on both sides of the case. In this corner, wearing the sanctimonious and confused trunks, are three kids with no clue what they're saying. And in this corner, wearing the belligerent and borderline pompous trunks, is the titan with an axe to grind. The kids never had a chance...

THE CANADIAN REPUBLIC

258

~

However incoherent the shouting was, the mere fact of this event is really a victory for our side, the freedom side; the fact that a 'debate' of this kind can still be staged in Canada, that after all the political positioning we can still give way to the arena of free speech to see what truth will come out in uncontrollable manner, is welcome. There are no doubt people in the sock puppet camp who would like to have all 'debates' reduced to some sort of ritualistic formula where everyone says only what is proper to say, as if one were engaged, say, in a friendly discussion on proper relations between Muslims and Dhimmis in the offices of the Egyptian state police.

THE COVENANT ZONE

~

Two of the students were women. One was born in Canada and one came here as a baby from India. The male had been born in Pakistan and had lived in Britain where he grew up before he emigrated to Canada. All of them were in western dress and had they not said they were Muslims there would be nothing about their appearance that would have tipped you off...

What impressed me was their lack of preparation (they came with some idea of a script that they would simply put out without challenge). This is not a good beginning for young lawyers... The second thing was, despite the fact that they have come of age and were educated in Canada, specifically in the legal tradition of Canada, they still don't understand the concept of free speech... They frequently complained that all Muslims in Canada were tarred with this extremist voice that rises in various parts of the Muslim community that Steyn featured in his book. But at no time did they take the opportunity to point to specific things and say as Canadian Muslims those things were wrong and those people who say them are wrong and are wrong to say them. In short, like nearly all other Muslims, they find themselves incapable of criticizing or taking issue with religious authorities... I am continually left with the impression that the only thing Muslims do not want discussed in any public forum is Islam.

DEAD RECKONING

I'm not the greatest fan of Steyn - I think for the topic he is covering, you're better off reading Bruce Bawer's book - but I think, regardless, that he is in the right on this matter... I found the students to be, well, whiny and childish. Now, they are young, so some of that is to be expected. But they kept reminding my close-personal-friend Steve Paikin that they wanted the exact same amount of time *as Steyn, and that they wanted Paikin to make sure Steyn wouldn't be* mean *to them... For the record, Steyn was polite and humorous. The students were polite and humourless.*

What really got me, was at the end of the show, Paikin said, 'Mark, I'll give you the last word', and all three students started shrieking, clearly seeing in that decision another slight and another excuse to wallow in victimhood. Unbelievable. Paikin - by his standards - showed a bit of temper, and said, 'Give me a break, will you?' or something along those lines...

Finally, watching the two women last night, reminded me somewhat of my experience at the PLO offices in Ramallah, in July of 2005, shortly before the Israeli disengagement from Gaza. The PLO officials we (a group of Canadian journalists) met with trotted out a very western looking woman - beautiful, as were the two on TVO last night - to join in on the meeting. By the end of the meeting, it became clear that the only thing western about her was her appearance. I don't think I can say entirely the same thing about the women last night, but there was something similar about the situation. Their looks were western, but their words didn't match up.

NATIONAL POST COLUMNIST RONDI ADAMSON

Wow, was that the longest hour in TVO history or what? You could tell Steyn was ready to blow a fuse during the first three seconds... Lots and lots of very 'unCanadian' yelling, which frankly I enjoyed enormously... I don't see how you can blame Steyn since this was his first face-to-face encounter with the twerps who are costing him six figures in legal fees.

My e-mail ranges from 'My TV set needs an exorcism and I need a Valium' to 'Best 60 minutes of Canadian television EVER!'

Unintentionally funniest line of the night:

Mohammed Elmasry declined our invitation to appear on tonight's program...

While Angry Chick on the Left takes home the We Don't Get The Whole 'Irony' Thing ribbon for:

What Mark Steyn really wants is to become a martyr!

Now I have to go clean the spittle off my TV screen.
KATHY SHAIDLE, CO-AUTHOR OF THE TYRANNY OF NICE

Steynposts, May 6th 2008

WELL, WE DID the TVO show and I doubt it was Must-See TV, even by the standards of Canadian public broadcasting. I succeeded in bouncing the Sock Puppets into agreeing to a face-to-face discussion, though it wasn't my finest hour or theirs. I believe the final words of the show were me saying, "Do you wanna go to dinner?", and Khurrum Awan yelling back, "No."

We didn't go for dinner, but we did have a relatively pleasant conversation after the broadcast that I thought was much more productive than the show. Khurrum was a bit chippy but the two ladies, Muneeza Sheikh and Naseem Mithoowani, are rather cute, even when they're damning me as a racist and hater. (Years ago, the BBC used to keep putting me up against humourless Marxist feminists only to find that on air I'd go all sweet on them and just make goo-goo eyes.) One confessed to finding me "mildly funny", which I took as a tremendous compliment until she remarked that she found "Little Mosque On The Prairie" funnier. Evidently by "mildly funny", she sets the bar down at world-champion limbo level. Heigh-ho. Still, even with dear old Khurrum, if I'd met him in an airport lounge on the other side of the world and we were stuck waiting for a flight, I think the conversation would go okayish. The post-show chit-chat was a useful reminder that everybody's media image is a reductio.

Nevertheless, we are stuck in our respective roles. I believe these Canadian Islamic Congress lawsuits - and, yes, I can hear the Socks yelling, "That's a lie! They're not 'suits', they're 'complaints'," but that's a distinction without a difference if you're paying lawyers' bills and you regard, as I do, the "human rights" commissions as a parallel legal system that tramples over all the traditional safeguards of Common Law, not least the presumption of innocence. Where was I? Oh, yeah. I believe these lawsuits are deeply damaging to freedom of expression. If they win (*when* they win) and the verdicts withstand Supreme Court scrutiny, Canada will no longer be a free country. It will be a country whose citizens are on a leash whose length is determined by the hack bureaucrats of state agencies.

And that leash will shrink, remorselessly. I was struck by something Naseem said to me on the sidewalk. I'd mentioned that I'd heard her on NPR saying that it was improper for me to attack "multiculturalism" because multiculturalism was officially embedded in Canada's constitution. And I said: So what? A free society shouldn't have an official ideology, but, if it has, I certainly reserve the right to object to it. If I'd lived in Italy 70 years ago, I would have objected to their official ideology (Fascism), and I object to Canada's, notwithstanding its touchy-feelier name. And she looked at me as if I was bonkers. I feel rather bewildered at meeting graduates of an elite institution in one of the oldest settled democracies on the planet who seem to think just because Pierre Trudeau cooked it up it's chiselled in granite. You can only marvel at what an amazing job he did of wiping a society's collective memory.

What was the most depressing part of the post-game show for me was realizing that for my accusers the assumption is that every defect in society can be corrected by government intervention. They said one reason they went to the "human rights" thought police is because they're worried Rogers might buy, for example, *The Toronto Star* and install Ken Whyte, yours truly and the rest of the Islamophobes. Well, maybe. But look: right now, I'm "excluded" from *The Toronto Star* and so's every other conservative. We're "excluded" from the CBC, which is paid for by the tax dollars of Canadian conservatives. But so what? Society is not perfectible, and for a government tribunal to order the *Star* to run one Steyn column for every Haroon Siddiqui column it runs would only make things worse.

There's some talk on TVO's part of getting us together for a more civilized discussion, so we'll see how that works out. My only real objection was when Naseem said "Mark Steyn wants to be a martyr." Actually, that's not true. I'd love to do as that alleged Islamic terrorist did, attempting to flounce out of his trial in Toronto the other day and shouting, "I'm outta here!" I'd like nothing more than never to appear on a single TV or radio show in the deranged Dominion ever again. But the "remedy" the Socks seek for *Maclean's* "Islamophobia" is incompatible with a free society. This is a point of principle. Here I stand. I can do no other. So on we go.

A few days after my appearance on "The Agenda", the Attorney-General of Canada broke his silence. And, to be honest, I wish he'd stayed in the Witness Protection Program. Instead, in a memorandum defending the constitutionality of state censorship, he unleashed 50 pages of sentimental and ahistorical twaddle:

> The triumphs of Fascism in Italy and National Socialism in Germany through audaciously false propaganda have shown us how fragile tolerant, liberal societies can be.

No Canadian who had a proper respect for the history of his country could write that sentence. Which is why it alone is a good example of why we need free speech. Nobody who gave it ten minutes' study would think that the Dominion of Canada, one of the oldest, peacefully evolved, constitutional democracies on the planet, is as "fragile" as the Weimar Republic or the Kingdom of Italy. So the most obvious "audaciously false propaganda" on display there is from the audaciously false propagandists on the Justice Department payroll. (As to the general accuracy of the thesis, see the preceding chapter on the proto-Trudeaupian "hate" laws of pre-Hitler Germany.) And how does the government's "audaciously false propaganda" strikes the fellows suing Ezra Levant and Maclean's? *If you were Elmo and his Sock Puppets, wouldn't you read the Justice Department's nonsense and feel the wind at your back? The Attorney-General's memorandum is a grim read, wallowing in Orwellian bilge such as this:*

> History teems with examples of times when lies, distortions and propaganda empowered groups like the Nazis to repress speech.

In other words, we need to "repress speech" because otherwise someone worse will come along and "repress speech". This horrible report is the product of a supposedly "Conservative" government but reads like the most cobwebbed clichés of any campus Marxist. Deborah Gyapong writes:

> I feel like a coup d'état has taken place and I have awakened to the aftermath.
>
> And this egregious affront to civil rights and to the freedom to speak the truth in Canada is being perpetuated now by the Conservative government.
>
> Woe is us. I have this awful, awful feeling that we're too late. The war has been won by the other side and there are just mopping up operations left...

I had a similar feeling on the TV Ontario show. At one point I looked across at the Sock Puppet Three and thought: It's not about who wins the argument. They're the future of this country, and that's that.

THE MULTICULTURAL PRESS
It's all relativist

IN TOM STOPPARD'S play *Night And Day*, the African dictator Mageeba explains his views on freedom of the press: "Do you know what I mean by a relatively free press, Mr Wagner?"

"Not exactly, sir, no," says the Fleet Street hack.

"I mean," says Mageeba, "a free press which is edited by one of my relatives."

Here in the citadels of western civilization, we have a slightly different problem: our relatively free press is a press edited by relativists.

Item: In 2007, six imams returning from a big conference of imams were removed from a plane at Minneapolis Airport after other passengers grew concerned about loud cries of "Allahu Akbar!", and the imams reseating themselves in the same configuration as the 9/11 hijackers and demanding seatbelt extenders, even though none was of sufficient girth to need them. Aside from Fox, America's national media showed little interest in the story. But nor, oddly, did the local media. After complaints, the managing editor of *The Minneapolis Star Tribune*, Anders Gyllenhaal, replied to at least one reader:

> *I don't think the paper dropped this story, but I do think it had run its course... I think this is one of those stories that runs for a couple of days, then subsides.*

Well, the reason he thinks this is one of those stories that runs for a couple of days is because he chose to run it only for a couple of days. Had it been something more consequential - like, say, fictitious stories about guards at Gitmo desecrating the Koran - he would have run it into the ground.

Why would a Minneapolis editor with a hot local story decline to cover it? Because the implications of that story - that those imams were deliberately probing the weaknesses of an airline system too craven to profile - is at odds with the orthodoxies of a free press edited by relativists.

When the Canadian Islamic Congress filed their multiple "human rights" complaints because a privately owned magazine had declined to let them hijack its content, cover and artwork, it quickly became clear that the broad mass of Canadian media were generally indifferent to the outrage. Had the CIC prevailed in their power grab, it would have reduced mainstream Canadian news publications to a maple-flavored variant of *Pravda*. However, as some leftie website put it, "Defending freedom of speech for jerks means defending jerks." Well, in a very narrow sense. But, in a far larger one, not defending the jerks means not defending freedom of speech for yourself.

Consider a cringe-making TV appearance by my old boss at *The Chicago Sun-Times*, John Cruickshank. Newly ensconced as the big cheese at CBC News, John was appearing on his own network to explain the particular sensitivity of Canada's national broadcaster on a certain topical subject. He posited a sophisticated equivalence between Muslim "extremists" and "extremists" who are "intolerant of any restrictions on speech rights". "To equate violent terrorists with free speech activists," pointed out Ezra Levant, "is grotesque." But, as the head of CBC News sees it, we're both just as "extreme" – on the one hand, people who threaten to (and actually do) kill you; and, on the other, people who point out there are fellows who want to kill you. A pox on both their extremist houses.

An alarming proportion of the Dominion's "media workers" seemed relatively relaxed about playing the role of eunuchs to the Trudeaupian sultans, if the alternative involved re-examining their complacent assumptions. Even when the Canadian Association of Journalists roused itself to apply for intervenor status at the trial in Vancouver, not every member was happy about the move. An esteemed – okay, self-esteemed - Ottawa journalist wrote back to the executive committee:

Hello all:

I would like to find out more from the CAJ executive about what we feel is at issue here, and what we plan to say before the tribunal. I am familiar with some of Steyn's work in the past and have written about it. It was not the sort of material that I was able to defend on a professional basis. At the time I believe I referred to it as 'obscene'.

It is one thing to say 'I don't agree with what you are saying, but I will fight to defend your right to say it' and quite another to say we will tolerate as professional journalists the most unprofessional sort of journalism just because someone wrote it.

Oh, my. I only wish my work were more "obscene" and preferably state funded: you know, crucifixes floating in my urine, or pictures of naked kids – I'd have a lot more defenders.

It's regrettable how few expensively educated members of the west's elites understand principle, but it's even sadder how few can even grasp basic self-interest. Were the Canadian Islamic Congress to get both the statutory penalty (the cease-and-desist order) and the remedy they applied for (a court-ordered right of reply), that would be a landmark legal precedent in advancing state regulation of the editorial content of Canada's mainstream magazines and newspapers. *That's* what you're defending, Obscenity Boy. I'll be long gone, a fading memory in the dimmest recesses of a few lonely right-wing madmen. But the BCHRT and the OHRC and the NSHRC and the CHRC and all the rest have made it plain that what you do is subject to their whims and the ambition of whatever fashionable lobby groups take their fancy. You'll be the poodle on their leash, not me.

A while back, I had lunch with Ken Whyte, my publisher at *Maclean's*, and mentioned en passant that one consequence of a year's worth of thought-police investigations was that it was no longer possible to avoid the painful truth that, for a profession that congratulates itself incessantly on its courage, bravery, fearlessness, etc (far more than, say, firefighters do) and hands out awards all year long for "speaking truth to power", most journalists are total pussies happy to suck up to state power as long as it's in PC clothing. A "journalism professor" boldly campaigning for the right of government bureaucrats to censor writers, would seem to be an almost parodic example of the phenomenon. Yet that was the role in which John Miller, a J-school ethics bore, chose to cast himself. Professor Miller attempted to intervene in the British Columbia trial on the side of the censors. Even after he was denied standing, he persisted in ever more obtuse attacks on me. Of course, even in Canada few journalists are willing to come out in favor of direct censorship, so instead they choose to defend the thought police as a kind of copy-editor of last resort: My writing, declared Professor Miller, was riddled with errors and thus unworthy of the protections accorded to "professional" journalism. I stand by the accuracy of my columns - although, given that truth is no defense at the "human rights" commissions, that's neither here nor there. But when the professor attempted to point out an actual example of factual inaccuracy he ran into a wee spot of bother. He ended up pinning an awful lot of his prestige on a nuttily obsessive determination to fact-check a joke. I thought Professor Miller's charges were so loopy they made a useful "case study", which begins on the page opposite. It illustrates the western media's commitment to the PC pieties: If it's a choice between illusions and the facts, they'll stick with the illusions, even as they're consumed by them.

THE SHAGGED SHEEP
Precepts of ejaculation

SteynOnline, November 30th 2008

OF ALL THE flagrantly Islamophobic Steyn material Elmo's Sock Puppets introduced in evidence, the allegation that most tickled my critics' fancy was this one, from page ten of the Canadian Islamic Congress dossier:

The representation that a large number of Muslims are 'sheep-shaggers'.

Oh, my. Let's examine this accusation in some detail. What follows is long, but it does have underage sex and bestiality in it. So enjoy!

The so-called "representation" arose from the following passage in my review of Oriana Fallaci's final book, *The Force Of Reason*:

Signora Fallaci then moves on to the livelier examples of contemporary Islam - for example, Ayatollah Khomeini's 'Blue Book' and its helpful advice on romantic matters: 'If a man marries a minor who has reached the age of nine and if during the defloration he immediately breaks the hymen, he cannot enjoy her any longer.' I'll say. I know it always ruins my evening. Also: 'A man who has had sexual relations with an animal, such as a sheep, may not eat its meat. He would commit sin.' Indeed. A quiet cigarette afterwards as you listen to your favourite Johnny Mathis LP and then a promise to call her next week and swing by the pasture is by far the best way. It may also be a sin to roast your nine-year-old wife, but the Ayatollah's not clear on that.

A cheap joke en passant. Indeed, insofar as I dwelt on the ovine fornication, it was to suggest to La Fallaci that, even for us flagrant Islamophobes, it was not perhaps the most useful avenue of attack:

I enjoy the don't-eat-your-sexual-partner stuff as much as the next infidel, but the challenge presented by Islam is not that the cities of the Western world will be filling up with sheep-shaggers. If I had to choose, I'd rather Mohammed Atta was downriver in Egypt hitting on the livestock than flying through the windows of Manhattan skyscrapers. But he's not.

And that's it. That's all I said. And no one would remember had not the Socks included the sheep-shagging line in their submission to the Canadian "Human Rights" Commission. Whereupon Dr John Miller …actually, I'm not sure he is a doctor: He calls himself "The Journalism Doctor", but the title seems to be entirely self-conferred. Anyway, at this point, Doc Miller, Prof Miller, Herr Baron von Miller or whatever he is got interested in the case and asked the British Columbia "Human Rights" Tribunal if he could intervene. Silly ol' me assumed that he wished to intervene to argue the cause of free speech. But no: he wanted to intervene to argue that I was not a "responsible journalist", and so it was entirely appropriate for the state to censor me. As Rory Leishman noted in the quaintly titled *London Free Press*, since this thought-police racket got going, "Most journalists have either condoned censorship or cowered in silence." Canadians who still value liberty should know that, if they rely on anemic PC flunkeys like Professor Miller, they'll lose their country. At any rate, the BCHRT declined to let him testify and gave him the bum's rush, so an aggrieved Prof Miller surfaced in the fall of 2008 and kept returning to the subject of the sheep-shaggers line. His complaint in those frantic weeks was in an apparently endless process of evolution. But let's go through the story so far:

1) First, insofar as I understand his initial argument, he advanced the curious line that the ruling from the Ayatollah was not widely cited, and therefore it was improper of me to use it. Apparently, one should only use familiar quotations in "responsible journalism".

After it was pointed out that in fact Khomeini's views on the post-bestiality buffet, child sex and other arcane points of Islamic law are known to many (especially those on the receiving end), a couple of weeks later he revised his line of attack:

> 2) Now his argument was that I'd concocted it out of whole cloth. The J-Doc declared boldly that Steyn "gave no citation for the quote, and I suspect it was made up."

In fact, as anyone who reads the passage above can see, I attributed it to Oriana Fallaci's book. The disinterested observer might conclude that Professor Ethics-Bore had never so much as glanced at the offending article but had simply taken the Sock Puppets' word for it. So the E-Bore was obliged to revise his argument yet again - and decided to accuse me of what he appeared to have done himself:

> 3) Now my sin was that I "clearly accepted someone else's word for it". Evidently, it wasn't all that "clear" when he was accusing me of making it up, but a drowning ethics prof can be forgiven for clutching at straw men.

At any rate, that makes three different complaints. As I commented at the time:

> *That's the great thing about the self-appointed 'Journalism Doctor': When he diagnoses you, he provides his own second opinion.*

A couple of weeks later, my crime was revised yet again. I received an e-mail from M J Murphy of Toronto, who blogs as "Big City Lib", saying only this:

> *I think you owe Dr Miller an apology.*

There followed a link to an Internet post by Mr Murphy headlined "Steyn Gets Punked By 28-Year Old Literary Hoax":

> Remember the kerfuffle between Mark Steyn and journalism professor Dr John Miller from a few weeks back? Dr Miller

accused Steyn of taking material for *America Alone* from illegitimate sources like the infamous *Little Green Book: Sayings Of The Ayatollah Khomeini*.

Actually, I don't think even Dr Miller has accused me of any such thing, although I admit, given his shifting accusations, that I'm no longer quite sure what he's accusing me of. Just to recap, said "kerfuffle" arose not from my book but from my review of La Fallaci's book in *Maclean's*. It's nothing to do with *America Alone*. There is no mention of sheep shagging in *America Alone*. There is no mention of any *Little Green Book* in *America Alone*. There is, indeed, no mention of Ayatollah Khomeini in *America Alone*. Prof Miller and Mr Murphy and their enthusiastic chorus boys at the website Law Is Cool are welcome to check for themselves, via the Amazon.com "Search Inside The Book" service.

But, leaving that aside and forgiving M J Murphy for confusing *America Alone* with a book review in *Maclean's*, if you return to the passage up above, you'll see that neither Oriana nor I refer to any *Little Green Book*. We cite a "Blue Book" - or "*Libro Azzurro*", in La Fallaci's original Italian. That's the color we're nailing to our mast. We're singing the blues, and it's you fellers who are smelling the green. Indeed, the guy who brought up the *Little Green Book* is Prof Miller in one of his attacks on me. I never mentioned any green book. Like I said, I'd rather be blue. So, if M J Murphy and the excitable schoolgirls at Law R Cool have proved *The Little Green Book* is a "literary hoax", they should take it up with Professor Miller.

Incidentally, I wouldn't describe *The Little Green Book* as a "hoax". It would be truer to say that it is a somewhat lurid and condensed version of the Ayatollah Khomeini's work. Nevertheless, if you read M J Murphy's post, you'll find that Marvin Zonis of the University of Chicago declined to provide an introduction for it. Professor Zonis is evidently regarded by M J Murphy as a greater authority in these matters than I am, so please keep his name in mind.

However, as it happens, I didn't take "someone else's word" for anything, whether it was the word of Oriana Fallaci or the compiler of

The Little Green Book. When it comes to the Ayatollah Khomeini's views on sheep shagging, my guide for many years has been a book called *Resaleh Towzih al-Masael.* The author is a chap called …Ayatollah Khomeini.

Let's go back to the original offending quotation from my *Maclean's* book review:

> *Signora Fallaci then moves on to the livelier examples of contemporary Islam - for example, Ayatollah Khomeini's "Blue Book" and its helpful advice on romantic matters.*

Prof Miller had great sport with this. Why, that birdbrain Steyn! He can't even get the color of the hoax book correct: It's not a "Blue Book", it's a "Green Book". Everyone knows that. Boy, that Steyn, he don't get nuttin' right. As the Credentialed Fact-Checker gleefully mocked:

> *There is no Blue Book, it's The Little Green Book. And it wasn't written by the Ayatollah at all, as you say, but by a source who was apparently at least three times, and three languages, removed.*

"There is no Blue Book": Thus saith the J-School Professor, and he surely wouldn't make such a baldly definitive statement if he hadn't fact-checked himself with the rigor Signora Fallaci and I are so deplorably lacking in.

Okay, I'm going to try to explain things very slowly for Doc Miller and M J Murphy, and with pictures, too. For personal reasons, which I'll return to in a moment, I happen to know that 30 years ago many Iranians did, indeed, refer to the Ayatollah's "Blue Book". Visiting Iran in the wake of the revolution, Oriana Fallaci would certainly have heard the *Towzih al-Masael* referred to both by Iranians and westerners as what she would call the *"Libro Azzurro"*. Are you wondering why? Well, here's a clue:

Hmm. Here's another clue:

Whoops, I see these are black-and-white pages. Okay, flip over to the inside flap of our back cover, which is in luxurious full color, and take a look. Do they appear to have a blue hue? How can that be? We all know: "There is no Blue Book." The Lord High Checker of Facts has pronounced. As it happens, *Resaleh Towzih al-Masael* has been published in Iran in several editions. But the most popular was the paperback edition published by Nashr I Sharia't of Teheran. It sold for 120 rials. It had some 350 pages, approx 5x7 inches, with a blue cover, featuring a picture of its ever more famous author. A souvenir hardback edition marketed as the perfect New Year gift was subsequently published by Rashidi with a plain blue cover. Since the old boy's death, the Khomeini *Resaleh* has got a bit like the Johnny Mathis Christmas album, re-released every year in a different color. But, as you can see on

274

the jacket flap of this very tome, many versions of the "Blue Book" are still out there.

In the relevant passage in her book, Oriana recalls first seeing excerpts from the "Blue Book" in 1979. That's what it was back then: A blue book. The blue book in revolutionary Iran. It certainly wasn't a "little green book" as no such thing was published till 1980. So when she and I refer to the Ayatollah's "Blue Book" we're referring to that Nashr I Sharia't edition of the *Resaleh*. It was translated into English, unabridged, by J Borujerdi and published in 1984 by Westview in London and Boulder, Colorado under the title *A Clarification Of Questions*.

I was given it a couple of decades ago by the Iranian gal I was then dating. She had a copy of the pocket paperback with the Ayatollah on the cover, and once, when she read out a bit to me, I expressed skepticism that it could really be that wacky. So a few weeks later she presented me with the English edition. As she explained, these were not just some personal musings from the Ayatollah but a kind of moral compass for the Islamic state. So I didn't need to "accept someone else's word for it" on having sex with nine-year-old girls, because, like anyone else who's taken even a cursory interest in the subject, I've known for a long time that, in the Islamic Republic of Iran, girls could be legally married at the age of nine. Article 1041 of the Civil Code states:

> *Marriage before puberty by the permission of the Guardian and on condition of taking into interest the ward's interest is proper.*

"Puberty" is defined as "nine full lunar years". In practice, girls as young as seven can be married on the say-so of a doctor. The justification for all this is in the highly elaborate rules of Islamic life. They may sound unlikely to M J Murphy or Prof Miller but the Ayatollah's "clarification of questions" doesn't strike most devout Iranian Shi'ites that way. Mr Borujerdi, the English translator, was an Iranian émigré living in Cleveland, and he gave an interview about the book to David Remnick (now the editor of *The New Yorker*) in *The*

Washington Post in 1985. M J Murphy and Prof Miller and the Law R Cool nellies are welcome to go to their local reference library and check it out. It's the Aug 21 issue, page B1:

> *"I did the translation because it gives a very close understanding of the Shiite view of the world," he said. "The Bantam Press published a very slight version five years ago called* The Little Green Book - *just six per cent of the original - but that was really a joke book, to poke fun at Khomeini and debunk Islam at the beginning of the hostage crisis. In Iran, this book is mandatory for every literate person, a kind of guide to living."*

So this is the real deal, not the sensationalist précis but a serious, scholarly "unabridged translation" designed to provide "a unique picture of the belief structure of Shi'ism". Mr Borujerdi had no difficulty finding eminent academics to provide an introduction – namely, Professors Mehdi Abedi and Michael Fischer of Rice University in Houston. But he also consulted on the translation and interpretation with many other scholars, among them Professor Wilfred Madelung of the Oriental Institute at Oxford University, Professor Wheeler Thackston of Harvard's Near Eastern Languages department, Professor William Darrow of Williams College, Professor Vincent McHale of Case Western, Professor Merlin Swartz of Boston University ...oh, and Professor Marvin Zonis of the University of Chicago. That would be the same Prof Zonis who was unhappy with *The Little Green Book*, and thus made M J Murphy unhappy, too. But Prof Zonis is cool with *A Clarification Of Questions*, so presumably M J Murphy will also be satisfied?

Resaleh Towzih al-Masael/A Clarification Of Questions consists of almost 3,000 "problems" for which Ayatollah Khomeini provides answers, plus a few follow-ups he dealt with in subsequent editions. Here is a page from Mr Borujerdi's translation:

> *#2631. It is loathsome to eat the meat of horse and mule and donkey and if somebody makes coitus with them, that is an*

intercourse, they become unlawful and they must be taken out of the city and sold elsewhere.

#2632. If they have intercourse with a cow and sheep and camel their urine and dung becomes unclean and drinking their milk will also be unlawful and they must be killed and burned without delay, and the person who had intercourse with them must pay money to the owner. Further, if he had intercourse with any beast its milk becomes unlawful.

I first read this book all those years ago with my Persian gal, and I take it off the shelf every once in a while because, like Oriana, I enjoy a good laugh: If you bonk your mule, you've gotta take him out the city and sell him. If you shag your neighbor's sheep, you've gotta write him a check. That's not me, that's not Oriana, that's not some compiler of some discredited anthology, that's the Ayatollah Khomeini. You can go to imam-khomeini.com and read it in the great man's original Farsi.

Now, it's true that La Fallaci's wording differs a little from Mr Borujerdi's. But so what? The King James Bible is different from the New International Version, or the *Reader's Digest* version. And the *Towzi* has been published in many different versions by the Ayatollah himself. For his translation, Mr Borujerdi looked at six different Farsi editions, some with supplemental questions, others with no answers to some of the original questions. In this instance, Oriana was translating into what she called "Fallaci's English" from an Italian version of the Ayatollah's Farsi that was excerpted in an Italian magazine under the headline "*I Dieci Khomeindamenti*", or "The Ten Khomeindments", which is a pretty funny title.

So, just to clarify, neither of us got "punked" by *The Little Green Book*, a book neither of us so much as mentioned. We both cited Khomeini's "Blue Book", because that's where we got it from. And Oriana's cited source for her Italian translation, "The Ten Khomeindments", was published in 1979, a year before Bantam released *The Little Green Book*, and at a time when the strictures of the

"Khomeindments" were among the research she took to Iran for her famous interview with the Ayatollah.

So I wonder what it is Professor Ethics-Bore thinks I should have "checked". That the Ayatollah disapproves of post-coitally chowing down on your barnyard sex partner? Check! Indeed, check mate. On the other hand, the E-Bore didn't check anything - not my original book review, not Oriana's original quote. He pronounced magisterially on the non-existence of any such "Blue Book" without checking a thing.

But, beyond all that J-school snoozeroonie stuff, what I find even more perplexing is why Prof Miller, M J Murphy and the nellies at Law Am Cool are so weirdly obsessed with insisting that somehow the Ayatollah's rulings about eating shagged sheep and having sex with nine-year olds must be some malicious rumor got up by Oriana and me and a couple of other neocon ignoramuses. No one who knows anything about Khomeini or Shia jurisprudence would be in the least bit surprised, so why would a prissy PC drone like Prof Miller be so cavalier as to expose himself as entirely ignorant of the subject he's loftily pontificating on? Not for the first time you realize that, for the lazy white liberal, driving around with a "CELEBRATE DIVERSITY" sticker absolves one from having to take the slightest interest in other cultures.

So, just to bring the deplorably unicultural Prof Miller up to speed, the easiest way to get a flavor of the Ayatollah's book is simply to sample the contents pages:

THE UNCLEANS
1&2. Urine and stool
3. Semen
4. Corpse
5. Blood
6&7. Dog and pig
8. Infidel
9. Wine
10. Beer

11. Sweat of an unlawful ejaculation
12. The sweat of a camel that eats uncleans

Hey, Multiculti Man, that would be you at big hit sound number 8: "Infidel" – right behind "Dog and pig" but, if it's any consolation, ahead of "Sweat of an unlawful ejaculation". But hang on: ejaculate-wise, the Ayatollah's just getting cranked up:

PRECEPTS OF EJACULATION
Things that are unlawful for an ejaculator
Things that are loathesome for an ejaculator
The bath of ejaculation…

I confess I was worried that Prof Miller, M J Murphy and Law R Cool might be in breach of the Ayatollah's "Precepts of Ejaculation" but, after thumbing through them, I can't find anything in there preventing you from doing it repeatedly all over the Internet.

In other words, anyone who had the most casual acquaintance with the Ayatollah's writings would be aware not only that it's not in the least bit surprising but entirely par for the course that the old boy had complex rules re using your embraceable ewe for the Friday night kebab special. But let's leave me and M J Murphy out of it, since we're merely the middle men in what is in effect Prof Miller's "fact check" of Oriana Fallaci. Could anything be more ludicrous than the tenured Ryerson bore presuming to lay down the law on Ayatollah Khomeini to the last western writer ever to interview him? In my (rigorously fact-checked) obituary of her for *The Atlantic Monthly* I wrote of Oriana's encounter with the Ayatollah:

After traveling to Qom and kicking her heels for ten days waiting for him to agree to see her, she was ushered – barefoot and wearing a chador - into his presence and found what she subsequently described as the most handsome old man she'd ever met. In his own way, he must have dug the crazy Italian chick: The meeting was terminated when she tore off 'this stupid medieval rag' and hurled her chador to the floor. But he agreed to return a day or two later to finish the interview.

279

It seems a fantastical encounter now: a man who'd just shoveled every female in supposedly the most modernized of Middle Eastern nations back into 'medieval rags' versus the apotheosis of the ballbusting western career woman. The phrase 'personality interviewer' is grossly devalued these days: look at Mike Wallace's cringe-makingly oleaginous encounter with today's Iranian must-get, President Ahmadinejad. Indeed, Wallace seems to have found Ahmadinejad more attractive ('very smart, savvy, self-assured, good looking in a strange way') than Fallaci found Khomeini. She was by that stage 'the greatest political interviewer of modern times' (Rolling Stone), and yet unlike so many of the bland bigshots jetting from foreign ministry to presidential palace she gravitated to power mainly for the opportunities it afforded to knee it in the crotch. She asked the Ayatollah indignant questions about the executions of prostitutes and homosexuals and he sneered at women like her for going around uncovered 'dragging behind them a tail of men'.

It's worth citing the "medieval rag" bit in full. La Fallaci had just raised with the Ayatollah the matter of "the condition of segregation into which women have been cast" in the Islamic republic. "They can't study at university with men, or work with men," she said, "or go to the beach or to a swimming pool with men. They have to take a dip apart, in their chadors. By the way, how do you swim in a chador?"

What a splendidly offhand question. Alas, the Ayatollah didn't care for it. "This is none of your business," said Khomeini. "Our customs are none of your business. If you do not like Islamic dress you are not obliged to wear it. Because Islamic dress is for good and proper young women."

"That's very kind of you, Imam. And since you said so, I'm going to take off this stupid, medieval rag right now. There. Done. But tell me something. A woman such as I, who has always lived among men, showing her neck, her hair, her ears, who has been in war and slept in the front line in the field among soldiers, according to you, is she an immoral, bold and unproper woman?"

That was 1979 - before any "literary hoax" called *The Little Green Book* was ever published. I had a thousand points of disagreement with Oriana Fallaci, but I adored her. She was a fearless woman, and when she went into a room with the dictators of the day she was full of facts. In a navel-gazing media forever congratulating itself on "speaking truth to power", she just got on and did it. In his soi-disant fact-check of me, Professor Miller wrote of Oriana:

When The New York Times *wrote her obituary on Sept. 15, 2006, the headline called her a 'writer-provocateur'. Sound familiar? Remind us of anyone we know?*

What a sad little man. He actually thinks he's insulting me by comparing me to the peerless Fallaci. But, of course, he's only doing it so he can go all J-school on us:

Journalists usually try to deal with primary sources (Writer-provocateurs seldom do).

Golly! I wonder if he has any idea quite what a Ryerson-atrophied pansy he sounds wagging his finger at Oriana Fallaci? "Writer-provocateurs" don't "deal with primary sources"? Well, her "primary source" on Ayatollah Khomeini is Ayatollah Khomeini. What have you got, Finger Boy? When she was hurling her chador at him in 1979, what were you doing? Retyping press releases from Ed Broadbent?

Unlike Signora Fallaci, I can't claim face time with the Ayatollah. But I've read his writings in the scholarly translations, and cross-referenced them with the original Farsi, and I am familiar with his rulings on camel sweat, touching one's beard after ejaculation, defecating in a dead-end street without the permission of its owner, and whether you can divorce your child bride before she's begun menstruating. It's unfortunate that the most influential Muslim of the late 20th century is a barbaric nutjob, but it happens to be the case.

So just to reprise:

Did I cite Oriana Fallaci accurately? Yes.

Did she cite Ayatollah Khomeini accurately? Yes.

Is there a volume by the Ayatollah commonly known as the "Blue Book"? Yes

Does it include rulings on sex with nine-year olds and what to do with a shagged sheep? Yes.

Did either of us mention a *Little Green Book*? No. In fact, the translation Oriana cites pre-dates *The Little Green Book* by a year.

I think Professor Waggy-Finger is doing what they call "projecting". He's accusing me of everything he's been doing himself:

I took "somebody else's word for it". Er, no. That would be you, taking the Sock Puppets' word for it on my book review.

I didn't check the "primary source". Er, no. That would be you, cavalierly announcing there's no such thing as a "Blue Book".

To be more charitable to you than you deserve, you assume that Oriana Fallaci and I so want to think the worst of Islam that we'll fall for any old hooey. Actually not. On the other hand, you so want to think the worst of us blowhard provocateurs that you assume we're as ignorant of Islam as you evidently are.

M J Murphy wrote: "I think you owe Dr Miller an apology." Au contraire, I think "Dr Miller" owes me and Oriana an apology. Since he decided to go to such kinky lengths to catch my eye, he has accused me of failing to provide a source for a quote: False. He's accused me of making up famous rulings of the Ayatollah: False. He's declared flat out that there is no such thing as a Khomeini "Blue Book": False. And people pay money to study "responsible journalism" with this guy? At least for his own ill-advised adventures in fact-checking, his unfortunate acolyte, M J Murphy of Toronto, isn't charging cash.

If I were celebrated toilet photographer Warren Kinsella or leading Canadian Internet Nazi Lucy Warman, I'd sue. But I'm not. Nor, despite a flying visit to the Falklands and a couple of wet weekends in Wales, have I ever been attracted to sheep-shagging. But I imagine it feels a bit like dealing with Messrs Miller, Murphy and the Law R Cool kids: No matter how often you roger them senseless, they keep on bleating. I wouldn't have bothered with this response were it not for the fact that Professor Waggy-Finger traduced not me but a great and courageous lady who is no longer here to laugh her magnificent scoffing laugh in his face. Oriana Fallaci is a hundred times the man John Miller is. Read her interviews with Arafat or the Shah and ask yourself whether she needs any posthumous lessons in "journalistic ethics" from an unread parochial poseur. And, if you are considering a career in journalism, think about what you'd like to be looking back on in 40 years' time: Oriana's resume or Professor Miller's.

Prof Miller came on like the Fact-Checking Ethics-Bore J-School Ayatollah and limps off like a poor little lamb who has lost his way, as they sing in the barnyards of Qom. Professor Miller, M J Murphy and Law Is Cool: The Shagged Sheep.

PRE-TRIAL
The stakes

Steynposts, May/June 2008

THE SOCK PUPPET Three's oft-heard cry is that this isn't about "freedom of speech" or "censorship"; they don't want to silence me personally, but are merely seeking the "right" to a reasonable response. The blogger Davin Burlingham addresses this point directly:

> *When I heard them repeat this position on television, I have to say I was shocked. Genuinely shocked. I will tell you why. These three are law students, correct? They are currently articling, which means they must have passed all their final exams, and are about to be called to the bar. Presumably they have demonstrated all the skills and their brains have imbibed all the knowledge needed to get through law school and find jobs. How, then, could they have failed to actually read the Code under which they are bringing a complaint? Take a look at s. 37(2) of the BC Human Rights Code, where it says:*
>
> > (2) If the member or panel determines that the complaint is justified, the member or panel
> >
> > (a) must order the person that contravened this Code to cease the contravention and to refrain from committing the same or a similar contravention
>
> *That is a mandatory injunction. An obligatory 'cease and desist' order. If the complainants win, the Tribunal has to order* Maclean's *to stop running 'Islamophobic' articles. Not just articles by Mark Steyn, mind you; they have to stop running those articles period. Goodbye Barbara Amiel. Now, you might*

respond that Steyn wouldn't be silenced, he would just have to pick his words more carefully. But think about it; the CIC is not just complaining about the excerpt from America Alone, *but about a whole sheaf of Steyn's articles. It's pretty safe to assume that whatever Steyn has written about Islam in the last seven or so years would be considered offensive by the CIC. In the face of an injunction, then, he would either have to stop writing about Islam or stop obeying the dictates of his conscience as a writer.*

The students may say they don't want to silence Mark Steyn or anyone else. Their complaint, if successful, will do just that. It can do no other.

Just so. I've tried to make that point in interviews. The BC tribunal's ruling will mean that I can no longer write for *Maclean's*, and that *Maclean's* itself will be highly circumscribed in what it can publish about the relationship between Islam and the west. On one of the central questions facing the world today, the editorial decisions of Canada's largest news weekly will be determined by a British Columbia "court".

Incidentally, lest you doubt that the intent of the Canadian Islamic Congress is to constrain dramatically the ability of *Maclean's* to discuss Islam, consider this clause of the BC Human Rights Code:

39 (1) If an order is made under section 37 (2) (a), (c) or (d) or (4) or 38 (2), the party in whose favour the order is made or a person designated in the order may file a certified copy of the order with the Supreme Court.

(2) An order filed under subsection (1) has the same force and effect, and all proceedings may be taken on it, as if it were a judgment of the Supreme Court.

My career in Canada will be formally ended next month. But don't break out the champagne and conga lines. If *Maclean's* decides to comply with the ruling, it will not be a "news weekly" in the sense that the term would be understood by any genuinely free society. And one day there will be plenty of Jews and gays and all kinds of other fellows who'll come to understand the damage this case has wrought.

PS With the trial only days away, a reader writes:

> *I have just heard you described on CBC radio as a 'controversial American journalist'.*
>> *The dreaded 'A' word. You are doomed.*

Oh, dear. Can I bring a "human rights" complaint against the CBC?

IN COURT

But we were getting along so well...

Maclean's, June 16th 2008

THE CHARGE levelled against *Maclean's* by the Canadian Islamic Congress is that, in publishing an excerpt from my book, this magazine exposed Muslims to "hatred and contempt". Alas, at the first day of the Great *Maclean's* Show Trial at the British Columbia "Human Rights" Tribunal, the well of my book excerpt's "hatred and contempt" pretty well ran dry in the first hour. So Faisal Joseph, counsel for the plaintiff Mohamed Elmasry, was forced to bus in a huge pile of miscellaneous generic "hatred and contempt" from all kinds of other sources. And even then much of it seemed less like "hatred and contempt" than "mild offhandedness and the occasional droll titter". A lot of it was from me, of course. Mr Joseph started with my article, but quickly moved on to my book, my columns, my sitcom review, my lame jokes, and no doubt (by the time you read this) my casual asides while muttering to myself on top of Mount Logan during a windstorm. At the end of the first day, m'learned friend was complaining that I had been rude to the three Osgoode Hall law students who've been fronting for the strangely shy and retiring Dr Elmasry these last six months. Not rude to them in the article in this space that triggered the complaint. No, apparently I was rude to them at TVOntario last month. Not rude to them on-air (although it was a somewhat raucous show), but rude to them off-camera. Geez, these days I don't seem to be able to step out the house without committing a hate crime.

Just for the record (and before it becomes chiselled in the granite of British Columbia "human rights" jurisprudence), I wasn't aware I was being rude to my accusers after the TVOntario show. The very last words on air were me saying, "You wanna go to dinner?", and Khurrum Awan yelling back "No!" But, as the host Steve Paikin and his producers reported at some length on their website, Khurrum and I and the two gals stuck around for an hour of relatively civil conversation. In fact, I got the impression one of the ladies was growing rather fond of me, which, to be honest, was the main reason I hung about. But, now I come to think of it, that was the way it went at high school. You figure you're doing great and then next morning you overhear her telling her best friend by the lockers that she thought you were a dweeby limpet with halitosis. Unfortunately, in today's fractious legal environment, if Khurrum Awan thinks you're a dweeby limpet with halitosis who can't dance and has dried sweat rings under his cheesecloth shirt, he can add it to the long list of actionable "human rights" grievances to be laid before multiple tribunals and commissions.

Even so, after six months of assurances from Canadian "human rights" commissars that if we don't police hatemongers like Steyn a new Holocaust will be upon us, I think witnesses were expecting a bit more red meat than the assertion that I can be a bit boorish over the green room Perrier. As was noted by scholars who'd attended the "trial" under the misapprehension that it bore some dim resemblance to conventional legal proceedings, it was hard to see what the post-show chit-chat after a television broadcast in 2008 had to do with a 2006 *Maclean's* cover story, which is, after all, supposed to be the hate crime under investigation. But it's even harder to see what any of this has to do with British Columbia or the "British Columbia Muslim community", on whose behalf this "human rights" suit is being brought. TVOntario is, despite its deceptive name, a TV network in Ontario. It is not broadcast in British Columbia. Khurrum Awan, the Osgoode Hall law student on the witness stand, is an alumnus of the Osgoode Hall in Toronto not some entirely different Osgoode Hall at

288

Fort Nelson. He lives in Mississauga, which is a suburb of Buckinghorse River. Whoops, my mistake. I mean Toronto. He works in Ontario, as an employee of the very barrister examining him in that Vancouver courtroom, fellow Ontario resident Faisal Joseph. Indeed, it is unclear whether Mr Awan had ever set foot in British Columbia until he and Mr Joseph and two other Ontario law students were flown to the west coast to testify to the pain and suffering of the British Columbia Muslim community they claim to represent. When the Ontarian Mr Awan and his fellow Ontarians agreed to appear on an Ontario TV show, there were no members of the British Columbia Muslim community present, either in the studio, the makeup room or the men's toilet (I cannot vouch for the ladies'). As they'd say in Hollywood, no members of the British Columbia Muslim community were harmed in the making of this program.

Yet, with the cheerful insouciance one has come to cherish from Canada's "human rights" regime, the troika of BC "jurists" had no difficulty permitting all this extraterritorial evidence from extraterritorial witnesses employed by the extraterritorial lawyer and the extraterritorial plaintiff to be entered in a case allegedly about "human rights" in British Columbia. The "chair" of the troika, Commissar Heather MacNaughton, sits under the coat of arms bearing the ancient motto of the Crown, symbolizing the robust threads of precedent and continuity that tie the Robson Square courthouse to 800 years of legal inheritance: "*Dieu et mon droit.*" "*Dieu*" doesn't seem to get much respect in the system these days, though Allah can still expect a modicum of deference. As to *mon* own particular *droit* - to due process, to the presumption of innocence, and to confront my accusers in a fair trial – that seems to have gone by the board.

So, as Faisal Joseph dredged up TV broadcasts from Ontario (which is not within British Columbia's jurisdiction), obscure blog posts from the Internet (which is not within this tribunal's jurisdiction), plus reports of his own press conference in Toronto (a well-known city in British Columbia, apparently) and snippets from the *Brussels Journal* (based in the capital city of the European Union, which British Columbia has presumably joined), *Maclean's* counsel Julian Porter, QC pointed out that, whatever the debate in these various fora, they had nothing to do with my article but rather were responses to the Canadian Islamic Congress' various "human rights" suits themselves.

At the opening of Tuesday's proceedings, Faisal Joseph announced that he wanted to devote that day not to me or *Maclean's* or the substance of my article but to the media and blogospheric reaction to the complaints. In other words, he was explicitly confirming Mr Porter's point – insofar as anything has exposed Khurrum Awan to "hatred and contempt", it's not the *Maclean's* cover story but his own lawsuit. Whether or not it is appropriate (or even legal) for Canadians to be "contemptuous" of the Canadian Islamic Congress' thuggish assault on ancient liberties, the fact is Mr Awan's lawsuit has earned him far more "contempt" than anything in my article. He should be suing himself. Which would be less wacky than most of the admissibility rulings by the BC troika.

Obviously I deeply regret that I offended my accusers in the TVOntario off-air banter, even though I thought we were getting along swimmingly. It just goes to show, even when you have no idea you're committing a hate crime, chances are you still are. On the other hand, it also suggests limited potential for conflict resolution with the plaintiffs. For six months, Khurrum and the gals had been telling readers of *The Globe And Mail*, *The National Post*, *The Toronto Star*, *The Ottawa Citizen*, *The Halifax Chronicle-Herald* and many other media outlets as far afield as the BBC, that all they wanted was an opportunity to "start a debate" with the Islamophobe Steyn. So we had a debate on TVOntario and now that turns out to be just the latest charge on the indictment. One can't help feeling that, if *Maclean's* had acceded to their demand for their own five-page cover story in the magazine and Mr Awan had turned up to issue his instructions to the printers, some perceived slight from the receptionist ("Sorry, we're out of decaf") could easily have triggered a fresh round of litigation.

Robert Frost once said that writing "free verse" was like playing tennis with the net down. The relationship of "human rights" tribunals to real courts seems to be like that: Julian Porter can whack some legalistic ace down the middle, but Faisal Joseph hurls back a box of golf balls he's flown in from Nunavut, and the umpires (three "judges" ignorant of law but expert in identity-group grievance) award him the point.

By the way, I see I've been nominated for one of the National Magazine Awards, to be handed out later this month. By then, Mr Joseph will have succeeded in getting the BC troika effectively to ban me from *Maclean's* and from all Canadian journalism. An impressive achievement. My book was a Number One bestseller in Canada, and the new paperback edition was at Number Four the other day, and President Bush, Vice-President Cheney, Governor Mitt Romney, Senator Joe Lieberman, Senator Jon Kyl and (at last count) six European Prime Ministers have either recommended the book or called me in to discuss its themes. But in Canada it's a hate crime.

One thing I've learned these last few months is that it's always worse than you expect. The willingness of the BC troika's social engineers to trample over every basic rule of English law has embedded at the heart of Canadian justice a soft beguiling totalitarianism. I'll be the first Number One bestselling author and National Magazine Award-nominated columnist to be deemed unpublishable in Canada.

But I won't be the last.

THE DEPARTURE GATE
Notes on a show trial

Steynposts, June 8th 2008

I SEE OMAR Sharif, of all people, says that, when he has a problem with some guy, he finds it far easier to go to the neighborhood sheikh to sort it out than to have to mess around with all that western legal mumbo-jumbo. He'll be happy to know they've introduced a similar system in British Columbia: The sheikhs sit on a "human rights" tribunal and sort it all out without any time-wasting rubbish about rules of evidence, presumption of innocence, etc. On the first day, the Canadian Islamic Congress lawyer, Faisal Joseph, says airily that freedom of speech is a "red herring". If it were, it would be on the endangered species list. On the other hand, the *New York Times* guy tells *Maclean's* Andrew Coyne he can't believe what he's seeing.

I don't have a lot to add to what Andrew Coyne, Ezra Levant and others have written on the British Columbia "Human Rights" Tribunal. Readers of this site have lived with the issues for six months and know most of the arguments - better, indeed, than the pseudo-judges in Vancouver. On Friday, the intervenor for the Canadian Association of Journalists referred *en passant* to constitutional challenges to Section 13 of Canada's Human Rights Code, and Chief Commissar Heather MacNaughton asked whether any such challenges were currently proceeding, and he replied: Yes. Warman vs Lemire. Most SteynOnline readers would be aware of Mr Lemire's constitutional challenge to the core "hate speech" weapon in the "human rights" armory, and know that it's intimately entwined with the *Maclean's* case. But Heather MacNaughton, British Columbia's chief "human rights" inquisitor, apparently wasn't.

Here are a few other observations:

1) When I arrived at the Robson Square courthouse, an officer of the BC Sheriff's Department intercepted me and said because of "security threats" he'd be sticking by me everywhere I went in the building. I found this rather reassuring for about 90 seconds. Then I realized he meant not that the court had been apprised of security threats against me but that I myself was the security threat.

~

2) With their usual low cunning, the "human rights" sheikhs chose a courtroom that only seats 40 people. So a big crowd (including CBC reporters) were wedged up peering through the glass in the door until the head sheikh (a judge best known for fining the Knights of Columbus for declining to rent their hall for a lesbian wedding) said the pressed faces of the people were distracting her and shooed them away. Typical. A third-rate bureaucracy that tells everyone from McDonald's to *Maclean's* how to run their affairs can't even organize a show trial with minimal competence.

Maybe the folks who can't get in should file a "human rights" complaint against the "human rights" tribunal for denying them the human right to attend a human rights trial.

~

3) Tuesday was devoted in large part to discussion of my review of the CBC sitcom "Little Mosque On The Prairie" and to in-depth joke exegesis by Chief Sock Khurrum Awan. To the best of my knowledge, he was not sworn in as an expert witness, a Professor of Humorological Studies from the University of Saskatoon or whatever. But he clearly felt many of my jokes were not funny, and actionably so. In my "Loose Ends" days at the BBC, we occasionally used to do the show on the road from Edinburgh, Belfast and so forth, and I'd find myself checking in to hotels with my pals Carol Thatcher, Craig Charles & Co. And Craig was occasionally wont to say to the fellow at reception things like, "I pre-booked a couple of hookers. Can you have them sent straight up?" And the clerk would give him a frosty stare, and Craig would turn around and say to us: "Uh-oh! Humor bypass operation." I never thought it was the greatest line, but it seemed oddly apt by the

time Mr Awan and Faisal Joseph were done discussing my "Little Mosque" review. To be humorless in complaining about a complaint that a humor show was insufficiently humorous is an achievement of almost Platonic perfection.

4) Less surprising were the usual Islamic scholars flown in from hither and yon to testify that to the "overwhelming majority" of Muslims the word "jihad" has nothing to do with killing infidels or blowing stuff up or anything like that, but is a benign concept meaning "healthy-lifestyle lo-fat cranberry muffin" or whatever it is. So it's nothing to be afraid of.

Years ago, I was on a BBC comedy quiz show with Stephen Fry and a question came up about Napoleon's mummified penis being sold at auction. And, upon hearing the word "penis", the audience tittered nervously. "Oh, come on," said Stephen. "'Penis' isn't a word to be afraid of. It's a *thing* to be afraid of." That's the way I feel about "jihad": pace the expert witnesses, whether or not it's a word to be afraid of, it's a thing to be afraid of.

5) I was very touched by the number of folks who came up to me in Starbucks, HMV and other Vancouver emporia and expressed support for me. On my first day at the hotel, I got into the elevator with two ladies, one of whom looked me over and exclaimed: "You're that dastardly troublemaker Mark Steyn!" They told me to stick it to the kangaroos and got off a couple of floors ahead of me. Whereupon the Eastern European bellman, intrigued by the conversation, said, "So what brings you to Vancouver, sir?"

I replied, "I'm on trial at the British Columbia Human Rights Tribunal for crimes against humanity."

"Oh," he said, with a nervous laugh. "You must lead a very interesting life."

Not lately.

6) I'm no legal scholar, so, when I think of courthouses, I think of buildings like the one in *Robin And The Seven Hoods*. It's Chicago in the Twenties, and, having been acquitted of this and that, Frank Sinatra emerges on to the courthouse steps and, accompanied by enthusiastic flappers, sings "My Kind Of Town". That's my kind of courthouse: steps and pillars. The Vancouver monstrosity was the exact opposite: A modernist hole in the ground, in which the courtrooms are windowless basements. Given the basic inversion of every fundamental legal principle, this seemed very appropriate. The only link with the outside world was a clock on the wall that was stuck at five past eight. And, as I gazed at its unchanging visage hour after hour, day after day, it struck – well, actually, it didn't strike, it having stopped some months or years back – but it struck me as an interesting glimpse into the big-government mindset, into the gulf between its ambitions and its capabilities. The Government of British Columbia regards it as an entirely feasible project to eradicate "hate" from society, even though hate is a human emotion that has been beat in the human heart for all eternity. But they can't get someone in to restart the clock.

7) I was flattered to see that the Government of British Columbia has chosen to mark the criminalization of my opinions by burying western civilization. From a local news report:

> *Tourists were shut off from the B.C. legislature's rotunda this week as work began to hide four historical murals behind walls.*
>
> *MLAs voted in 2007 to remove the murals and display them elsewhere, because some people find the colonial depictions of aboriginal people to be offensive... The four murals were commissioned in 1932 as a gift to the province from Provincial Secretary S L Howe. They were completed by artist George Southwell to depict Howe's desire to illustrate the 'establishment of civilization' in B.C.*
>
> *• 'Labour' shows the building of either Fort Langley in the 1820s or Fort Victoria in the 1840s.*

- *'Justice' shows colonial Chief Justice Matthew Baillie Begbie holding court in Clinton during the Cariboo gold rush in the 1860s.*

- *'Courage' depicts the meeting of captains Vancouver and Quadra at Nootka Sound in 1792 to turn over Vancouver Island territory from the Spanish to the British.*

- *'Enterprise' shows Hudson's Bay Company official James Douglas landing at Clover Point to select the site of Fort Victoria in 1843.*

Perhaps it would be quicker just to wall me up with the buried "Justice" mural.

8) Finally, skedaddling out of Vancouver on Saturday, I got to the airport to find my flight had been delayed two hours. So I did what I normally do in such circumstances - went to kill time by heading to the gift shop to buy some crummy souvenir knick-knacks for my kids. And, as soon as I got to the first amusing "Beautiful BC" T-shirt, I thought: Why the hell would I want any souvenirs of the lousy jurisdiction that wants to end my career in Canada? So I put the bills back in my pocket and made a mental note to buy a couple extra "Live Free Or Die" T-shirts back in New Hampshire.

Steynposts, Thursday, June 12th 2008

The Canadian state's assault on free speech has never made the front page of the Dominion's leading liberal newspaper, *The Toronto Star*, nor of *The Globe And Mail*, nor even of *The Vancouver Sun*, when the show trial was happening right under their noses.

But it is on the front page of today's *New York Times*, and above the fold, too, which is a once-a-decade event. Never mind the goofy pic of me auditioning for the opening titles of the next Bond movie; here's how the piece ends:

Mr Steyn, the author of the article, said the Canadian proceedings had illustrated some important distinctions. 'The problem with so-called hate speech laws is that they're not about facts,' he said in a telephone interview. 'They're about feelings.'

'What we're learning here is really the bedrock difference between the United States and the countries that are in a broad sense its legal cousins,' Mr Steyn added. 'Western governments are becoming increasingly comfortable with the regulation of opinion. The First Amendment really does distinguish the US, not just from Canada but from the rest of the western world.'

For as long as that lasts.

THE SECOND VERDICT

The 'roos jump for the exit

Steynposts, June 27th 2008

O N THURSDAY, the Canadian "Human Rights" Commission (very quietly) dismissed the Canadian Islamic Congress complaint against *Maclean's* re *America Alone* - and without even giving the Socks the consolation of an Ontario-style drive-by verdict. The decision of the Jennifer Lynch mob includes the following:

> *The Steyn article discusses changing global demographics and other factors that the author describes as contributing to an eventual ascendancy of Muslims in the 'developed world', a prospect that the author fears for various reasons described in the article. The writing is polemical, colourful and emphatic, and was obviously calculated to excite discussion and even offend certain readers, Muslim and non-Muslim alike.*
>
> *Overall, however, the views expressed in the Steyn article, when considered as a whole and in context, are not of an extreme nature as defined by the Supreme Court in the Taylor decision. Considering the purpose and scope of section 13 (1), and taking into account that an interpretation of s. 13 (1) must be consistent with the minimal impairment of free speech, there is no reasonable basis in the evidence to warrant the appointment of a Tribunal.*
>
> *For these reasons, this complaint is dismissed.*

Here's the official reaction from my colleagues:

Maclean's *magazine is pleased that the Canadian Human Rights Commission has dismissed the complaint brought against it by the Canadian Islamic Congress. The decision is in keeping with our long-standing position that the article in question, 'The*

Future Belongs To Islam', an excerpt from Mark Steyn's best-selling book America Alone, *was a worthy piece of commentary on important geopolitical issues, entirely within the bounds of normal journalistic practice.*

Though gratified by the decision, Maclean's *continues to assert that no human rights commission, whether at the federal or provincial level, has the mandate or the expertise to monitor, inquire into, or assess the editorial decisions of the nation's media. And we continue to have grave concerns about a system of complaint and adjudication that allows a media outlet to be pursued in multiple jurisdictions on the same complaint, brought by the same complainants, subjecting it to costs of hundreds of thousands of dollars, to say nothing of the inconvenience. We enthusiastically support those parliamentarians who are calling for legislative review of the commissions with regard to speech issues.*

Faisal Joseph, lawyer to the CIC and Mohamed Elmasry's vicar on earth, is not happy. He accuses the Canadian "Human Rights" Commission of caving in to "inappropriate political pressure". And he's entirely right about that. Had *Maclean's* and I been as impoverished and poorly connected as the average victim of the Section 13 thought police, we'd have wound up just like them: guilty, fined, subject to lifetime speech bans, and damned in public as Haters with a capital "H". So dear old Faisal is quite right to be cheesed off.

We now await the decision from the pseudo-judges of the British Columbia tribunal.

ISLAM vs FREEDOM
The trend

Maclean's, May 26th 2008

MANY YEARS ago, I proposed a feature to an editor about a new trend – as I recall, it was celebrities wearing cravats. I wanted us to be first with the big "The Cravat Is Back!" weekend pictorial. Anyway, she demanded to know the evidence for this trend. And I cited Ted Danson wearing one to the Emmys and Roger Moore wearing one to go snorkelling in Belize. Or possibly vice-versa.

"And…?" she said coldly.

"Er, what do you mean - 'and'?"

"Mark, Mark, Mark," she sighed. "How many years have you been in journalism? It takes three to make a trend." And she sent me away with a flea in my ear and an undertaking not to return until Prince Edward had been spotted wearing a cravat at a gala performance of *The Phantom Of The Opera*. Or vice-versa. I'm making a general point here, so let's not get hung up on details.

Here's the thing: Two years ago, the Supreme Islamic Council of Canada took *The Western Standard* to the Alberta "Human Rights" Commission for republishing the Danish Mohammed cartoons. A few months back, the Canadian Islamic Congress took *Maclean's* to the Canadian, Ontario and British Columbia "Human Rights" Commissions for publishing an excerpt from my bestselling hate crime, *America Alone*. Last week, the Centre for Islamic Development took *The Halifax Chronicle-Herald* to the Nova Scotia "Human Rights" Commission for publishing an editorial cartoon of a, ah, person of an Islamic persuasion.

Have we got a trend yet?

This is the way it's going to be in Canada, this year, next year and beyond.

300

A few days back I found myself on a TV Ontario show with the three Osgoode Hall sock puppets whom the media have promoted as the "complainants" in the suits against *Maclean's*. (They're not: Mohamed Elmasry, the head of the Canadian Islamic Congress, is the complainant.) It was not the most agreeable of encounters, at least on camera. I believe the very last words of the show were me saying to the sock puppets "Wanna go to dinner?" and one of their number, Khurrum Awan, yelling back, "No!" But off-air the chit-chat went rather more pleasantly, and, in the course of it, Mr Awan observed that Jews had availed themselves of the "human rights" commissions for years but it was only when the Muzzies decided they wanted a piece of the thought-police action that all these bigwigs started agitating for reining in the commissions and scrapping the relevant provisions of Canada's "human rights" code.

He has a kind of point. Which is why some of us consistently opposed the use of these commissions even when it was liberal Jews using them to hunt down the last three neo-Nazis in Saskatchewan. Yet, accepting that the principle is identical, there is a difference. For the most part, the Canadian Jewish Congress, B'nai Brith and the other beneficiaries of the "human rights" regime went after freaks and misfits on the fringes of society, folks too poor (in the majority of federal cases) even to afford legal representation. These prosecutions were unfair and reflected badly on Canada's justice system, but liberal proponents of an illiberal law justified it on the assumption that it would be confined to these peripheral figures nobody cared about. You can't blame Muslim groups for figuring that what's sauce for the infidel is sauce for the believer – and that, having bigger fish to fry, they're gonna need a lot more sauce.

The first three organizations taken by Jewish groups to the federal "human rights" commission were the Western Guard, the Church of Jesus Christ Christian-Aryan Nations and the Manitoba Knights of the Ku Klux Klan. Despite their fearsome names, none of these clear and present dangers to the peaceable kingdom had an in-house legal department, or a spare thousand bucks to retain outside counsel, or indeed a buck-and-a-quarter for the bus ride to the hearing. By contrast, the Muslim lobby groups' first three fish are Canada's newest political magazine (*The Western Standard*, whose print edition has since ceased publication); Canada's oldest and biggest-selling news weekly (*Maclean's*); and the biggest daily newspaper in the Maritimes (*The Halifax Chronicle-Herald*). This is an entirely different scale of project. Muslim lobby groups have very shrewdly calculated that the "human rights" commissions are the quickest, cheapest and most coercive means of applying pressure to mainstream publications in order to put Islam beyond discussion – or at least beyond all but the most pink-marshmallow celebrate-diversity discussion.

When it was yours truly and Ezra Levant, the publisher of *The Western Standard*, taking the heat, it was easy to write us off as a couple of rightwing blowhards. Mainly because we are. But the Islamophobe du jour is the *Chronicle-Herald*'s Bruce MacKinnon, a cartoonist who's won an Atlantic Journalism Award and is the very soul of moderation. Alas for him, the head of the Nova Scotia "Human Rights" Commission is a fellow called Michael Noonan, last heard from comparing his job to that of the South African blacks who stood up to "the jackboots of the state" in the Sharpeville massacre. In other words, he seems just the sort of vainglorious stooge who'll be happy to do the Centre for Islamic Development's bidding and place *The Halifax Chronicle-Herald*'s editorial content under government regulation – or, as he would say if he were less hilariously un-self-aware, under "the jackboot of the state".

Discussing the *Maclean's* case recently, the blog Dead Reckoning observed of our complainants:

> *They think they are entitled to force Maclean's to simply allow them to publish whatever they want, and if they can't get it by bullying Maclean's they will get a government agency to do it for them.*
>
> *This is so Muslim. If you want to accuse somebody in an Islamic country of offending Islam, you go to an Imam and get*

him to issue a fatwa against the offender. In effect, the human rights commissions substitute for the Imams and issue the fatwas.

There's something in that. The Ontario "Human Rights" Commission's drive-by conviction of *Maclean's* was, indeed, a kind of fatwa – a pronouncement from doctrinal authority, which is why the Sock Puppets hailed it as an "historic victory". If, as the Canadian Islamic Congress does, you look at the OHRC as, in effect, a proto-Sharia court enforcing the official state doctrine, its verdict seems entirely natural. In this case, the doctrine is political correctness, but, if only for the moment, its interests presently align with the Muslim lobby's. Many of us regard the "human rights" commissions as a parallel justice system at odds with 800 years of Canada's legal inheritance and dispensing with all the distinguishing features – due process, the presumption of innocence, etc. We should have realized earlier that its chief characteristics are also the closest our system comes to the capricious and authoritarian aspects of Islamic law. This week, in a brief objecting to a constitutional challenge to Section 13 of the Dominion's human rights code, Canada's Justice Ministry declared:

*Mr Lemire complains that the prohibition against disseminating hatred via the Internet is not accompanied by the defences of truth and fair comment that are available to traditional news media in torts ranging from defamation to seditious libel. This argument is misleading. **The defences of truth and fair comment remain available to torts such as defamation and seditious libel, regardless of the medium in which they occur. However, none of the traditional media can avail themselves of these defences in cases of alleged hate propaganda,** whether the communication appears in print, on television or on a website.*

*As the Federal Court has explained, **defences that may be available in tort actions are not available in cases of hate propaganda because the prohibition is concerned with adverse effects, not with intent.***

My emphasis. Also my sprayed coffee. And my steaming pants and scalded crotch.

The government rarely expresses it that brazenly. Especially the Justice Minister of a supposedly Conservative government. By the way, by "adverse effects", they mean not anything that's actually happened but something that might potentially theoretically hypothetically happen maybe a decade or four down the road. If you create a justice regime predicated as a point of principle on disdain for objective reality, it's no big surprise to find perpetually aggrieved Muslim lobby groups eager to avail themselves of it – big time.

If you're an editor or a publisher in Canada, the "human rights" regime is building a world in which the only choice on key issues of public debate is between state censorship or self-censorship. True, not everyone sees it that way. In Toronto last week, I had lunch with an old editor of mine in a fashionable eatery on King Street, and she couldn't see what all the fuss was about. "You need to lighten up," she said. "Write about a movie." Soon, I'll have no choice. Although the Osgoode Hall sock puppets protest that all they want is a "right of reply", when the British Columbia "Human Rights" Tribunal finds us guilty, its pseudo-judges are statutorily obligated to issue a cease-and-desist order which will have the effect of preventing *Maclean's* running any writing on Islam by me or anybody of a similar bent – even though the plaintiffs have not challenged the accuracy of a single fact or statistic or quotation.

So I'll be gone from the Canadian media, which will undoubtedly be distressing to my loyal reader (I use the singular advisedly). But a year or two down the line, many other subscribers to *Maclean's* and the *Chronicle-Herald* and eventually the *Globe* and *The Toronto Star* will be wondering why there are whole areas of debate that no longer seem to get much of an airing in the public prints. In 1989, Muslims who objected to Salman Rushdie burned his novel in the streets of England. Two decades on, they've figured out that it's more efficient to use the "human rights" commissions to burn the

304

offending texts metaphorically, discreetly, off-stage …and (ultimately) pre-emptively.

Pace my old editor, I don't need to see a movie because I'm in one. We're at that point in the plot where the maverick investigator takes the call saying a third example of the strange spore has been found in a field in Idaho, and he pushes another pin in the map and goes "Hmm" thoughtfully.

But he still can't get his colleagues to see that something's going on.

THE THIRD VERDICT

Free at last! (For now)

National Review Online, October 10th 2008

MARK HEMINGWAY is right to say that free speech in Canada "does not exist in any meaningful way". As the British Columbia "Human Rights" Tribunal's rambling and incoherent decision makes plain, *Maclean's* and I were acquitted of "flagrant Islamophobia" for essentially political reasons - because neither the court nor its travesty of a "human rights" code could withstand the heat of a guilty verdict. Jay Currie puts it well:

> *The way I read this decision is that it imposes a two part test: a) are your words offensive and hurtful? b) are you a major media organization with deep pockets represented by serious lawyers. If 'a' and not 'b' you are a hate monger; if 'a' and 'b' you are engaged in political debate.*

Just so. Because we spent a ton of money and had a bigshot Queen's Counsel and exposed the joke jurisprudence and (at the federal "human rights" commission) systemic corruption, the kangaroo courts decided that discretion was the better part of valor. The Ontario "Human Rights" Commission ruled they weren't able to prosecute the case because of a technicality - I offered to waive the technicality, but the wimps still bailed out. If you have the wherewithal to stand up to these totalitarian bullies, they stampede for the exits. But, if you're just an obscure Alberta pastor or a guy with a widely unread website or a fellow who writes a letter to his local newspaper, they'll destroy your life.

I sympathize with the Canadian Islamic Congress, whose mouthpiece feels that, if the British Columbia pseudo-judges had applied the logic of previous decisions, we'd have been found guilty. He's right: Under the ludicrous British Columbia "Human Rights"

Code, we are guilty. Which is why the Canadian Islamic Congress should appeal, and why I offered on the radio an hour ago to chip in a thousand bucks towards the cost thereof.

National Review Online, November 24th 2008

ON FRIDAY I had the honor of addressing the Federalist Society in Washington on the matter of my free-speech travails up north. And, in response to a question on whether the Canadian "Human Rights" Commission were surprised that I'd pushed back against them, I quoted that great line from the Kevin Bacon film *Tremors*, about the giant mutated killer worms terrorizing some town in Nevada. As you'll recall, Michael Gross and Reba McEntire play a couple of gun nuts with more firepower down in their basement than the average EU army, and when the killer worms come to call they wind up blasted to smithereens and splattered all over the walls. And here comes the great line:

Looks like they picked the wrong rec room to break into.

The giant killer worms of the Canadian "Human Rights" Commission picked the wrong rec room to break into. Ezra Levant and I and a few others went nuclear on the Dominion's thought police and gave them the worst year of publicity in their three-decade existence. The result is that, earlier this month, over 99 per cent of delegates to the Conservative Party convention voted to abolish Section 13 (the "hate speech" provision) of the Canadian Human Rights Act, and a brave principled Liberal, Keith Martin, renewed his private member's motion in the House of Commons to do the same.

This morning, the CHRC issued the so-called Moon Report on free-speech issues. Most of us expected it to be a whitewash. Instead, Professor Moon says:

1. The first recommendation is that section 13 of the Canadian Human Rights Act (CHRA) be repealed so that the CHRC and the Canadian Human Rights Tribunal (CHRT) would no longer deal with hate speech, in particular hate speech on the Internet.

This is a great tribute to what Ezra calls his campaign of "denormalization" of Canada's Orwellian "human rights" racket. They're not yet ready to throw in the towel completely, but the argument's been entirely reframed. And, if the pressure can be kept up, the deranged Dominion may yet rejoin the ranks of free nations.

THE INDESTRUCTIBLE CLICHÉ
Blowing smoke

FOR THE FIRST three months of my battle with the "human rights" enforcers, I received an e-mail approximately every minute and a half from sensible moderate reasonable *bien pensants* protesting that, while of course they're all in favor of freedom of speech, it's a question of striking a balance, drawing the line and whatnot. At which point they usually trot out the old favorite that "there's no right to shout 'Fire!' in a crowded theatre." Darren Lund does it at the drop of a hat. He's not a homosexual but he plays one at the Alberta "Human Rights" Commission, getting offended on behalf of gays and lesbians and then filing homophobia complaints. He succeeded in getting the peculiarly thuggish Alberta tribunal to impose a lifetime speech ban on the Reverend Stephen Boissoin, and for his totalitarian pains was the inaugural recipient of the Alberta "Human Rights" Award. So, given that he lives and breathes censorship, you'd think he would come up with a slightly less stale cliché. But no. Whenever *The Globe And Mail* or anybody else asks him for his thoughts on free speech, he dusts it off one mo' time. Defending the thuggery of the Boissoin decision in *The Calgary Herald*, he trotted out the bromide about "falsely shouting 'fire' in a crowded theatre" and then added that the Alberta pastor's letter "didn't just shout fire; I suggest that those words had the effect of setting the fire and locking the theatre door."

I wonder how many of these liberal Canadians fretting about conflagrations spreading from orchestra to proscenium know they're quoting:

a) an American;

and, better yet,

b) an American judge upholding espionage charges against an anti-war protester.

"The most stringent protection of free speech would not protect a man in falsely shouting fire in a theatre and causing a panic," wrote Justice Oliver Wendell Holmes, supporting the indictment of Charles Schenck for distributing leaflets urging draftees not to serve in the First World War.

That's the "fire": Cindy Sheehan at a weekend protest in Berkeley.

As *The National Post*'s Colby Cosh pointed out, by that standard thousands of Canadian liberals would have been rounded up for protesting the war in Afghanistan.

Many of my leftie critics also say that my interest in the politico-cultural aspects of demographics makes me a eugenicist. Er, no. Again, that's your boy: Big Government enforced-sterilization eugenicist Oliver Wendell Holmes.

My critics then say, okay, even if you're not a eugenicist, you are a Broadway theatre critic and therefore can't be expected to understand demography and other geopolitical issues more complicated than the ingenue's Act Two tap solo. Fair enough. But, it's precisely because I'm a musical comedy bore who was fifth row central for the opening night of *Hitchy Koo Of 1917* that I'm fully aware the analogy was already ridiculous by the time Justice Holmes delivered it. Gas-lit 19th century playhouses were fire-risks; the electrified Winter Garden on the Broadway of 1919 wasn't. The fragrant Victorian allusion was obsolescent even at first utterance.

Colby Cosh makes two further points about Holmes' metaphor: "Anyone who uses it is openly comparing a mass public contemplating a political argument to a rampaging herd of terror-stricken animals." Aside from the fundamental condescension therein, it would seem the herd mentality is most evident among those brain-dead sophisticates who stampede to recite the fire-in-a-theatre line as if it's the most penetrating insight ever articulated. Even if it were, it's entirely irrelevant in a Canadian context. Note Holmes' words: "*falsely* shouting fire in a theatre." Under the "hate speech" provisions of Canada's Criminal Code, truth is no defense: even if the theatre really is ablaze, you're still guilty.

And, needless to say, today half the folks who think it's wrong to shout "Fire!" in a crowded theatre think it's okay to shout "Allahu Akbar!" on a crowded commuter plane taking off from Minneapolis. In 2008, the BBC reported on some Scandinavian disturbances under the following headline:

Swedish City Hit By Youth Riots

"Youths", huh? Like the "youths" in the French riots of 2005. Youths of no other discernible characteristics. Let's take a wild guess here. Would the "Swedish city" happen to be "Malmö"? Why, amazingly, yes. As the BBC reported:

> *Dozens of youths have rioted in the southern Swedish city of Malmö for a second consecutive night, setting cars on fire and clashing with police.*

While we're on a roll, would it happen to be the part of Malmö known as "Rosengard"? Why, right again! From a Reuters picture caption:

> *Police extinguish burning barricades on the main road in the immigrant-dominated suburb of Rosengard in Malmö in southern Sweden, early December 19, 2008. The fire department considered the area to be too risky to enter with their personnel.*

"Immigrant-dominated", eh? Is that a way of saying it's the most heavily Muslim neighborhood of Sweden's most Muslim city? Ah, well, let's not go that far. All the BBC is prepared to suggest is that the otherwise non-specific youths' riotous activities were "linked to the closure of an Islamic center".

Not only is there no freedom to shout "Fire!" in a crowded theatre, but in a burning city feel free to shout "Go back to sleep!" for another decade or three.

In a splendidly barristerial wind-up to the Vancouver show trial, *Maclean's* counsel Julian Porter, QC stood before the three pseudo-judges of the kangaroo court and declared:

> *Against the argument that you cannot cry fire in a crowded theatre: Oh yes, you can - you must, if in your considered view there is a fire. In that case there is a duty to cry fire.*

Well said. The theatre is burning. And the best evidence of that is a kangaroo court in a citadel of the west bending over backwards to insist otherwise.

EPITAPH

Pompey now desired the honour of a triumph, which Sylla opposed...
Pompey, however, was not daunted; but bade Sylla recollect that more
worshipped the rising than the setting sun.

PLUTARCH

75 AD

EXIT MUSIC

The song of civilizational self-loathing

Maclean's, May 12th 2008

A COUPLE OF years ago, an Australian reader wrote to say he was beginning to feel as Robert Frost did in "A Minor Bird":

> *I have wished a bird would fly away*
> *And not sing by my house all day.*

My correspondent's unceasingly cheeping bird was Islam. He was fed up waking every morning and reading of the latest offence taken by the more excitable Mohammedans. If memory serves, this exhaustion was prompted by a Muslim protest outside Westminster Cathedral demanding death for the Pope. It was organized by a fellow called Anjem Choudhary, who says that "whoever insults the message of Mohammed is going to be subject to capital punishment." But then again it might have been some other provocation entirely – say, the chocolate swirl on the top of a Burger King dessert carton that an aggrieved customer complained bore too close a resemblance to the Arabic script for "Allah" (the offending menu item was subsequently withdrawn). If you're that eager to take offence, it's not difficult to find it. Or as President Bush said to me around the same time: "If it's not the Crusades, it's the cartoons."

Which would make a great bumper sticker. It encapsulates perfectly not only the inability of the perpetually aggrieved to move on, millennium-in millennium-out, but also the utter lack of proportion.

Anyway, my *New York Times* bestseller (and Canadian hate crime) *America Alone: The End Of The World As We Know It* is released in paperback across the Dominion's bookstores this week, and, if a mere excerpt in *Maclean's* was enough to generate two "human rights" prosecutions, the softcover edition should be good for a full-blown show trial followed by a last cigarette and firing squad – although, this being Canada, there'll be no last cigarette. (To mark the paperback launch, I'll be in Toronto at the Bay & Bloor branch of Indigo on Wednesday May 7th with my old pal Heather Reisman. So do come along if you're interested in hearing what the book's about, or if you're an Ontario "Human Rights" Commissar and you'd like to arrest me.) In any event, with a new round of promotional interviews looming, several readers wrote to ask if I ever felt like my Australian pal: Don't I wish the Islamic bird would just fly away? Wouldn't it be nice not to be up to your neck in jihad 24/7?

I'm using "up to your neck" metaphorically, but a lot of chaps are more literal. Naeem Muhammad Khan, the unemployed Torontonian whose website urges that the "apostasy" of *Maclean's* contributor Tarek Fatah and other Muslim moderates be punished by death, says of one of his targets: "Behead her!!! And make a nice video and post it on YouTube." There is no point wishing Mr Khan would fly away and not sing by our house all day. He's here to stay, and anyone who advocated, say, his deportation would find himself assailed by moderate reasonable Canadians horrified at such a betrayal of our multicultural values.

Which is the point. For as Robert Frost's poem continues:

> *The fault must partly have been in me.*
> *The bird was not to blame for his key.*
> *And of course there must be something wrong*
> *In wanting to silence any song.*

In the case of an enfeebled west at twilight, the fault is wholly in us. After September 11th 2001, many agonized progressives looked at America and its allies' relations with the Muslim world and argued that we need to ask ourselves: Why do they hate us? As Brian Dunn, a Michigan blogger, put it, a more relevant question is: Why do *we* hate us? After all, if all our institutions, from grade school to public broadcasting to Hollywood movies to Canadian "human rights" commissars, operate from the basic assumption that western civilization is the font of racism, imperialism, oppression, exploitation and all the other ills of the world, why be surprised that the rest of humanity takes us at our word?

"Multiculturalism" is a unicultural phenomenon. It exists only as a western fetish, and we don't believe in it, not really. Most people, given the choice, want to live in an advanced western society. That's why even impeccably PC lefties refer carelessly to other cultures as "developing nations": the phrase assumes they're "developing" into something closer to ours, because that's the direction of progress. Even hardcore multiculturalists want to live in a western society. For one thing, that's the only place you can make a living as a multiculturalist. The general thinking was summed up in an email I got the other day from a reader arguing that there was no point getting irked by the Archbishop of Canterbury's call for the introduction of sharia in the United Kingdom. We are, said my correspondent, "rich enough to afford to be stupid."

I wonder if it's quite that simple. We are encouraging of certain forms of assertiveness: I am woman, hear me roar! Say it loud, I'm black and proud! We're here, we're queer, get used to it! But the one identity we're enjoined not to trumpet is the one that enables us to trumpet all the others: our identity as citizens of a very specific kind of society with a very particular inheritance, built on the rule of law, property rights, and freedom of speech. Heaven forbid we should assert any of that: I am western, hear me apologize! Say it loud, I'm Dutch and cowed! We're Brits, we're shits, awf'lly sorry about that!

If you no longer know what you stand for, how can you know what you stand against? That's why Swedish cabinet ministers say we should be nice to Muslims now so that when they're in the majority they'll be nice to us, and Dutch cabinet ministers say they'd have no objection to sharia as long as a majority of Dutch electors voted for it, and Canadian Prime Ministers say things like: "I believe that once you are a Canadian citizen, you have the right to your own views and to disagree."

That was Paul Martin, and he was reacting to the news that the youngest Khadr boy and his mum had landed at Pearson to renew their OHIP cards. Junior had been paralyzed in the shootout with Pakistani forces that killed his dad, the highest-ranking Canuck in al-Qaeda (at least until Osama's Canadian passport turns up in the back of the cave). And, not fancying a prison hospital in Peshawar, the kid and his mum flew "home" to enjoy the benefits of Ontario health care. Would it have killed Mr Martin to express mild distaste at the idea of your tax dollars paying for the treatment of a man whose Canadian citizenship is no more than a flag of convenience but unfortunately that's the law, blah blah blah? Apparently so. Instead, his reflex instinct was to proclaim this as a wholehearted demonstration of the virtues of a multicultural state so boundlessly tolerant it even lets you choose what side of the Afghan war you're on: When the draft card arrives, just check "home team" or "enemy" according to taste. We'll still be congratulating ourselves on our boundless tolerance even as the forces of intolerance consume us.

Which is more likely? That the Ontario "Human Rights" Commission will investigate Naeem Muhammad Khan for his explicit incitement to murder? Or that it will rebuke *Maclean's* for being so "racist" and "Islamophobic" as to quote such chaps? Well, they've already done the latter. So have Her Majesty's constabulary in England. After Channel 4 broadcast an undercover report showing imams in British mosques urging the murder of gays and apostates and whatnot, the West Midlands Police launched an investigation …into the TV network for its insensitive "Islamophobia". As Bruce Bawer, a gay American who lives in Scandinavia, writes in the current *City Journal*:

> *Those who, if given the power, would subjugate infidels, oppress women, and execute apostates and homosexuals are 'moderate' (a moderate, these days, apparently being anybody who doesn't have*

explosives strapped to his body), while those who dare to call a spade a spade are 'Islamophobes'.

"Islam is a fighting creed," wrote John Buchan, Canada's former Governor-General (incredible as that seems), "and the mullah still stands in the pulpit with the Koran in one hand and a drawn sword in the other." That's from his novel *Greenmantle*, which the BBC had commissioned a new dramatization of, only to cancel it in the wake of the London Tube bombings. And just because the novels of the man who gave us the Governor-General's Literary Awards are beyond the pale in these sensitive times doesn't mean Buchan's wrong: Islam *is* a fighting creed, but it doesn't need to be, not when it's up against a culture so turned on by self-flagellation.

To cite Bruce Bawer again on what he calls "the anatomy of surrender":

The key question for westerners is: Do we love our freedoms as much as they hate them? Many free people, alas, have become so accustomed to freedom, and to the comfortable position of not having to stand up for it, that they're incapable of defending it when it's imperiled - or even, in many cases, of recognizing that it is imperiled.

Indeed. The bird that needs to fly the coop is the one that's been chirruping away with the Song of Civilizational Self-Loathing for two generations now. To quote another landmark of ornithological versifying:

Spread your tiny wings and fly away.

IN MEMORIAM
Look around

National Review, November 6th 2006

O N THE TOMB of the great architect Sir Christopher Wren at St Paul's Cathedral is a famous inscription: *Si monumentum requiris, circumspice.* If you seek my monument, look around. Conversely, if you're seeking the tomb of western civilization, look around at the monuments. Not the old ones to generals and potentates, but the new ones.

A year ago, London's Mayor "Red Ken" Livingstone unveiled a new statue on the famous "empty plinth" in Trafalgar Square. Sharing the heart of the capital with King George IV, General Sir Charles Napier and Major General Sir Henry Havelock these days is Alison Lapper, an armless woman heavily pregnant. At the unveiling, Miss Lapper said the new statue would force Britons to "confront their prejudices" about disability. As my old editor, Charles Moore, pointed out, Trafalgar Square already has a monument to persons who've overcome disability: the one-eyed one-armed Admiral Lord Nelson standing on his column and no doubt bemused by the modish posturing below. Red Ken became weirdly obsessed, as is his wont, by the dead white males clogging up the square and was anxious to even up the score. He professed never to have heard of General Napier or General Havelock, which is a sad comment – not that he should be so ignorant, but that he should be so boastful of his ignorance. (*National Review* readers who wish to bring themselves up to speed on Sir Charles Napier will find him on page 193 of my new book.) So the point of the fourth plinth was to send a message that warmongering white males no longer had the square to themselves: the statue of Miss Lapper is a monument not to disability so much as to the psychological self-crippling to which so many Britons are prone.

Another monument: the Arizona 9/11 Memorial. It is a remarkable sight. Five years after the slaughter of thousands of Americans, one had long ago given up all hope that the nation might rouse itself to erect, as James Lileks put it at National Review Online, "a classical memorial in the plaza with allegorical figures representing Sorrow and Resolve, and a fountain watched over by stern stone eagles". But, even so, the Arizona memorial is an almost parodic exercise in civilizational self-loathing, festooned in slogans that read like a brainstorming session for a Daily Kos publicity campaign: "You don't win battles of terrorism with more battles." "Foreign-born Americans afraid." "Erroneous US airstrike kills 46 Uruzgan civilians." And this is the *official* state memorial. Governor Napolitano called it "great" and "honorable". It isn't. It's small and contemptible. Assuming it survives, future generations will stand before it and marvel – either that the United States is still around or that such an obviously deranged country even needed an enemy to lose to.

A third monument, a third country: France. This one was unveiled at the end of October in Clichy-sous-Bois. If that name rings a bell, it's the bell on the fire truck racing through the streets to douse the flaming Citröens and Renaults in last year's riots. They began when two of France's legions of – what's the word? – "youths" were fleeing the cops and decided to hide out in an electrical sub-station. Bad choice. They were electrocuted. Their fellow "youths" blamed the police and launched a three-week orgy of destruction. Now Clichy-sous-Bois has put up a monument to the unfortunate Zyed Benna and Bouna Traore. As in Arizona and London, this is an official memorial. That's to say, the Mayor of Clichy-sous-Bois unveiled the monument to Messieurs Benna and Traore in the front of their school and then led a "silent march" to the sub-station where he laid a wreath commemorating their death – or, indeed, manslaughter, if some of the complaints against the pursuing *gendarmes* come off.

Now let's take it as read that the deceased were as they're portrayed – lovable rogues who were alienated only by the lack of employment opportunities, etc. Granted all that, is it still necessary to put up a formal monument to them? Weren't the thousands of newspaper columns saying these riots were nothing to do with Islam and were all about the need for more public spending monument enough? Wasn't Prime Minister Dominique de Villepin's "raft of measures" – the creation of an anti-discrimination agency, 20,000 job contracts with local government agencies, an extra 100 million euros for community associations – monument enough? Weren't the French government's desperate entreaties to A-list imams to serve as interlocutors with the "youths" monument enough?

No, no, no. They had to go and build an actual monument.

America, Britain and France are not peripheral members of the developed world but its heart. They're the west's three permanent representatives on the Security Council, the three nuclear powers. But if these monuments truly represent the spirit of each nation as those monuments to Nelson and Napier did in their day then you would have to be an unusually optimistic sort to bet on the long-term prospects of all three countries. The poseur diversity of Trafalgar Square slips easily into the self-loathing of Arizona, and from there it's but a short step to the open appeasement in Clichy-sous-Bois. If you seek our monument, look around: We cannot state who we are, what we believe, why we fight.

COLLECT THE SET!

THE FACE OF THE TIGER
Steyn on war
and the world

BROADWAY BABIES SAY GOODNIGHT
Steyn on stage – a classic romp
through a century of showbiz

MARK STEYN FROM HEAD TO TOE
Steyn on everything –
from the crowned
heads of Nepal to
Fergie's toe, via
Sinatra's voice,
Kosovar lungs and
Bill Clinton's
"executive branch"

MARK STEYN'S PASSING PARADE
Steyn on people,
from Artie Shaw and
Ray Charles to the
Princess of Wales
and Idi Amin

AMERICA ALONE: THE END OF THE WORLD AS WE KNOW IT
Steyn on demography,
civilizational confidence,
and a glimpse of the day
after tomorrow –the international bestseller, and the
Canadian Number One
the Islamists tried to stop

MARK STEYN'S AMERICAN SONGBOOK
Steyn on composer Jule
Styne, lyricist Dorothy Fields,
plus a Cole Porter classic

A SONG FOR THE SEASON
Steyn on song - a musical calendar
from "Auld Lang Syne" to "White
Christmas" via "My Funny
Valentine", "Summertime",
"Autumn Leaves" and more

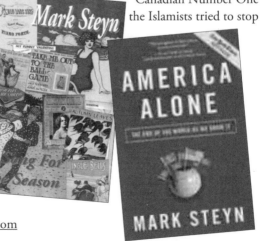

MARK STEYN RETURNS...

...in the next issue of National Review;
...in his weekend syndicated column;
...every day at SteynOnline.com;
...and across Canada each week in Maclean's, *state censors permitting*